SOFT

'Homeless', Oscar Gustav Rejlander, 1857

SOFT

A Brief History of Sentimentality

FERDINAND MOUNT

BLOOMSBURY CONTINUUM
LONDON · OXFORD · NEW YORK · NEW DELHI · SYDNEY

BLOOMSBURY CONTINUUM
Bloomsbury Publishing Plc
50 Bedford Square, London, WC1B 3DP, UK
Bloomsbury Publishing Ireland Limited
29 Earlsfort Terrace, Dublin 2, D02 AY28, Ireland

BLOOMSBURY, BLOOMSBURY CONTINUUM and the Diana logo are trademarks of
Bloomsbury Publishing Plc

First published in Great Britain 2025

Copyright © Ferdinand Mount, 2025

Ferdinand Mount has asserted his right under the Copyright, Designs and Patents Act, 1988, to be
identified as Author of this work

For legal purposes the Picture credits and Permissions on pp. 269–71 constitute an extension
of this copyright page

All rights reserved. No part of this publication may be: i) reproduced or transmitted in any form, electronic or mechanical, including photocopying, recording or by means of any information storage or retrieval system without prior permission in writing from the publishers; or ii) used or reproduced in any way for the training, development or operation of artificial intelligence (AI) technologies, including generative AI technologies. The rights holders expressly reserve this publication from the text and data mining exception as per Article 4(3) of the Digital Single Market Directive (EU) 2019/790

Bloomsbury Publishing Plc does not have any control over, or responsibility for, any third-party websites referred to or in this book. All internet addresses given in this book were correct at the time of going to press. The author and publisher regret any inconvenience caused if addresses have changed or sites have ceased to exist, but can accept no responsibility for any such changes

A catalogue record for this book is available from the British Library

Library of Congress Cataloguing-in-Publication data has been applied for

ISBN: HB: 978-1-3994-2188-1; eBook: 978-1-3994-2186-7; ePDF: 978-1-3994-2185-0

2 4 6 8 10 9 7 5 3 1

Typeset by Deanta Global Publishing Services, Chennai, India
Printed and bound in Great Britain by CPI Group (UK) Ltd, Croydon CR0 4YY

To find out more about our authors and books visit www.bloomsbury.com and sign up for
our newsletters

For product safety related questions contact productsafety@bloomsbury.com

In memory of Tristram

But vain the Sword and vain the Bow,
They never can work War's overthrow.
The Hermit's Prayer and the Widow's Tear
Alone can free the World from Fear,
For a Tear is an Intellectual Thing,
And a Sigh is the Sword of an Angel King,
And the bitter Groan of the Martyr's woe
Is an Arrow from the Almighty's Bow.

          WILLIAM BLAKE

Contents

Introduction: The Unforgivable Sin — ix

CHAPTER ONE: The First Sentimental Revolution — 1
Inventing Love — Passionate about the Passion — This Vale of Tears — The Power of Soft

CHAPTER TWO: The New Stony Age — 43
A Lament for Walsingham — The Dowsing Rod — Chilling with Michelangelo

CHAPTER THREE: The Second Sentimental Revolution — 63
The Man Who Invented Me Too — Love Divine, All Loves Excelling — The Continental Version — The Dawn of Toleration — The Three Scottish Sympathizers — Movers, Shakers and Quakers

CHAPTER FOUR: Manliness Rules OK — 123
Reacting into Reaction — Women Can Be Manly, Too — The Dry Imperial Eye

CHAPTER FIVE: Mr Popular Sentiment — 147
The Case of Charles Dickens — Uncle Tom and Aunt Phillis — Victor Hugo, Hélas!

CHAPTER SIX: The Great Estranging — 187
The Dilemma of The Doctor — On or About December 1910 — The Revolt Against the Masses

CHAPTER SEVEN: The Third Sentimental Revolution   215
1963 and All That — *It's a Private Matter* — *It's a Crime to Discriminate* — *Murdered for a Song* — *Tears on the Turf* — *6 September 1997*

Picture Credits and Permissions   269
Notes   272
Further Reading   285
Acknowledgements   292
Index   293

Introduction

THE UNFORGIVABLE SIN
'What's wrong with being sentimental? Sentimental means liking stuff.'

It's hard to forget the shock of hearing Paul McCartney give this answer to a radio interviewer a year or so ago. I can't remember the interviewer's response. He was probably as gobsmacked as I was. Only the most famous living songwriter in the world (according to the music critic of *The Times*, Lennon and McCartney were the greatest songwriters since Schubert) could have got away with so blithely contradicting the entrenched shibboleth of modern high culture: that sentimentality is the ultimate unforgivable crime. For critical theorists, the slightest hint of sentimentality is enough to disqualify from serious consideration any novel, or artwork, or piece of music, political or philosophical argument or even remark in ordinary conversation. It is an insult more damning to the work in question than dismissing it as leaden, ill-constructed or confused.

As the editors of the Oxford World's Classics edition of the eighteenth-century sentimentalist bestseller *The Man of Feeling* remark: 'Of course, the word "sentimental" and its cognates these days always has a derogatory sense, a sense of an undesirable and sometimes embarrassing excess of feeling'.[1] In their collection of essays, *Faking It:The Sentimentalisation of Modern Society*, Digby Anderson and Peter Mullen, both priests in the Church of England, declare: 'There is a word for the decadent disposition in our culture which falls for the fake: it is "sentimentality". The sentimentalist is a person in denial, and what he avoids or denies is reality.'[2] Twenty years on, the exasperated laments for the decline of the British character are as loud as ever. In a recent *Spectator* cover piece, the screenwriter Gareth Roberts complains that 'we have entirely lost our aversion to glutinous sentimentality ... we are drowning in a sea of syrup.'[3] Paul McCartney is by no means the only pop star to have been accused of being sentimental. But he may be unique in so boldly embracing the description. For there is no doubt that if there were a modern sin against the Holy Ghost, sentimentality would be it, and it's a brave man who isn't ashamed to own up to it.

Weeping for the misfortunes of strangers, especially people who are far distant from us in time or place, comes in for a special thumping. Our age is denounced as a 'society of spectacle', in which we are prurient perpetual onlookers wallowing in other people's misery, usually to demonstrate our own virtuousness. The implacable Jean Baudrillard thunders that 'in the new Sentimental Order, the affluent become consumers of the ever more delightful spectacle of poverty and catastrophe, and of the moving spectacle of our own attempts to alleviate it'.[4]

But is it really illegitimate or phony to be touched by the misfortunes of strangers? We are, after all, often berated at the same time for our deafness to miseries suffered far away, and even those on our doorsteps, too. Over the past 200 years, the impact of sympathy, not least long-range sympathy, on the treatment of slaves, excluded minorities of all sorts and the wretched of the earth, has been memorable and cumulative.

Would it have been better, for example, if *Uncle Tom's Cabin* had been suppressed, as some outraged Southerners demanded? It was the second-bestselling book in the United States in the entire nineteenth century, after the Bible. No other book did a tenth as much to make the continuance of slavery in the South seem loathsome and intolerable. Abraham Lincoln himself is said to have remarked on being introduced to Harriet Beecher Stowe after the outbreak of the Civil War, 'And this is the little lady who started this great war' (and if he didn't say it himself, lots of other people thought it). Yet if ever a novel could be fairly described as sentimental, Uncle Tom's Cabin is it. And there were plenty of critics at the time ready to denounce it as sentimental tosh – 'a derivative piece of hack work', designed to appeal to 'women's sloppy emotions'.

Those stern Victorians who loathed Uncle Tom's Cabin would have loathed another tear-jerking bestseller published a decade later. The Revd Charles Kingsley called his story The Water Babies, A Fairy Story for Land Babies (1863). But as well as being a fairy tale for children, it is a didactic moral exercise and a telling plea for social reform. Tom is a poor orphaned chimney sweep who slaves for the horrible Mr Grimes. 'He cried when he had to climb the dark flues, rubbing his poor knees and elbows raw; and when the soot got into his eyes, which it did every day of the week; and when his master beat him, which he did every day in the week; and when he had not enough to eat, which happened every day in the week likewise.'[5] After Tom manages to escape, he goes to live with the water babies, perfectly formed human babies with tails who live in the ponds and streams, and there he is washed clean of all the dirt and the germs which brought so many sweeps to an early grave. The story is preachy and amusing and whimsical by turns, upsetting those who like their books cut and dried. It was hugely popular and became part of the campaign, led by Lord Shaftesbury, to regulate the employment of boy sweeps. The Chimney Sweepers Act of 1864 was further tightened, by Shaftesbury again, in another Act of 1875. By now, the employment of children was increasingly controlled, not only up the chimneys but in the factories and down the pit, where their lives had been no less miserable and unhealthy and the injuries they suffered no less fatal or crippling.

The Shaftesbury Society for the protection of children continues to this day. For a hundred years it used as its poster child to highlight the plight of homeless children a photograph taken in 1857 by the pioneer Swedish photographer Oscar Gustav Rejlander (1813–75) (which is the frontispiece of this book). This photograph, variously known as Homeless or Poor Jo or Night in Town, was one of the intensely emotional and varied works which earned Rejlander the title of father of art photography. He also made memorable portraits of Tennyson, Darwin and Lewis Carroll, and provided nine illustrations for Darwin's *The Expression of the Emotions in Man and Animals* (1872), six of which he posed for himself. If anyone embodied the idea that art is about feeling, it was Rejlander.[6]

Were the Victorians uniquely susceptible to appeals to sentiment? Could a photograph, or a children's story, or a popular novel have such an effect in our own day? We need look no further than *Cathy Come Home*, the celebrated *Wednesday Play*, first screened to 12 million viewers in 1966. This powerful and affecting drama about a homeless mother who, after a series of disasters, loses custody of her three children essentially because she is homeless, written by Jeremy Sandford and directed by the indefatigable Ken Loach, brought the plight of homeless families to the forefront of public attention, although the problem had been there ever since the war. The furore led eventually to the Housing (Homeless Persons) Act of 1977. It also inspired the founding of the charity Crisis and gave wings to another charity directly aimed at the homeless, Shelter, which happened to have started up at exactly the same time. This is not to say that the problem has now been cured, but ever since the issue has never ceased to nag at the public conscience. Some sterner spirits remain unmoved. As recently as 2023, Suella Braverman, then Home Secretary, asserted that 'we cannot allow our streets to be taken over by rows of tents occupied by people, many of them from abroad, living on the streets as a lifestyle choice'.[7]

Or you could take the film *Victim* (1961), in which Dirk Bogarde plays an agonized gay barrister who is being blackmailed by a former boyfriend. The theme of homosexuality had never been seriously tackled in a commercial film before. Bogarde's harrowing performance, perhaps his finest ever, lent a powerful thrust to the campaign to liberalize the severe laws on homosexual conduct. The campaign had been running strongly since long before the publication of the Wolfenden Report in 1957, but the Tory government still shrank from acting, fearing a violent public reaction. In fact, public opinion was already shifting, and *Victim* gave it a powerful nudge. The Homosexual Law Reform Act of 1967 changed everything.

What sentimental fiction – books, TV programmes, plays – can do is to make the victims' voices heard at one remove, ultimately to legitimize their agency. Peter Nichols's play *A Day in the Death of Joe Egg*, first produced at the Glasgow Citizens Theatre in 1967, turns his own experiences of bringing up a handicapped daughter into something approaching a surreal comedy. It would perhaps be too much to claim that this much revived play led to the formation of the British Cerebral Palsy Society in 1969, or the beginnings of the Cerebral Palsy Games a few years later. One could also point to Christy Brown's memoir of growing up with cerebral palsy, *My Left Foot*, which had come out back in 1954. What we can perhaps discern, though, is the growth of a climate in which the public was readier to hear the voices of the afflicted and to treat them on equal terms. Similar misfortunes are increasingly the subject of plays, books and films: the diseases of old age, such as dementia, in the film *Away from Her*, starring Julie Christie, and Florian Zeller's *The Father*, brilliantly acted by Anthony Hopkins among others. The stony hearts who find this sort of thing uncomfortable write it off as 'Criplit', or, in the case of the numerous tales of appalling childhoods now filling the bestseller lists, 'Mislit'. But they are outflanked when the victims happily adopt these generic titles for themselves.

All such breakthroughs must rely to some degree on emotive, heart-wrenching language, in short, on sentimentality. What its critics deride as 'excess of emotion' is precisely what is needed to shift public opinion. It is the weight of feeling that carries the ball over the line.

And if sentimentality is still to be considered a heinous sin, what precisely is the nature of this sin? The overwhelming consensus of the critics is that sentimentality is fake, inauthentic, because it is *unearned*. Oscar Wilde tells us in *De Profundis* that 'a sentimentalist is one who desires to have the luxury of an emotion without paying for it'. In James Joyce's *Ulysses*, Stephen Dedalus sends Buck Mulligan a telegram declaring that 'The sentimentalist is he who would enjoy without incurring the immense debtorship for a thing done.' The critic and the true creative artist condemn sentimentality for being cheap, because the sentimentalist hasn't paid for it properly.

But this sweeping indictment is rather bizarre, perhaps itself even a little cheap. Why do emotions have to be paid for? What sort of transaction is in question? Surely when we talk about feelings, we usually think of them springing up naturally in response to experience, not as commodities to be bought and paid for.

And who exactly is this 'sentimentalist'? Wilde and Joyce and plenty of other critics make him sound like a person who practises the stuff regularly, perhaps even professionally, like a violinist or a devout Catholic. But most people are only intermittently sentimental, and only about some things and not about others. The same person may be sentimental about babies or Arsenal Football Club, and witheringly hard-headed and cynical about the Labour Party or the royal family. Right-wing conservatives pride themselves on being hard-nosed about most things, but they swoon at the thought of the Nation. One's emotions about a single thing may be a confused mixture, too. In *De Profundis*, Oscar is sentimental, almost mawkish (a favourite epithet of the critics) about his love for darling Bosie, but brutally realistic about the selfishness and self-indulgence of the real-life Lord Alfred Douglas (Douglas went on to become almost as nasty as his appalling father, Lord Queensberry). In fact, Wilde himself acknowledges this potential confusion in his equally famous *bon mot*, that 'the sentimentalist is always a cynic at heart. Indeed, sentimentality is merely the bank holiday of the cynic.'[8] Wilde famously declared that 'one must have a heart of stone to read the death of Little Nell without laughing'. But Wilde's own stories such as *The Happy Prince* are soaked in sentiment. His sons recalled their father's eyes filling with tears as he read them *The Selfish Giant*.[9]

And what precisely gives the Critic (let us award him a capital letter, since he clearly has such a good conceit of himself) the right to question the quality of other people's emotions? A reaction to some traumatic event which seems to him 'maudlin' (another favourite epithet of the Critic's) or excessively effusive may seem to others a natural human response.

There, upon her little bed, she lay at rest.

'The Death of Little Nell' by George Cattermole, from The Old Curiosity Shop, 1902

Nor is the Critic's own language beyond criticism. 'Woke', for example, that contentious term that right-wingers are so fond of flinging at the nearest target, had its origins far back in President Lincoln's day when 'The Wide Awakes' were founded in Hartford, Connecticut, as a militant pressure group in support of Lincoln and abolition. Woke received its modern revival in the 1938 Lead Belly song 'The Scottsboro Boys', about the trials of nine black teenagers wrongly accused of raping two white girls and sentenced to death. The legal battles went on for years, all the way to the Supreme Court, partly inspiring Harper Lee to write To Kill a Mockingbird. Lead Belly advises 'everybody, be a little careful when they go along through there [Scottsboro] best stay woke, keep their eyes open' – that is, watch out for lurking white racists. Today, Woke has been taken up by the Aggrieved Right as a term of abuse, to describe over-zealous efforts to eliminate various sorts of injustice and inequality. In fact, 'wokery' has become a synonym for sentimental do-goodery, along with 'virtue-signalling'. But if we look back over the honourable history of the term, we might 'be a little careful' about flinging it around as an insult.

As we tiptoe through these choppy waters, we may begin to suspect that the Critic's position may not be as secure as he or she (far more often he) thinks. Yes, of course, we are justified in deriding the gross commercial motives of TV producers, who set up their peep shows of someone being confronted with their long-lost daughter or their estranged brother. This has been a staple of popular entertainment since the mid-1950s when This Is Your Life started – and was immediately denounced by 'Cassandra', pen name of William Connor, in the Daily Mirror as 'a ghastly, cloying, repulsive stunt' and 'a preposterous, sniveling charade'. But of course the reactions of the actual participants in the show are mostly heartfelt and authentic. We would be taken aback, shocked even, if such traumatic reunions provoked no more than a cool handshake and a 'nice to see you again'. But what of the audience both in the studio and at home? Aren't they being exploited for profit? Yes, they are, but that does not mean that they are also being degraded. Nor is their instinctive sympathy with the agonizing life stories of total strangers something to be ashamed of. Is it any more disgraceful to be moved by such spectacles than to be moved to tears by King Lear or Brief Encounter, which cannot even claim to be based on real people?

One begins to sense that the Critic is basically hostile to all displays of emotion. His world view is like Brighton rock, hard all the way through, with only the sticky-sweet coating of irony that you find in the works of Andy Warhol and Jeff Koons. More unappealing still, his denunciations seem driven at least in part by a wish to show himself superior to the soppy herd. I think the American philosopher Robert Solomon is right to detect a certain lurking snobbery, both social and intellectual. As he points out, '"cheap" means "low-class". And the suggestion is that we should be "above" such sentiments ... Irony and skepticism are the marks of the educated; sentimentality is the mark of the uneducated ... the "high" class of many societies associate themselves with emotional control and reject sentimentality as an expression of inferior, ill-bred beings, and male society has long used such a view to deride the "emotionality" of women.'[10]

There's an embarrassing gap, too, in the Critic's analysis: the total absence of a historical dimension. The reality is that people have thought very differently in different centuries about the uses and abuses of emotional display. This reality offends our strongly felt intuitions. We instinctively resist the idea that emotions could have a history. It would seem ridiculous to many people that there should exist a Centre for the History of the Emotions at Queen Mary University, London. But it does exist, and its director, Professor Thomas Dixon, has written an excellent history of crying in this country, *Weeping Britannia* (2015), which I shall draw on heavily. We prefer to think that grief and joy, hatred and love, come naturally to our hearts and minds, without being shaped by outside pressures. Yet this is not so. As Denis de Rougemont put it many years ago, in his extraordinary, shocking and still highly contentious book *Love in the Western World*,[11] '"Everything changes except the human heart," say the old sages, but they are wrong. Metaphorically speaking, the human heart is strangely sensitive to variations in time and space.' To put it in concrete terms, displays of emotion, whether in public spaces or in private between individuals, are partly governed by fashion and convention. The outward expressions of every type of emotion, and the rituals governing them, respond to historical shifts of which people at the time may scarcely be aware. Conversely, at the same time these pressures on emotional display also interact with and impact back upon social and political actions and trends. It's a two-way exchange between the hearts and minds of individual men and women and the pressures of society.

What we shall find repeated through the cultural history of Europe over the past millennium is a movement between feeling and unfeeling, between passion and dispassion, from melting to hardening and then eventually back again. This movement seems to run through the whole of society, through literature and art, influencing politics and legal systems, saturating morality and religion and family life. Sometimes people seem vaguely or even fully aware of what is happening around them, and embrace or recoil from it, according to taste and temperament. Sometimes the movement appears to flood over them while they are barely conscious. But the surge in one direction or another is extraordinarily powerful, and so is the reaction, which is often instantaneous and simultaneous, producing ferocious clashes. 'Culture wars', as we call them today, are nothing new. In fact, Western culture often seems to exist in a state of permanent internal conflict.

What we shall find too is that the new shift does not develop gradually or naturally out of the old orthodoxy. On the contrary, it is propelled by a furious revulsion against the old stuff. The history of culture typically proceeds by *backlash*. The prophets and gurus of the New, whether in art, literature, politics or religion, define themselves *against* the Old. Nothing could exceed the scorn of the New Critics like Cleanth Brooks and Robert Penn Warren for Shelley's skylark and Wordsworth's daffodils. In politics, the New Left is scorching in its critique of the Neoliberalism of the 1980s, just as scorching as the Neoliberals in their day were of the Socialists of the 1940s. In art, the torchbearers of Modernism like Clive Bell and Clement Greenberg deplore the Victorian Realists; in fact they deplore figurative artists altogether, just as Luther and Cromwell deplored the saints and ceremonies of the old Catholic Church which were so dear to the ignorant peasants. They all insist that the old stuff is not simply stale and outdated, it is meretricious and pernicious, and, of course, sentimental; there is not a shred of merit to be found in it. Only rarely will you find a critic with the breadth of sympathy to seek out the virtues in the discarded, someone like Frederick Pottle, the great Boswell scholar of Yale. He could understand why Edgar Allen Poe and Robert Browning thought Shelley's Indian Serenade 'exquisite' and 'divine', while Brooks and Warren thought it was tosh, and why Dr Johnson and Thomas Gray thought Dryden was a great poet and Matthew Arnold and A. E. Housman thought he wasn't. 'I shall maintain that all critical judgments are relative to the age producing them' was Pottle's guiding rule.[12] He was happy to call himself a 'relativist', which in the zealot's lexicon is a vile insult, almost as bad as being called an 'indifferentist'. In the Catholic Church, 'indifferentism'; the idea that there are many different roads to salvation, is officially a heresy, and heresy has to be stamped on wherever it rears its hoary head.

These shifts and counter-shifts tend to accompany and illuminate the most seismic social developments – the Crusades, the Reformation, the Enlightenment, Imperialism, Modernism. To know what British or Western life was 'really like' at any particular period, it's helpful to know the prevailing conventions about showing or not showing grief and joy, about the importance (or lack of it) attached to sympathy and empathy, above all, about when and how much to weep for the misfortunes of others. If we can understand a little more about how emotional display is, to quite a large extent, historically conditioned, then we may feel more inclined to question our own assumptions and inhibitions about such things.

This understanding of the connections between our history and our emotions suggests another task, of a still more daunting nature. If the conventions governing emotional display can impact upon politics, and they can, then we need to form a judgement as to whether this impact is benign or malign. We cannot just dismiss emotional display as deplorable sentimentality on purely aesthetic grounds – it's icky, it's over the top, it's fake – we have also to judge, in each particular case, whether or not it's good or bad for human flourishing. And that is what SOFT is ultimately about.

This book offers a very rough sketch of the ups and downs of sentimentality over the past millennium. It might also be called a map of the bumpy road to love.

ONE

The First Sentimental Revolution

INVENTING LOVE

Even today, it remains a difficult idea to swallow, that love had a starting date. Yet C. S. Lewis had no doubt of it: 'Everyone has heard of courtly love, and everyone knows that it appears quite suddenly at the end of the eleventh century in Languedoc.'[1] Quite why this momentous event should have happened then and there, and not somewhere else and at some other time, he was less certain. 'The new thing itself, I do not pretend to understand. Real changes in human sentiment are very rare – there are perhaps three or four on record – but I believe that they occur and that this is one of them.'[2] Even those historians who are less confident about identifying such an epochal shift, like the great medievalist Colin Morris, do not deny that something remarkable happened in southern France around AD 1100: 'An almost complete silence was followed by the beginning of a love literature which challenged in quality and surpassed in volume that of any earlier civilization.'[3] The troubadours, that motley crew of hangers-on at the courts of Aquitaine, an assortment of aristos, peddlers and wandering minstrels, really were the pioneers: 'For all their limitations, these men were the observers of the human heart in love, perhaps the first in the new Europe.'[4]

Where did it all come from? Denis de Rougemont, in *Love in the Western World*, argues that 'the cultivation of passionate love began in Europe as a reaction to Christianity (and in particular to the doctrine of marriage) by people whose spirit, whether naturally or by inheritance, was still pagan.'[5] He, too, was in no doubt about the uniqueness of the event, and its huge significance for posterity: 'that all European poetry has come out of the Provencal poetry written in the twelfth century by the troubadours of Languedoc is now accepted on every side.'[6] And this phenomenon was not confined to the dalliance of bored courtiers waiting for the next Crusade. 'Courtly love comes into existence in the twelfth century during a complete revolution of the human *psyche*. It sprang up out of the same movement which forced upwards into the half light of our human consciousness, into lyrical expression by the human spirit, the feminine principle of *Shakti* [the creative power of the godhead in Hindu myth, always conceived of and personified as female], the worship of woman, of the Mother and of the Virgin.'[7] The knight's passionate love for his lady and the Christian's passionate veneration for Our Lady took off at exactly the same period and faced the same intense hostility from the Church authorities.

By contrast, if we look back to earlier centuries, 'we must conceive a world emptied of that ideal of "happiness" – a happiness grounded in successful romantic love – which still supplies the motive of our popular fiction'.[8] The great classical authors had no elevated notion of love between a man and a woman. Ovid's *Ars Amatoria* is little more than a playboy's handbook. For the ancients, passionate love was a form of madness, usually punished by the Fates: see the sticky ends of Medea, Phaedra and Dido; it was certainly not to be regarded as the noblest of human emotions. Men's deepest feelings were to be reserved for their fatherland and for their friends and comrades. Heroes of the sagas dream of the fame they will win in battle, not of their sweethearts back home. In the *Song of Roland* (c. AD 1040), Roland's betrothed, Alde, is a shadowy figure compared with his loyal comrade Oliver. She expires at the feet of the Emperor Charlemagne on hearing of Roland's death, but the whole episode is dealt with in a line or two: 'Alde the beautiful has gone to her end' (l. 3723). Handled by a Provençal troubadour a century or so later, Roland's love for Alde and her tragic death would have covered pages.

That is the difference between the old *chansons de geste* and the new *chansons d'amour* of the twelfth century onwards. There are plenty of brave deeds in the new romances by Béroul and Chrétien de Troyes: knights errant whack each other from dawn to dusk, shattering lances, shields and usually skulls, too. But what they are truly pursuing is the unique, unrepeatable love that alone can give meaning to their lives.

This then is the novelty. As Johan Huizinga declares in his wonderful study *The Waning of the Middle Ages*, 'When in the twelfth century unsatisfied desire was placed by the troubadours of Provence in the centre of the poetic conception of love, an important turn in the history of civilization was effected.'[9] To be in love became the summit of human experience – an idea which would have struck Aristotle or Ovid as outlandish in the extreme. And if you had never known love, you had not really lived at all.

In the words of Bernart de Ventadorn, one of the finest troubadours and one of the humblest-born (his father was a baker's oven minder):

That man is dead who has no sense
Of love's sweet savour in his heart.[10]

And if you lost your love, you were nothing but a shrivelled, desperate creature. Bernart again: 'She has taken my heart, she has taken my self, she has taken from me the world, and then she has eluded me, leaving me with only my desire and my parched heart.'[11]

Or take the declaration of Héloise to Abelard (the legendary nun and the monk met for the first time in 1118):

'God knows that I never wanted anything from you, but you yourself; desiring, not what was yours, but you alone. I did not look for the bonds of marriage nor any dowry, nor did I even consider my wishes and desires, but I endeavoured to satisfy yours, as you well know ... I call God to witness that if Augustus, the governor of the whole world, offered me the honour of marriage and granted me the entire earth to be mine for ever, I would esteem it dearer and more noble to be called your prostitute than his empress.'[12]

The troubadour's lyrics in the local language of Occitan are often of memorable beauty. Almost the first recorded troubadour, William of Aquitaine or Poitiers (he was Duke of one and Count of the other), had origins as grand as Bernart's were humble, but in poetic skill they were equals. Here's some of William's famous *Ab la dolchor del temps novel*, rendered into modern French:

> Par la douceur du temps nouveau
> Les bois verdissent, les oiseaux
> Chantent chacun en son langage
> Les versets de leur chanson neuve:
> Il faut bien qu'on se mette en quête
> De ce qu'homme désire le plus!

...

> Ainsi va-t-il de notre amour
> Comme de la branche de l'aubépine
> Tant que dure la nuit sur l'arbre,
> Elle tremble à la pluie, au gel.
> Mais l'endemain le soleil luit
> Sur la feuille et le rameau vert.[13]

Or, in A. S. Kline's English translation:[14]
> This love of ours it seems to be
> Like a twig on a hawthorn tree
> That on the tree trembles there
> All night, in rain and frost it grieves,
> Till morning, when the rays appear
> Among the branches and the leaves.

Sounds even better in the plaintive, metallic Occitan. There were women troubadour poets, too, the trobairitz. Far fewer of their songs survive, 20 or 30, as against more than 2,000 of the troubadours' lyrics. Which may be why they are scarcely mentioned by the older writers on medieval love. But they are just as candid, sassy and lyrical as the men. The best-known trobairitz is probably Beatriz, Comtessa de Dia. Here's a sample from her song, 'Estat ai en greu cossirier' ('I've been in great distress of ... mind'):

> Oh how I wish that one fine night
> My cavalier would lie naked in my arms
> And use me as his pillow,
> And find himself in paradise,
> For I love him far more deeply
> Than Floris loved Blancheflor.
> My heart, my love are his,
> My sight, my senses and my life.
>
> My lovely friend, so tender and so good,
> When will you come to my embrace,
> So I can lie beside you all night long
> And bewitch you with an amorous kiss?
> You can be sure, I'd be so happy
> To hold you in my husband's place,
> If only you will promise me
> To do everything I want you to.

The brief biography attached to her songs, the *vida*, tells us that she is singing about and in love with Raimbaut of Orange, another famous troubadour. If so (the *vidas* are not entirely reliable), she was in for a rocky ride, as Raimbaut tells us in one of his bitterer songs that the way to win women is to 'punch them on the nose', because that is what they like, although in other moods Raimbaut can be as sentimental as any of his fellow warblers. But then it sounds as if Beatriz has enough self-confidence to call the shots. She is the only trobairitz for whom the original music survives.

But even Beatriz's range pales beside that of a later woman poet in Wales, Gwerful Mechain (d. 1502). She came from the gentry of north-east Wales, but there is nothing genteel or constricted about her verse. She is capable of writing a skilled and touching ode on Christ's Passion, and at the same time she produces a reckless, rollicking 'Hymn to the Vulva', 'Cywydd y cedor':

> Let songs to the quim grow and thrive,
> Find their due reward and survive.

The rest of the poem is even more uninhibited. In fact, it was so scandalous that in later, more censorious times it was attributed to the father of medieval Welsh poetry, Dafydd ap Gwilym, who lived a century earlier, on the grounds that he had written an 'Ode to the Penis'. But 'Cywydd y cedor' is Gwerful's work all right.

It should be said, of course, that there are medieval Latin lyrics which are very beautiful, too, as shown in Peter Dronke's great collections, and there are beautiful fragments among the Old English verse that has survived, such as *The Wanderer*, in which an exile dwells on the past glories and sorrows of his life, on his lost lord and lost comrades. Also preserved in the precious tenth-century *Exeter Book* is *The Seafarer*, with its similar mixture of melancholy and nostalgia. But there's no love interest in either of them. Only in the ballads of the troubadours and the trobairitz, in their sad, salty Occitan and in the romances in Old French produced in the north of the country, notably at the court of Marie de Champagne, do we find this obsession with man–woman love and its elevation to an all-consuming passion.

We have already seen, too, how wrong we would be to assume that these poets and romancers churn out naive and slushy stuff. On the contrary, they are by turns mordant, joyful, sarcastic, mournful, erotic and even unrestrainedly coarse. Love may be the passion that drives these rollicking dialogues and verse-tales, but not without generating deceit, mendacity and cruelty, often on a shocking scale.

Take one of the earliest workings of the story of Tristan and Yseut (Isolde to Wagner), by the Norman poet Béroul, of whom little is known beyond the fact that he wrote in the middle of the twelfth century. The surviving portion of his irresistible poem, which first enchanted me 60 years ago, begins with a thumping lie told by the heroine Yseut, in an elaborate set-up designed to deceive her husband King Mark. The evil court dwarf, Frocin, has discovered Yseut's affair with the King's nephew, Tristan, and has arranged for Mark to eavesdrop on their midnight meeting in an orchard. Mark hides in a tree, but both Tristan and Yseut catch sight of his shadow and begin a staged dialogue of the ripest falsity. Yseut kicks off with a riff which I'll quote at some length to give its flavour: 'The King thinks that I have been wicked enough to love you. But before God I swear I have been loyal; may He scourge me if anyone has had my love except the man who had me as a maiden [which was, of course, Tristan] ... I would rather be burned and have my ashes scattered to the winds any day of my life than love someone who was not my rightful lord.'[15] Tristan responds, equally deceitfully, 'God, why is the King so foolish? I would let him hang me before I became your lover.'[16]

When they are finally found together, the King first threatens to burn the guilty couple on the pyre. But a local leper, Ivain (several of the leading characters in these romances are of Welsh origin), has a better idea: 'Look, here I have a hundred companions. Give Yseut to us and we will possess her in common. No woman ever had a worse end. Sire, there is such lust in us that no woman on earth could tolerate intercourse with us for a single day.'[17] After a pause for thought, Mark hands her over to the lepers, suggesting that he's not a very nice character either, but as they take her away, Tristan leaps out of a bush and rescues her.

After sundry twists and turns, Tristan reappears, himself disguised as a leper, and at Yseut's request carries her across a ford, thus enabling her at the subsequent trial of her honour to swear on the holy relics that 'no man ever came between my thighs except this leper who carried me on his back across the ford and my husband, King Mark'.[18]

At the same time, *The Romance of Tristan* contains lovely passages, for example when the couple go to sleep together in a wood, only to be discovered, again, by King Mark:

'The bower was made of green branches with foliage in places, and the ground was well covered with leaves. First Yseut lay down;

then Tristan drew his sword, put it between their bodies and lay down himself. Yseut was wearing her tunic – if she had been naked that day, dreadful harm would have come to them – and Tristan kept his trousers on. The queen had on her finger the gold wedding ring set with emeralds the king had given her. Her finger was woefully thin, the ring all but slipping off. Hear how they were lying: she had put one arm under Tristan's neck and the other, I think, over him; her arms were clasped tightly around him. Tristan in his turn had his arms around her, for their affection was not feigned. Their mouths were close together, yet there was a space between them and their bodies were not touching. There was no wind and the leaves were still. A ray of sunlight fell on Yseut's face where it shone like glass. So the lovers went to sleep, not thinking of any harm that might befall them.'[19]

Béroul himself intrudes here, not for the first time, to tell us: 'Nor, as the story says where Béroul saw it written down, did two people ever love each other so much, nor pay for it so dearly.'[20] These authorial intrusions make it clear that Béroul is firmly on the side of the lovers. He never stops denouncing the evil dwarf Frocin and the three barons, who are, after all, only trying to convince Mark of the truth about his erring wife. For the Romancers, love not only conquers all, even if it brings death in its train as it does eventually for Tristan and Yseut (Tristan interposing the sword and keeping his trousers on secures him only a temporary reprieve), but it justifies the most flagrant lies and impostures.

The story of Tristan and Yseut is, if not the very first, the archetypal love story in Western culture. Yet there is something incurably odd about it. For what sparks off the whole long tragedy is not a spontaneous surge of passion between the couple. The passion has to be artificially engineered by a love potion, and, what's more, a potion which is drunk by the wrong couple. Brewed by Yseut's mother to be given to her daughter and King Mark of Cornwall to be drunk on their wedding night, during the voyage to Cornwall by mistake Yseut's maid hands it to Tristan who drinks it and passes it on to Yseut who also drinks. Béroul tells us that 'neither knew that the potion held for them a lifetime of suffering and hardship and that it was to cause their destruction and their death'.[21] Thus at the very beginning of romantic love, we are told that it is a kind of *mistake*. This ominous intimation is to reverberate down the centuries into our own day.

'Tristan drinking the love potion' from Le Livre de Messire Lancelot, by Gautier de Moap, 1470

Even Yseut's deceits pale beside the ingenious fabrications of Fenice (Phoenix) in Chrétien de Troyes's romance *Cligès*. Fenice is besotted with the irresistible young knight who gives his name to the tale, but she is married off willy-nilly to his uncle the Emperor. To avoid yielding her virginity to this unwanted spouse, her maid Thessala gives him a magic potion. As soon as the Emperor has drunk it, Thessala tells her, 'they will share the same bed, but no matter how often she is with him he will be as safe as if there is a wall between them. "But don't let it upset you if he takes his pleasure of you in his dreams, for when he's fast asleep he'll have his sport with you, and will firmly believe he took his pleasure while awake. He'll never suspect it was a dream, deceit or lie".'[22] This useful drug does its stuff, but Fenice remains miserable, and she concocts a further plan with Thessala to steal the urine of a dying woman and present it as her own, so that she can convincingly fake her own death and be buried in a tomb specially constructed to allow her to escape and join Cligès for a life of uninterrupted sexual bliss in a secluded tower. Chrétien recounts these extraordinary manoeuvres with total sympathy and not a hint of disapproval. These romances are soaked in transgression – it is the adultery that generates the whole drama – but they are also driven, to a remarkable degree, by the ruthless cunning of women in love. Female agency is flourishing in the fiction of the twelfth century.

But what makes Chrétien remarkable is not so much the ingenuity of his plots as the pulsating richness of the interior lives of his characters. As C. S. Lewis points out, 'the space devoted to action that goes forward only in the souls of his characters was probably beyond all medieval precedent. He was one of the first explorers of the human heart, and is therefore rightly to be numbered among the fathers of the novel of sentiment.'[23] Entire pages of *Cligès* and Chrétien's Lancelot romance, *The Knight of the Cart*, and his *Erec and Enide* are indeed filled with the clashing of indomitable knights and with the elaborate costumes and processions of tournaments. But even more space is given over to the self-explorations of hero and heroine, the two sexes treated in emotional terms as equally suffering and sensitive souls. In *Cligès*, for example, five pages, 3,000 words or more, are devoted to the tortured ruminations of Alexander and Soredamors (= She Who is Gilded by Love), before either of them dares confess their love.[24] Later on in the same romance, the second pair of lovers, Cligès and Fenice, are equally tongue-tied at length:[25]

'... both were so fearful of being rejected that they dared not open their hearts. ... Yet in spite of this the eyes of each revealed their secret thoughts, had they only known to look! Cautiously they conversed with their eyes, but they were so fearful of their tongues that they dared not put into words the love that tormented them. It is no wonder that Fenice did not begin, for a maiden should be reticent and shy. But what made Cligès hesitate? What was he waiting for? He, whose every deed was emboldened by her, afraid of her alone? God! What was the source of this fear, that caused him to cower only before a maiden, a weak and fearful creature, simple and shy?'

Or take Lancelot's trance-like state when a girl gives him Guinevere's comb with the bright beautiful strands of her golden hair still entangled in its teeth: 'first he removed the hair, being careful not to break a single strand. Never will the eye of man see anything receive such reverence. For he began to adore the hair, touching it a hundred thousand times to his eye, his mouth, his forehead and his cheeks. He expressed his joy in every way imaginable and felt himself most happy and rewarded. He placed the hair on his breast near his heart, between his shirt and his skin.'[26]

Chrétien is the first poet to introduce us to Camelot, to Lancelot and Guinevere, to Perceval (another Welshman, Wagner's Parzival), to Gawain and the rest of the characters who have haunted Arthurian romance ever since, from Sir Thomas Malory to Richard Wagner. But even more, if anyone can be said to be the originator of the modern love story, from *La Traviata* to Mills & Boon, it is Chrétien de Troyes.

What he also introduces us to is full-blown female sexuality (known to the ancients, too, of course, but never before treated with such candour or intensity). In *The Knight of the Cart*, the Queen is told, falsely, that the King's men have murdered Lancelot on her account. She breaks down in desolate anguish: 'Ah God! Will I be forgiven this murder, this sin? Never! All the rivers and the sea will dry up first! Oh misery! How it would have brought me comfort and healing if I had held him in my arms once before he died. How? Yes, quite naked next to him, in order to enjoy him fully. Since he is dead, I am wicked not to kill myself.'[27]

The theme is treated even more explicitly in the *Roman de la Rose*, the most popular of all medieval romances (the number of surviving manuscripts far exceeds those of Chaucer's *Canterbury Tales*). Here, for example, is the 'Advice of the Old Woman' to would-be lovers:

'And when they go to work, they should both exert themselves so conscientiously and to such good effect that both together experience pleasure before the work is finished; they should wait for each other so that they may come to a climax together. One should not abandon the other, nor should either cease his voyage until they reach port together; then they will have delight in all its fullness.

'If she feels no pleasure, she should pretend to enjoy the experience and simulate all the signs that she knows are appropriate to pleasure; in this way, he will imagine that she is glad of it, when in fact she cares not a fig.'[28]

The *Roman de la Rose* is an extraordinary work, nearly 22,000 lines long, or 335 densely printed pages in Frances Horgan's brilliant translation for Oxford World Classics (1994). The first 4,000 lines were composed by Guillaume de Lorris sometime in the first half of the thirteenth century, the poem being edited and completed 40 years later, in a very different spirit, by the mordant polymath Jean de Meun. Part of it was translated into English as *The Romaunt of the Rose* by Geoffrey Chaucer, or someone in Chaucer's circle, but it is Jean de Meun who has left his inimitable stamp on the whole enterprise. The poem is a gigantic allegory. The young man who sets off to pluck the rose from the enchanted garden, outwitting all its defenders, remains unnamed throughout, and all the characters he meets with are Qualities not Persons: Courtesy, Idleness, Fair-seeming, Pleasant Conversation, plus the God of Love, who shoots the Narrator with his five deadly arrows: 'He has inflicted five wounds on my body, and their pain will never be relieved unless you give me the rose-bud that is more beautifully shaped than the others: it is my death and my life and there is nothing that I desire more.'[29] The Narrator tells us that 'No one has suffered who has not tried love; do not imagine that anyone who has not loved knows what anguish is.'[30] And what does he gain by it? 'The pain is immeasurable, and the joy lasts only a short time.'[31] Echoes here of Lord Chesterfield's earthy verdict on sex 500 years later: 'The position is ridiculous, the pleasure momentary and the expense damnable.'

But the Narrator is hooked nonetheless. The figure of Reason attempts in vain to dissuade him from the quest, by using arguments which would have been familiar to the ancients: 'Love is a mental illness afflicting two persons of opposite sex in close proximity who are both free agents. It comes upon people through a burning desire, born of disordered perceptions, to embrace and to kiss and to seek carnal gratification.'[32]

C. S. Lewis, in his thorough study of the *Roman*, is worried that the poem may not strike modern readers as irresistibly as it did the romance-hungry public of the thirteenth century: 'We have to reckon not only with unfamiliar erotic psychology, but with the unfamiliarity of allegory in general; and, to speak plainly, the art of reading allegory is as dead as the art of writing it.'[33] I am not so sure. Even today, the *Roman* is curiously alluring, so light on its feet, so innocent seeming, so naughty, and in parts so beautiful. We are still easily transported along with the Narrator into this enchanted garden of songbirds, all minutely listed, and all familiar to us today: 'in one place were nightingales, in another jays and starlings, and elsewhere were great flocks of wrens and turtledoves, goldfinches and swallows, larks and titmice. In another place were assembled calandra larks, tired from the effort of outdoing one another in song; there were blackbirds and thrushes, trying to sing more loudly than all the other birds, and elsewhere parrots and many birds throughout the groves and woods where they lived, taking pleasure in their lovely singing.'[34] Not to mention the flautists in the garden, and the jongleurs and the ladies performing with their castanets and tambourines. Or the considerable psychological insights that Guillaume slips into this beguiling pastoral. Lewis says that 'it is arguable that Guillaume, even more than Chrétien, deserves to be called the founder of the sentimental novel. A love story of considerable subtlety and truth is hidden in the *Romance*. It would be a work not of creation, but of mere ordinary dexterity, to strip off the allegory and retell this story in the form of a novel.'[35] But, he rightly argues, this would not be an improvement. We could try renaming Courtesy and Idleness with familiar medieval names such as Louis or Christine, but we might not lose ourselves so easily as we do in Guillaume's allegorical realm. Rather than acting as a barrier to our pleasure, it is, I think, the allegory that helps to seduce us.

In *The Waning of the Middle Ages*, Johan Huizinga declares: 'Few books have exercised a more profound and enduring influence on the life of any period than the *Romaunt of the Rose*.'[36] Its popularity lasted for at least two centuries, and it helped to determine the conception of love, and especially in Jean de Meun's continuation it did serious damage to the Church's hold on the popular imagination. 'By blending with Christian conceptions of eternal bliss the boldest praise of voluptuousness, he had taught numerous generations a very ambiguous attitude towards Faith.'[37] The sexual motif is placed in the centre of love poetry, but enveloped by symbolism and mystery and presented in a guise of saintliness. 'It is impossible to imagine a more deliberate defiance of the Christian ideal.'[38]

No wonder Jean Gerson, the redoubtable Chancellor of the University of Paris, again and again denounced the pernicious influence 'of the vicious romaunt of the rose'. If he had possessed the sole copy, and it was worth a thousand pounds, he would rather burn it than sell it to be published.[39] What helped to give Jean de Meun's work such a mesmerizing grip were, paradoxically, his long digressions on psychology, biology and philosophy, making the poem almost an encyclopaedia as well as a romance. He was interested in everything. His summary of the arguments on free will versus necessity would pass muster in a philosophy seminar today and are certainly easier reading than the original version on offer in Boethius' *Consolations of Philosophy* (Jean translated Boethius into French and also the letters of Héloise and Abelard, the first great erotic correspondence in Western history). His insatiable curiosity reaches into the everyday, so that at times the later pages of the *Roman* read like a modern lifestyle supplement. In the person of the Old Woman, he offers advice on bad breath, table manners and make-up (how to conceal spots), also on when it is permissible to go begging, or to use words like 'testicles' in company, or when it is proper to weep. Above all, Jean, through his allegorical characters, gives an entirely naturalistic, non-moral view of sex in all its aspects.

The Old Woman, for example, writes of domestic violence and why women put up with it in a way that is recognizable to any reader of newspaper confessions today:

'Women have very poor judgment, and I was a true woman. I never loved a man who loved me, but if this wretch had hurt my shoulder or cracked my skull, I tell you I would have thanked him for it. However much he beat me, I would still have had him fall upon me, for he was so good at making peace, whatever hurt he might have done me. However badly he treated me, beating me and dragging me about, hurting my face and bruising it, he would always beg my forgiveness before he left. However humiliating his language to me, he would always sue for peace and then take me to bed, and so there was peace and harmony between us once more. And so he had me on the end of a rope, the false, thieving traitor, because he was so good in bed.'[40]

In Guillaume's section of the poem, the erotic metaphor of the rose with its tightly folded buds is kept within the limits of discretion. But as the quest draws near its conclusion, Jean's metaphors go into a kind of allegorical overdrive, unleashing what can only be described as a rhapsody in praise of rough sex:

'Plough, barons, plough for God's sake, and restore your lineage. Nothing can restore it if you do not put your minds to ploughing vigorously. Tuck your clothes up nicely in front of you as though to take the air, or go quite naked if you like, but do not get too cold or too hot. Lift the stilts of your ploughs with your bare hands, support them firmly on your arms and make an effort to thrust the ploughshare straight along the right path, the better to penetrate the furrow. As for the horses in front, for God's sake do not let them slow down, but spur them on harshly and give them the most violent blows you possibly can, if you want to plough deeply.'[41]

The final plucking of the rose is a violent business, prolonged over several lurid pages of which I must give some samples (simply to talk of Jean de Meun's 'obscene' or 'pornographic' imagination does not convey the full effect of it):

'... having done so much and wandered so afar with my unshod staff, I knelt without delay, full of agility and vigour, between the two fair pillars, for I was consumed with desire to worship at the lovely and venerable shrine with devout and reverent heart ...

'... I partly raised the curtain that screened the relics, and drawing near to the image that I knew to be close to the sanctuary, I kissed it devoutly. Next I wanted to sheathe my staff by putting it into the aperture while the scrip hung outside. I tried to thrust it in at one go, but it came out and I tried again, to no avail because it sprang out every time and nothing I did could make it go in. There was a barrier within which I could feel but could not see ...

'...when I could not immediately break the barrier, I struggled so hard and with such violence that I was drenched with sweat and I was, I believe, quite as weary as Hercules ...

'I know at least that at that time the path had not been opened up or trodden. Therefore I forced my way into it, for it was the only entrance, in order duly to pluck the rose-bud.'[42]

After all that (and there is a lot more of it on the same lines), the Narrator wins his bright red rose. 'Then it was day and I awoke.'[43] Phew! The reader, too, can be forgiven for wiping a few beads of sweat from his or her brow. Notice that, even at the extreme moments of the Narrator's efforts, the religious imagery of 'shrine', 'sanctuary' and 'relics' is still being deployed.

About a century after Jean de Meun completed his lion's share of the *Roman*, the young Geoffrey Chaucer collaborated on translating it into what we call Middle English. We know that he was part of the team, because he tells us so in his *Legend of Good Women*. Nobody is quite sure which section of the text that has come down was his work, or even if *The Romaunt of the Rose* is his version at all. But he certainly picked up a huge measure of Jean de Meun's irony, salty language and capacity to surprise.

Although Chaucer continues to enjoy an imperishable reputation as the Father of English literature, it is still easy to underestimate his tragic depths and take him at face value as a teller of rollicking romances and satires. *Troilus and Criseyde*, his long verse romance, is immediately enchanting. Who can forget the first appearance at the temple of Criseyde, the widowed Trojan princess?

> ... among these, in widow's black, and yet
> Unequalled in her beauty, came Criseyde;
> Just as an A now heads our alphabet,
> She stood unmatchable; she glorified
> And gladdened all that crowded at her side ...
> And yet she stood there, humble and alone
> Behind the others, in a little space
> Close to the door, for modesty ...[44]

Like all memorable beauties, Criseyde had one peculiar feature:

> Often enough it was her way to wear
> The heavy tresses of her shining hair
> Over her collar, down her back, behind.
> These with a thread of gold she used to bind.
> Save for the fact her eyebrows joined together,
> There was no fault that I can recognize;
> Her eyes they say, were clear as summer weather.[45]

Criseyde is a monobrow, perhaps the first in world literature. More to the point, she seems to be as virtuous as she is beautiful. And when the fine, upstanding knight Troilus falls in love with her as soon as he sees her, she is slow to accept his advances and also reluctant to give up 'her darling liberty' and her good reputation.

But the quiet tenor of her life is rudely interrupted. Her father Calchas has defected to the Greeks, and at his insistence Criseyde is to be traded for the Trojan Antenor, who is held captive at the Greek court. After finally persuading her to let him make love to her, Troilus tries to forestall this prisoner exchange by suggesting that they run away together, but she refuses because it would ruin her reputation. She does, however, promise to return to Troy to see Troilus within ten days, but of course she is powerless to escape her Greek escort Diomede, who immediately begins to make advances to her as well.

Troilus is desperate. He haunts the gates of Troy and her shut-up palace in the hope of seeing her again. Quite soon, however, Criseyde accepts her new situation and accepts Diomede, but without any illusions about what people will think of her betrayal of Troilus:

> No good, alas, of me to the world's end,
> Will ever now be written, said or sung.
> Not one fair word! No book will be my friend ...[46]

The distraught Troilus plunges into battle, determined to seek out Diomede and kill him. Despite repeated encounters, he never succeeds and is eventually himself killed by the spear of Achilles.

It is an affecting tragedy, but to the eyes of modern readers it is much more than a tale of sundered lovers and the fickleness of women. For though Criseyde thinks Troilus a handsome fellow, she does not immediately fall in love with him, as he does with her, and she is quite prepared to remain a widow for the foreseeable future. It is her uncle Pandarus who devises the nasty trick which brings them together, by staging a business meeting at his house to discuss how to protect Criseyde's widow's estate from fraudsters. Pandarus then coaches Troilus to pretend to be dying in his bedroom and manages to persuade Criseyde that only her kisses can revive him. Even then, the actual scene of their lovemaking is rather repellent:

> What is there for the hapless lark to do
> When taken in the sparrowhawk's fierce foot ...
> Criseyde, on feeling herself taken thus ...
> In the enfolding arms of Troilus
> Lay trembling, like an aspen leaf she shook ...
> And then this Troilus began to strain
> Her in his arms and whispered, 'Sweetest, say,
> Are you not caught? We are alone, we twain,
> Now yield yourself, there is no other way.'[47]

Only then does Criseyde begin to respond and her terror abate '... so, free of all alarms, / They wound and bound each other in their arms ... Criseyde, now that her fears were still, / Opened her heart to him and showed her will.'[48]

There follows a remarkable erotic stanza about their lovemaking:

Her delicate arms, her back so straight and soft,
Her slender flanks, flesh-soft and smooth and white
He then began to stroke, and blessed as oft
Her snowy throat, her breasts so round and slight,
And in this heaven taking his delight,
A thousand, thousand times he kissed her too,
For rapture scarcely knowing what to do.[49]

But their eventual mutual delight does not disguise the fact that she has been tricked into it. She has yielded to 'pity sex'. It is thus ultimately a tragedy not of love thwarted by social pressures, but of woman's powerlessness in the face of exploitation by powerful men. It's pretty much an early case of 'Me Too'. Whatever you choose to call it, the story is a dark one.

Chaucer is so often subtler than he seems. *The Canterbury Tales* opens with 'The Knight's Tale', which is usually described as 'a classic courtly romance'. In the Prologue, the Knight himself is famously called 'a verray, parfit, gentil, knight' ('verray' meaning 'true'), a phrase which has become proverbial and is even today deployed in obituaries of worthy men, and most readers have taken this description at face value. But is the Knight really 'a man of unsullied ideals', as alleged by Michael Murphy in *Canterbury Quintet*?[50]

Terry Jones, who was also a considerable medieval scholar as well as a star of *Monty Python*, gives us a very different picture in *Chaucer's Knight* (1980). In this contrarian study, which has convinced many keen Chaucerians, such as the novelist Anthony Powell,[51] Jones points out that all the engagements listed to the Knight's credit – Alexandria, Lithuania, Prussia, Algeciras and so on – were in fact massacres carried out by brutal gangs of wandering mercenaries. The Knight was obviously prepared to fight for anyone who would pay him, including heathen sultans. Conspicuously absent from his battle honours are any of the great English victories of the time, such as Crécy and Poitiers. It's like chalking up one's service at My Lai, Srebrenica, Chechnya and Congo.

As Powell points out, 'the Knight is an ominous figure in Chaucer's picture of the world round him, with its Lollards, peasant revolts, bands of mercenaries, the last in certain cases exceeding in size a medieval national army.'[52] Nobody could be less like the reassuring figure of a decent country gentleman which modern scholars have so often misread him as.

Not merely is the Knight a shabby thug, without loyalty or a coat of arms to his back; his Tale is a sour inversion of the classic courtly romance. The cousins Palamon and Arcite are discovered lying wounded on the battlefield and imprisoned by Duke Theseus, where they both catch glimpses of and instantly fall in love with Theseus's sister-in-law Emily. Far from competing for her hand in loving brotherhood, as they do in the original Boccaccio tale which Chaucer used as his source, each claims bitterly that 'I saw her first.' They swear undying hatred for each other and fight ferociously until they are both wounded, Arcite fatally, and Emily is more or less thrust into the arms of the surviving Palamon. The end is decorated with philosophical reflections, which only highlight what a sour tale it is, although it has taken six centuries for a reader as sharp as Terry Jones to point out quite how sour.

'The Knight's Tale' is followed by the rough intervention of the Miller, a 16-stone drunk, who insists on telling his tale next. His contribution has become a byword for bawdiness, with the lovers thrusting their bare arses out of the bedroom window, one of them letting out an enormous fart and being branded with a hot ploughshare for his pains. But seen from another point of view, 'The Miller's Tale' is an altogether more innocent affair than the Knight's, with its own lyrical passages such as the description of Alison, the pea-brained carpenter's saucy wife:

She was a fair young wife, her body as slender
As any weasel's, and as soft and tender;

> She used to wear a girdle of striped silk;
> Her apron was white as morning milk
> Over her loins, all gusseted and pleated.
> White was her smock, embroidery repeated
> In a pattern on the collar, front and back.

Alison, too, has memorable eyebrows:

> And she had plucked her eyebrows into bows,
> Slenderly arched they were, and black as sloes;
> And a more truly blissful sight to see
> She was than blossom on a cherry-tree.[53]

There is a lawless gaiety about 'The Miller's Tale'. In order to have his way with Alison, Nicholas, the gallant harpist-astrologer, deludes the poor carpenter by claiming to have predicted an impeding Noah-scale Flood which they can only escape by taking refuge in tubs hung in the eaves, from which implausible scam the series of misadventures follow. The contrast between the Miller's and the Knight's Tales is only one of the bewildering mood switches in the book. You never know what Chaucer has up his sleeve next. He is capable of being both affectingly sentimental and bitingly anti-sentimental within the space of a single tale. Only Laurence Sterne in *Tristram Shandy* manages to pull off the same trick quite so effortlessly.

But then the whole tradition of courtly romance is never as stereotyped or as single-voiced as posterity imagines. No tale that has come down to us is more endearing than *Aucassin and Nicolette*, by an unknown author working in northern France at roughly the time that the troubadours were singing in Provence. The author uniquely calls it a *chante-fable*, that is, a prose narrative interspersed with singable verse. Uniquely, too, we even have the music for it, possibly the first score for a musical comedy to survive. You might think we would be in for a typical chivalric romance. But from the start, our expectations are subverted. Yes, Aucassin is a handsome young fellow 'with laughing grey eyes', and he is the heir to Count Garin of Beaucaire, but as soon as he sees Nicolette, a Saracen prisoner, who also has laughing grey eyes among her other beauties, he is 'so smitten by all-conquering love that he would neither be a knight, nor take up arms, nor go a-journeying, nor do any of those things he ought'.[54] In total contrast to her pacifist admirer, Nicolette is a resourceful tomboy. She is held captive in a tower, but the singing of the nightingale makes her think of her love for Aucassin and she instantly knots her towels and bed linen together to make an escape rope, then clambers over walls and up ditches, covered with scratches and blood, to reach Aucassin to tell him how much she loves him. After her brief secret visit, Aucassin gallops after her into the woods, but, typically clumsy, falls off his horse and dislocates his shoulder – which Nicolette quickly manipulates back into place and heals the bruise with a poultice made of a strip from her shift. He puts her in front of him on his horse, and off they gallop together, kissing and embracing as they ride, until after many adventures they reach the Castle of Torelore or Topsy-Turvey – where the King is lying in childbirth and the Queen has gone off to lead her troops in battle. On arriving at the battlefield, Aucassin discovers that the battle is being fought with rotten crab apples and eggs and fresh cheese as missiles. Now at last Aucassin puts his hand to his sword, wades into this weird melee and starts slaying the enemy in numbers, until the King appears, having given birth, and tells him to stop it, saying, 'Sir, you have already overdone it. It is not our custom here to kill each other.' Aucassin and Nicolette have a blissful time together in Topsy-Turvey Land, until a Saracen fleet appears, takes the castle by storm and seizes Nicolette, taking her prisoner back to Carthage, where she turns out to be the daughter of the King. Naturally the Saracens want to marry her to one of their own princes, but once more Nicolette escapes, this time disguising herself as a male minstrel. She strums her viol all the way back to Beaucaire, where this extraordinary tale of gender-swapping and battles fought with vegetables finds its appointed happy ending.

You might think that this surreal pacifist fable would be out of place at the height of the Crusades. But as Terry Jones points out, anti-crusade and anti-war feeling were rather common among Chaucer and his friends. The poet John Gower was emphatic on the subject:

> And for to slay the heathen all,
> I know not what good there might fall,
> No matter how much blood be shed.
> This find I written: how Christ bid
> That no man should another slay ...[55]

One of the Twelve Conclusions that the Lollards nailed to the door of St Paul's was that 'Knights, who run to the "hethenesse" [the heathen equivalent of Christendom] to get themselves a name for slaying men are greatly blamed by the Prince of Peace.' The same lesson is taught by Chaucer's own 'Tale of Melibeus', and by John Wycliffe, too: 'Lord! what honour is it to a knight that he kills many men?'[56]

By Chaucer's day, chivalry and the crusading movement were already beginning to seem rather obsolescent, and open to mockery by the rising middle class (who also resented the expense). Of course, the most celebrated of all satires on the pretensions and delusions of the Crusaders does not appear until more than two centuries later. Miguel de Cervantes's novel *The Ingenious Gentleman Don Quixote of La Mancha* was originally published in two parts, in 1605 and 1615. The book has had a glorious afterlife. It has been translated into English at least 26 times. It is frequently described as the first modern novel and was voted the best work of fiction ever by a panel of 100 celebrated authors quizzed by the Nobel Institute in 2002. Above all, it has been credited with destroying the whole world of Spanish chivalry by the power of its ridicule.

For those who see it as the mission of literature to destroy our illusions about the world, it is the classic, the greatest ever exercise in debunking, and hence the unmistakable precursor to the modernism of the Flaubert tradition. Gustave Flaubert himself adored the book ever since he had had a children's edition read to him: In a letter of 1852, he wrote: 'Je retrouve toutes mes origines dans le livre que je savais par coeur avant de savoir lire, *Don Quichotte*.' When he set out to depict and mercilessly deride the romantic illusions of Emma Bovary, he always had Cervantes's foolish knight in mind.

And yet. Is *Don Quixote* really as original or as great as all that? Hadn't much of the debunking work already been done, back in Chaucer's day? Even in backward-looking Spain, chivalry had been a dead letter for a century or more. And doesn't Cervantes's exact contemporary William Shakespeare do it all just as well, or better? There is a depth of sympathy in the character of the cowardly pisshead, Sir John Falstaff, which is rather hard to find in the portrayal of Quixote. Where in Cervantes is there anything to match Mistress Quickly's account of Falstaff's death towards the beginning of *Henry V*:

'... he's in Arthur's bosom, if ever man went to Arthur's bosom. A' made a finer end and went away an it had been any christom child; a' parted even just between twelve and one, even at the turning o' the tide: for after I saw him fumble with the sheets and play with flowers and smile upon his fingers' ends, I knew there was but one way; for his nose was as sharp as a pen, and a' babbled of green fields.'[57]

For all its delights, *Don Quixote* is the product of a harder age. The ferocious giants whom Quixote attacks turn out to be workaday windmills, new technology in Cervantes's day as they are again in our own. His ladylove Dorothea is in reality a slaughterhouse worker who is a dab hand at salting pork. Cervantes's great gift is to disenchant us in the most enchanting way, which particularly appeals to literary modernists. *Don Quixote*, in fact, is not the first but the last peak in the chain reaction against the First Sentimental Revolution – that reaction which each such revolution provokes and which we shall see repeated in future centuries. Romance does not die of its own accord. It has to be killed off. And what Cervantes administered was the *coup de grâce*.

PASSIONATE ABOUT THE PASSION

But romantic love between a man and a woman is only half the story of the First Sentimental Revolution. The other half is the overflowing of human passion into the story of the Passion of Christ. That boundless *expressiveness* which we have seen displayed in the erotic realm flowered just as freely in the religious sphere, too. Nor are the two unconnected. There is an undeniable interpenetration of language and thought between them, and it is an entirely conscious process. Jean de Meun knows perfectly well what he is doing when he uses the sacred vocabulary – sanctuary, shrine, pilgrimage – to describe the sexual pursuit. So, a couple of centuries later, does St Teresa of Ávila when she uses the language of romantic love to make us understand the depth of her passion for Jesus. The Freudians had a field day uncovering her unconscious motives and her sublimated sexual urges. But 'Saint Teresa was unaware of nothing.'[58] In her girlhood, she doted upon the romances of chivalry, and once thought of writing one herself in collaboration with her brother. As Gaston Etchegoyen put it in *L'Amour divin: essai sur les sources de sainte Thérèse*:[59] 'In Spain, the authors of romances of chivalry display the same realism as those of treatises on mysticism, sacrificing a sense of the marvellous in favour of a more familiar and moving intimacy, as they tend to treat the human and the divine on one plane, either by contemplating the divine from a secular standpoint or by giving the human a divine interpretation. Above all, divine and courtly love encourage one another to a similar heroic notion of moral obligation, of action, and of faith.'[60] See, too, how the Arthurian romances take on a Christian tinge with each retelling. When we first encounter the 'grail' in Chrétien's *Perceval*, it seems to be a fairly ordinary serving dish, worth mentioning only because there was a holy wafer in it. By the turn of the century, it has become the Holy Grail, brought to England by Joseph of Arimathea on his legendary visit to Britain. Then it becomes the chalice from which Jesus drank at the Last Supper, and the ultimate object of knightly quest, its aura undiminished to this day, as all sorts of places from Valencia to Aberystwyth claim that their Grail is the real thing.

Just as men become emotionally and erotically alive to the women in their lives – and vice versa – so Christians become personally attached to the central personages in their faith story, and exhibit an increasingly fervent devotion to them as individuals. The sufferings of Christ's Passion are now felt – and depicted – with an intensity quite unknown in the first millennium of Christianity. Colin Morris points out that the typical crucifix of the Dark Ages shows Christ alive and upright. His eyes are open, his arms straight and he shows no sign of suffering. 'It is a remarkable fact that in the first thousand years of the Church's history, years in which death was often close and threatening to most men, the figure of the dead Christ was almost never depicted. The crucifix was conceived as an expression of the triumph of Christ, the Lord of all things ... "He looks like a Greek God, Great Pan rather than the Man of Sorrows".'[61] In fact, it is only in the eleventh and twelfth centuries that he begins to be called the Man of Sorrows, although that title has good scriptural authority, being drawn from the foretelling of the Messiah in Isaiah 53.3: 'He is despised and rejected of men: a man of sorrows, and acquainted with grief: and we hid as it were our faces from him; he was despised and we esteemed him not.'

For the next 500 years, though, the agonies of Christ dying on the Cross, his gaping wounds, his tortured face, his lolling head, are portrayed with ever increasing force, reaching their climax, I think, in Matthias Grünewald's Isenheim altarpiece (1512–16). There the crucified Jesus is depicted, not only with the cruel nails piercing his hands and feet but with ghastly plague sores down his body. The monks at the monastery of St Anthony at Isenheim specialized in the treatment of sufferers from the plague and other grievous skin diseases. Nothing could make it plainer that, during his time on earth, Jesus was one of us, vulnerable to the worst of mortal ills. Nothing could have been further from the view of Christ risen in glory which prevailed in the early Church, for example, in the wonderful sixth-century mosaic in Ravenna, where a radiant, beardless young Jesus smiles down from the dome, looking as though he had never known a moment's unhappiness.

As a student in Freiburg 60 years ago, I cycled across the Rhine to nearby Colmar where the altarpiece now hangs. I have never seen a work of art more deeply affecting or more unashamedly gruesome. The sickly, pale flesh of the dying Christ against the darkened sky of Golgotha afflicts you in every sense. But this dark vision is itself, in artistic terms, a dying one. For Grünewald's work is as remote from the new classicism of the Renaissance as it is from the triumphalism of the Early Church, as equidistant from the mosaics of Ravenna as it is from the serenity of Raphael (1483–1520), although Raphael was almost an exact contemporary of Grünewald (1470–1528).

The Isenheim altarpiece by Matthias Grünewald, 1512–16

The Isenheim altarpiece also shows the Virgin Mary beside the Cross, ashen-faced and fainting with grief into the arms of St John. It is also in the early years of the twelfth century that the cult of the Virgin really begins to take off. From this period, she begins to be called *Regina Coeli*, the Queen of Heaven. And when the poets have cleared their throats, she becomes the subject of ever more adoring odes. No poem devoted solely to the Virgin is known until the second half of the thirteenth century. It's Petrarch who first devotes his later poems to Our Lady instead of his lady, to Mary rather than to Laura.[62]

The human story of the Nativity begins to take centre stage, as it does in the richly sentimental and poignant paintings being made at the same time in Flanders and Florence. That single verse in St Luke's gospel provides the setting for a thousand Madonna and Childs and also myriad odes to the Virgin: 'And she brought forth her first-born child, and wrapped him in swaddling clothes, and laid him in a manger; because there was no room for them in the inn.'[63] Among the earliest poems in *The Oxford Book of English Verse* and Dame Helen Gardner's *Faber Book of Religious Verse* are lyrics dedicated to Mary, all dating from the 1300s: *A Hymn to the Virgin* – 'lovely flower of all things, *Rosa sine spina*'; Friar William Herebert's *Orison to the Blessed Virgin*, one of the earliest Middle English poems by a named author; and *Our Lady's Song* (1375), which is sung by Mary to her baby:

Jesu, sweete son dear,
On porful [wretched] bed liest thou here,
And that me grieveth sore,
For thy cradle is as a bere [byre];
Ox and ass be thy fere [companions],
Weep I may therefore.

In this song, Mary 'has no clout nor cloth' to swaddle her baby in:

But lay thy feet to my pap,
And wite [keep] thee from the cold.

New doctrines and institutions spring up spontaneously to honour the Virgin in ways that the Church had never countenanced before and didn't much like the look of now.

At Lyons in 1140, the canons set up their own Feast of the Immaculate Conception of Our Lady, defying the vociferous protests of St Bernard of Clairvaux against 'this new feast of which the custom of the Church knows nothing, which reason does not approve, and that tradition does not authorise'.[64] A hundred years later, Thomas Aquinas was equally hostile, arguing that 'if Mary had been conceived without sin, she would not have needed to be redeemed by Jesus Christ'.⁶⁵ But the arguments from orthodoxy were futile. If the Church was to counter this dangerous new cult of Eros, it had to go along with the popular veneration of the Virgin. As Johan Huizinga remarks with barely concealed disdain, religious customs tended to multiply in an almost mechanical way. A special office was instituted for every detail of the worship of the Virgin. There were particular Masses, later abolished by the Church, in honour of her piety, of her seven sorrows, of all her festivals, of her sisters, the two other Marys, not to mention all the saints in Our Lord's family tree. In 1233, seven cloth merchants in Florence left their patrician families to live a life of poverty and penance on nearby Monte Senario, dedicating themselves to the service of the Virgin. The Servites, as they came to be called, prospered, despite the efforts of Pope Innocent V to suppress the order. Their mission responded so exactly to the sentimental adoration of the Virgin that there was no use pointing out the lack of justification in Holy Writ for any such cult, let alone the amazing assortment of saints who came to be venerated in her wake.

As Émile Mâle tells us in *The Gothic Image*, 'The people never wearied of seeing their protectors and friends, for they felt to be on more familiar terms with them than they could be with an omnipotent and far-off God.' All human life came to be represented in that great company deemed worthy to sit at the right hand of God: Popes like St Gregory, knights-errant like St George, kings like St Louis, but also shoemakers like St Crispin, beggars like St Alexis, not to mention shepherds, carters, cattle drovers, serving men of all kinds. There was even a canonized lawyer. The hymn in honour of St Yves registered good-humoured surprise: 'A lawyer and not a thief, a thing that amazed the populace.'⁶⁶

The saints who were honoured were primarily perceived as friends and helpers, and neighbours, too, 'people like us'. The mystic Julian of Norwich wrote of St John of Beverley, 'our lorde shewed hym full hyly in comfort of us for homelynesse, and brought to my mynde how he is a kind neyghbour and of our knowing'.⁶⁷ They were often seen as country people themselves, wearing sensible boots and floppy hats, or accompanied by farm animals, like St Anthony with his pig. Sensible Church leaders left it to local clergy and local people to promote their own saints. Sir Thomas More said, 'I believe this devotion so planted by God's own hand in the hearts of the whole church, that is to wit, not the clergy only, but the whole congregation of all Christian people, that if the spirituality were of the mind to leave it, yet would not the temporality suffer it.'⁶⁸

The guilds were free to choose their patron saints on the basis of the slightest connection. The porters recognized St Christopher because he had borne Christ on his shoulders; perfume sellers chose Mary Magdalen because she poured a vase of precious ointment over the Saviour's feet. Perhaps the most tenuous but charming connection was that of the sawyers who celebrated the feast of the Visitation, because on that occasion the Virgin and St Elizabeth bent towards one another as do two workmen when using a saw.⁶⁹ If you were looking for a patron saint, you had only to consult the pages of *The Golden Legend*, the bestselling compilation of saints' lives by Jacobus de Voragine, the thirteenth-century Archbishop of Genoa, which was translated into virtually every European language, and acted as a sort of mail-order catalogue for choosing your own patron.⁷⁰ The Church authorities were in two minds about their cults. There was undeniably something dangerously do-it-yourself and a frivolous tinge to these cults, but if they brought ordinary working people to the Mass, they had to be tolerated.

The cult of the saints provided opportunities to appeal to women and speak to their concerns and anxieties, nowhere better than in the marvellous series of paintings over the Lady Altar in the church at Ranworth, Norfolk, so full of colour, with all the sinuous, flowing rhythms of international Gothic, justly known in Germany as the 'weicher Stil', the soft style. It was the custom after childbirth for women, when they came to be churched, to present themselves and their babies before the principal image or altar of Our Lady, and to light a candle in thanksgiving for their safe delivery. In *The Stripping of the Altars*, his great prolonged elegy for the vanished pre-Reformation England, Eamon Duffy takes us through the iconography of the Lady Altar. All four of its paintings deal with childbirth, portraying the extended family of Jesus: first the three daughters of St Anne – the Blessed Virgin with the Christ child, then, next to her Mary Salome with her sons, the apostles James and John, and on the other side of the Virgin, Mary Cleophas with her four sons, James and Joses (or Joseph), Simon and Jude. And completing the quartet there is St Margaret of Antioch, who burst out of the dragon's belly while in prison, making her the patron saint of women in childbirth, or 'our lady's prison', as it was often called.[71] There was a strong cult of St Anne in Norfolk. With her three marriages and her three daughters, whose daughters in turn gave birth to six Apostles and Our Saviour, she symbolized fertility as well as family life. Duffy points out that the figures in the painting are not merely sacred emblems. They are mothers and children of flesh and blood: one of the toddlers blows bubbles from a pipe, another clutches a toy windmill.[72] It is hard to imagine a more intimate and sympathetic illustration of the intercessory power of the saints.

THIS VALE OF TEARS

What also united the sacred and profane realms in the later Middle Ages was the recourse to tears, amounting to an addiction. We have seen the lovers in the romances weeping a storm in every kind of situation, when they fall in love, when they fall out of love, when they are separated, when they are reunited, tears of joy, tears of frustration, tears of despair. The same was true in the hour of death, and in the long rituals of mourning and commemoration that followed. Seneca's warnings against excessive mourning were utterly forgotten, the Stoics' insistence on controlling your emotions seemed hard-hearted. People wept at the slightest provocation, in church or out of it. As Huizinga declares, 'No other epoch has laid so much stress as the expiring Middle Ages on the thought of death. An everlasting call of *memento mori* resounds through life.'[73] This very night, our souls may be taken from our bodies, and all that will be left will be the tears that those who survive us are duty bound to shed.

The weepers had the highest approval ratings for their shows of lachrymosity. It was axiomatic that the genuine religious sensibility always showed itself by copious weeping. Devotion, says Denis the Carthusian, is a sort of tenderness of heart which easily provokes tears of piety. We should pray God to have 'the daily baptism of tears'. According to St Bernard, tears were 'the wings of prayer' and 'the wine of angels'. We should get ready to give ourselves up to the grace of weeping, especially during Lent, so that we may say with the Psalmist, 'my tears have been my meat and drink'. St Vincent Ferrer wept so copiously every time he consecrated the Host that the whole congregation burst into tears along with him, so that a general wailing was heard as if in the House of the Dead.[74]

But people also wept at processions and public hangings (sometimes the hangman wept, too), in fact at almost any large public occasion. Medieval mystics were notorious for their tearfulness, especially Margery Kempe, who infuriated her fellow pilgrims to the Holy Land in 1414, according to her own account, 'because she wept so much and spoke all the time about the love and goodness of our Lord'. When she actually got to the holy sites of Jerusalem, she 'wept and sobbed as plenteously as though she had seen our Lord with her bodily eyes suffering his passion at that time', and when she came to Mount Calvary, the site of the Crucifixion, she could not stay standing, or even kneel, but 'writhed and wrestled with her body, spreading her arms out wide, and cried with a loud voice as though her heart would have burst apart'.[75] Margery shed tears of joy, too. Trying to re-enact Christ's entry into Jerusalem, she almost fell off her donkey from crying so much over the joy and sweetness of the moment.[76] At home in King's Lynn, in bed with her brewer husband (she often cried when he pestered her for sex), she 'heard a melodious sound so sweet and delectable that she thought she had been in Paradise', and jumped out of bed, exclaiming, 'Alas, that ever I sinned, it is full merry in Heaven.'[77]

Kings were not ashamed of weeping. Henry III scarcely stopped crying from the moment that, as a golden-haired boy of nine, he was told that he had succeeded his father King John to the throne. He broke down in tears whenever he said goodbye to his beloved wife Eleanor of Provence or his son, the future Edward I, both of them far tougher nuts. After his blood row with Edward in 1260, he at first refused to see him, because 'if he appears before me, I could not stop myself kissing him'.

Henry III by Matthew Paris

Henry's emotionalism expressed itself in his piety and charity, which went hand in hand together. He had an instant sympathy for victims of injustice. He deplored the 'cruel and inhuman' treatment of Richard of Bletchingdon, who had been forced to attend court despite his blindness, and he took pity on 'the poor little woman' from his royal manor of Ludgershall, whose husband had been hanged and her daughter burned for homicide. He was as generous with his handouts as his father had been stingy. On his royal progresses, he visited every hospital and friary en route, giving them timber for their building works and rich cloths for their altars and vestments.[78]

When he married Eleanor, for whom he developed a lasting affection rare in royal marriages of that or any period, he began the practice of feeding 500 paupers at court every day, a sort of miniature welfare state.[79] When the Dominicans and Franciscans arrived in England, in 1221 and 1224 respectively, he welcomed them and showered them with gifts of money, food, clothing and building timber, helping them to establish dozens of houses across the country, 17 gifts alone to the Franciscans of Winchester (his birthplace), including the ground on which to build their monastery.[80] On Maundy Thursday, he washed the feet of hundreds of lepers, and at Christmastide, too, a spiritual chore that even his saintly friend Louis IX of France shrank from doing.[81] When the Patriarch of Jerusalem sent him a crystal cup containing a drop of the blood that Jesus had shed upon the Cross, he received the cup at St Paul's, dressed as a pauper, and walked carrying the cup the whole way along the filthy road to the Abbey. After the ceremony in the Abbey, seated on the throne, he spotted the chronicler Matthew Paris and beckoned him to sit on a lower step and write a full account of the day's doing for posterity, which Paris duly did – an early example of royalty's skilful use of the media.

There was an equally intense competition in piety between Henry and Louis: Henry loved to hear Masses, Louis loved sermons. On his visit to France to see Louis in 1260, Henry would first hear Mass at his lodgings in the monastery of Saint-Germain-des-Prés, then stop at every church on the way to hear a Mass at each, making him so late for the meeting that there was no time for business. After a couple of days of this, Louis had the churches on the route closed until Henry had passed by. The next day, Henry turned up on time, declaring that he could not possibly attend the talks because all the churches were closed, which must mean that Paris was under a papal interdict. Louis confessed his ruse, and asked Henry why he insisted on hearing so many Masses, to which the English King riposted, 'why do you delight in so many sermons?' 'It seems to me delightful and healthy to hear often about my Creator,' Louis answered. 'And to me it appears even more delightful and healthy to see him frequently than to hear about Him.' Can anyone ever have taken transubstantiation more seriously?[82]

When in France, on an earlier visit, in 1254, Henry had visited the tombs at Fontevraud Abbey of his mother Isabella of Angoulême, of his grandparents Henry II and Eleanor of Aquitaine and of his uncle Richard the Lionheart. He must have been deeply moved, for he bequeathed his heart to Fontevraud in his will. Of all the remarkable monastic houses founded across Europe in the Middle Ages, none was more extraordinary than Fontevraud or its founder Robert d'Arbrissel. Born the son of a priest around 1050, he became a wandering preacher and later a hermit who attracted flocks of devotees with his denunciations of the blind ignorance of the people and the fornications and corruptions of priests and princes. His young followers tramped after him in their thousands, barefoot and heavily bearded ('barbarum prolixitate notabiles'). Like the Eastern mystics, he tested his immunity to temptation by inviting his female followers to share his bed (cf. Mahatma Gandhi in our own day). Eventually in 1101 he settled down and established 'a colony of huts' at Fontevraud around a great church (dedicated to the Virgin, of course). This soon blossomed into a mighty abbey with thousands of monks and nuns, a large hospital and an equally large leper colony. But its key feature was that the women ran the place. Robert wrote: 'You know that everything I have built in this world I did for the nuns, and it is to them that I have offered all the strength of my talents. What is more, I have submitted to them, me and my disciples, for the good of our souls.'[83] For hundreds of years, it was the Abbess who ruled. Nearly two centuries later, when Henry III died, it was the Abbess who came all the way to London to collect his heart. Robert's charisma attracted women of all sorts to Fontevraud, from prostitutes to princesses, including the estranged wife and the daughter of William of Aquitaine, who gave the land for the Abbey at his wife's urging.

We have already met William as the first of the great troubadours, but he was also the most powerful prince in the lands of modern-day France. He was an incorrigible womanizer and warrior, went on a ruinous crusade, was twice excommunicated. No less likely a patron of a great religious institution can be imagined. The desertion of his womenfolk to a place devoted to chastity and piety was such a slap in the face that he immediately founded a sort of little counter-abbey ('habitacula quaedam quasi monasteriola'), 60 miles to the south at Niort, but inhabited by unreformed courtesans and with a super-madame as 'Abbess'. This precursor of many a latter-day porno paradise was obviously a riposte to his wife, but his modern admirers argue that this juxtaposition of the sacred and the profane may have added an extra dimension to his poetry, injecting a secular mysticism which is equally part of what I have called the First Sentimental Revolution. Even today, after being bashed up by the Huguenots and despoiled and dissolved in the French Revolution, the surviving buildings at Fontevraud still give one a sense of purposeful peace as well as of undimmed beauty. I don't know what happened to the little counter-abbey at Niort.

THE POWER OF SOFT

Worldly, hard-headed men such as the chroniclers and Henry's great enemy Simon de Montfort thought little of Henry and did not hesitate to describe him as 'simple-minded', 'senseless and useless', *simplex, insipiens, inutilis*. After his dismal performance at the Battle of Saintes in 1242, Montfort said to his face: 'It would be a good thing if you were taken and shut away, as was done to Charles the Simple. There are houses with iron bars at Windsor that would be good for imprisoning you securely.'[84]

Yet the long view of posterity suggests a rather different conclusion. Henry's combination of generosity, pacifism and assiduous piety produced results. He wept buckets, but he gave buckets, too. His donations left an indelible mark on the country, and so did his practical achievements in peace-making and law-making, most of them undervalued in his lifetime and ever since. Most glorious of all was Westminster Abbey, which was Henry's personal pride and joy. Throughout his reign he fussed over every detail of the building of the triforium and the installation of the Cosmati pavements, above all over the shrine of Edward the Confessor, his hero, whose body he had translated in the crowning moment of his long reign.

Under Henry's personal rule, new fairs and markets opened all over the country. The population of England doubled or trebled between 1180 and 1330, from two million to six million. And coinage in circulation rose even faster, from £125,000 to about £1,100,000. Agriculture boomed along with the growing population to feed. In southern England, the ploughed area was already as large in 1086 as it was on the eve of the First World War.[85] At the same time, the legal underpinning of the market system was increasingly organized. The common law was growing fast, and so was recourse to the courts by all sorts of people down to individual peasants. The old idea of a stagnant Middle Ages is out of favour. Historians now agree that England was a rapidly commercializing society, in which the bonds of feudalism were slackening, though they still disagree about how fast. Sheep were cropping the downs across southern England, and their wool was feeding the Flemish cloth trade. Old mining industries and new ones were booming, too — Cornish tin, lead in the Peak District, silver in Durham and Devon, bell pits for new coal finds were being dug all over the country.

The profits and the products of these enterprises helped to make the thirteenth century a great age of church-building, the heyday of the Early English style — Salisbury, Wells, Lincoln and innumerable glorious parish churches. The soaring steeples of the East Midlands, the graceful towers of Somerset first hit the skyline. Westminster Abbey was only the culmination of a unique flowering of the 'soft style'.

Westminster Abbey, the interior

But the building of so many magnificent churches and monastic houses was not simply a tribute to the glory of God; it had huge practical consequences for the welfare of the sick and the poor. If the thirteenth century was perhaps the greatest age for building cathedrals, it was also the greatest age for building hospitals. Right up to the Dissolution of the Monasteries and the confiscation of their endowments, the Church offered an enormous amount of assistance to the sick. Most monasteries had their 'infirmaries', and the constitution of all religious bodies made the care of the sick one of the abbot's or abbess's most important duties. St Benedict declared in his Rule: 'Before all things and above all things, special care must be taken of the sick, so that they be served in every deed, as Christ himself, for he saith: "I was sick, and ye visited me"; and "what ye did to one of the least of these my Brethren, ye did to me".' It has been calculated that up to the Dissolution there were some 800 charitable institutions in England, which provided services to the sick and destitute, each with up to 100 beds for anyone in need. They were also supported by the charitable bodies which sprang out of the Military Orders formed for the Crusades: the Order of St Lazarus of Jerusalem, for example, and the Knights of St John of Jerusalem, which had and still has its HQ at the hospital of St John in Clerkenwell. Not a stone's throw away still stands the huge complex of St Bartholomew's Hospital, an offshoot of the Priory founded by Rahere in the twelfth century. Modern historians have pointed out that these institutions did not usually offer much in the way of trained medical staff, but they provided comfort and refuge, and a chance of regaining health, and sanity, too. According to contemporary accounts, 'the "poor mad men of Bethlehem" were splendidly looked after and often restored to reason'. Any such institution could look forward to a generous dollop of Henry's charity whenever he passed their way.[86]

In England and France, too, the First Sentimental Revolution was a period of social progress, buttressed by the peace treaty eventually concluded between the like-minded Henry and St Louis. The Treaty of Paris of 1260 was much deplored by hawks in England, because Henry had conceded so many of his French possessions, but it endured for 30 years and more. It is no accident that this period also saw the first experiments in what we would recognize as parliamentary government, with knights and burgesses represented alongside the aristocracy. These experiments were wracked by civil war – Henry was virtually deposed for a time and carted around the country as Montfort's prisoner. In the equally violent counter-revolution, Montfort's army was destroyed at the murderous Battle of Evesham (1265), which so shocked contemporary observers by its ruthless disregard of the conventions of chivalry. Montfort himself was killed and dismembered, his testicles being hung either side of his nose, then stuffed into his mouth. But the legacy of parliaments which represented a far wider section of the people than the nobility endured. There was a new sense of freedom for women (relative, true, but undeniable): in the upper echelons, the redoubtable Eleanors – of Aquitaine, Provence and de Montfort – made their voices heard and their writ run. In the next century, women are just as likely to be the narrators of the bestselling tales – three of the *Canterbury Tales*, seven out of ten in Boccaccio's *Decameron* are told by women. Sir Maurice Powicke, the great historian of the thirteenth century, thought that in those years, more than at any other time in the medieval period, 'England was able to cope with herself ... I mean that the tempo is more even, that the measure of agreement was greater ... that the response to fresh influences or new tasks was clearer, and, if I may use the word, happier.'[87]

Henry's practical sentimentality took the edge off the old feudal aggro, softened relations between the classes, as it did relations between the English, Scots, Welsh and Irish, to an extent seldom repeated in later centuries. The violent quarrels with the Welsh were to be renewed into the age of the Tudors, with the Scots into the eighteenth century, with the Irish until the Good Friday Agreement. Henry reached a live-and-let-live arrangement with them all. Feudalism wasn't quite dead, but cash wages were beginning to replace feudal services. People of both sexes were just beginning to be valued for what they could do rather than for who they were. We can discern the beginnings of what Sir Henry Maine famously dubbed 'the movement from Status to Contract'. In that still disputed formulation, sentimentality can be seen as a kind of cheerleader, insisting that we see our fellow men and women as individuals rather than as indistinguishable members of a caste or class. The educated classes, mostly clerics, begin to write their autobiographies, recounting their depressions, dreams and changes of heart with a candour which has no real precedent beyond the *Confessions* of St Augustine. The practice of confession in church becomes more regular, and the emphasis switches from the priest's absolution to the sincerity of the person confessing. Intention becomes key in the assessment of conduct more generally, among theologians as among jurists.[88] Painters and sculptors begin to produce recognizable images of their subjects. The sculpture in Cosenza of Isabel of France, wife of Philip III, shows her face gashed and distorted from the fall which killed her on the way back from the Tunis Crusade in 1270.[89] The statue of Henry III in Westminster shows his droopy left eyelid (as does his portrait by Matthew Paris reproduced on p. 33), and may well have been worked from his death mask. The art of portraiture is born. We are seeing what Colin Morris calls 'the discovery of the individual'.

And Henry was at the heart of it all, with his pacific nature, his hatred of hunting and tournaments, his love of Gothic architecture, and his instinctive sympathy for underdogs. If anyone deployed 'soft power' centuries before the term was thought of, it was Henry III. If he could ever have persuaded his parliaments to vote him the taxes he needed, he might have fought more wars, but I doubt it. It was the same with his taking the Cross for the Crusades. Again and again, he announced a date on which he would set off for the Holy Land, but he never did. He preferred to make his pilgrimages at home and feed his own paupers.

There is never any shortage of hard-nosed, self-styled 'realists' who insist, along with Niall Ferguson, that 'the trouble with soft power is that it's, well, soft'.[90] Butter is never any substitute for guns. The sustained exercise of hard power is the only way for a nation to achieve its goals, whether at home or abroad. Actually that isn't what Ferguson himself thinks; he tells us also that diplomacy and moral power, including religion and ideology, can be decisive, too. But those things, too, are part of what Joseph Nye, a former Assistant Secretary of Defense under Bill Clinton, who originally coined the term, means by 'soft power'; he wasn't just talking about cultural and commercial strength. And as Nye points out, history repeatedly shows that hard power alone, even when applied over a long period and at great cost in blood and money, is by no means sure to deliver: see Vietnam and the Middle East, *passim*. Ferguson, as it happens, was writing in Foreign Policy, in January/February 2003, on the eve of the Second Iraq War, which rather painfully illustrates the point. By contrast, soft power, whether deployed as an adjunct to hard power or as a substitute for it, has often produced surprisingly good outcomes: the end of the Cold War, the Good Friday Agreement in Northern Ireland, the end of apartheid in South Africa. And the thirteenth century of Henry III has plenty of similar examples to offer: the enduring peace deal with France, the tolerable rubbing-along relations with Scotland, Wales and Ireland and, not least, the eventual redemption and rehabilitation of the rebels after the ghastly civil wars of the 1260s. Henry's first impulses were often mistaken, but he was humble enough to alter course and seek out any available path of conciliation. Again and again, his generosity and practical piety redeemed his initial false moves. If posterity has underrated him, it is because the historians who create our images of the past tend to be over-impressed by hard power.

TWO

The New Stony Age

A LAMENT FOR WALSINGHAM

Bitter, bitter, O, to behold
The grass to grow
Where the walls of Walsingham
So stately did show.
Such were the works of Walsingham
While she did stand;
Such were the wracks as now do show
Of that holy land.
Level, level with the ground
The towers do lie,
Which with their golden glittering tops
Pierced once to the sky.
... Weep, weep, O Walsingham,
Whose days are nights,
Blessings turned to blasphemies,
Holy deeds to despites.
Sin is where Our Lady sat,
Heaven turned to hell.
Satan sits where Our Lord did sway;
Walsingham, O farewell.[1]

Ruins of Walsingham Abbey

Today only a single soaring arch survives of the great Augustinian Priory of Our Lady to point the way to heaven for the flocks of pilgrims, among them almost every English king up to and including Henry VIII. The shrine was dismantled and the Priory demolished under the orders of Thomas Cromwell. The Sub-prior refused to agree and was charged with conspiring to rebel against the Dissolution. He was hanged outside the Priory walls. The Prior was more compliant and actually helped the Commissioner to remove the figure of Our Lady and the gold and silver ornaments. He received a decent pension of £100 a year. The site was sold to one Thomas Sidney for £90 and a handsome private mansion erected on the spot, probably employing the stone from the Priory. The valuable lead from the roof would have been flogged to the highest bidder. There were often juicy rewards for collaborators. A nun at Wilton Abbey complained of the ready acquiescence of her abbess Cecily Bodenham: 'Methinks the Abbess hath a faint heart and doth yield up our possessions to the spoiler with a not unwilling haste. Master Richard Neville, the Sub-Seneschal informeth me that His Majesty's Commissioners do purpose to reward her with a fair house at Fovant and a goodly stipend withal.' Which is precisely what Cecily got.

Ever since, it has been impossible to erase entirely from the national memory, as Shakespeare himself could not, 'those bare ruined choirs where late the sweet birds sang'. Similar bitter echoes haunt once sacred sites all over England. Shaftesbury Abbey was reduced to the ground. Only the foundations remain to spark the visitor's imagination. Yet that sturdy atheist Thomas Hardy could not resist musing in *Jude the Obscure*:

'Vague imaginings of its castles, its three mints, its magnificent apsidal Abbey, the chief glory of South Wessex, its twelve churches, its shrines, chantries, hospitals, its gabled freestone mansions – all now ruthlessly swept away – throw the visitor, even against his will, into a pensive melancholy, which the stimulating atmosphere and limitless landscape around him can scarcely dispel.'

Not many miles away once stood Amesbury Abbey, founded by Queen Ælfthryth long before the Conquest, and reformed by Henry II as one of the English outposts of Fontevraud. Henry's widow Eleanor of Aquitaine went to live there, as did Henry III's widow, Eleanor of Provence, who died there. All this royal heritage did not protect the Priory, which was brutally destroyed like the rest. Not far away again, at Glastonbury, the Abbot, Richard Whiting, put up a sturdy fight and, though he had been a signatory to the Act of Supremacy which made Henry VIII head of the Church of England – so you might think the King owed him one – he was hanged, drawn and quartered as a traitor on Glastonbury Tor. The same fate met the last Abbot of Reading. Hugh Faringdon is said in fact to have complied with the suppression, but was hanged, drawn and quartered in front of the Abbey gatehouse on suspicion of having aided the northern rebels. As a mitred abbot, Faringdon was entitled to be tried by Parliament, but Thomas Cromwell had the death sentence carried out before the trial could begin. Stalin's show trials were but a pale reflection of Cromwell on the rampage.

The ground had been prepared for these brutal acts by the harsh and uncompromising tone of Thomas Cromwell's second set of Royal Injunctions, issued in September 1538, which doubled down on the first set issued two years earlier. Even at this distance in time, the assertion of the King's authority makes the flesh tingle: Cromwell salutes Henry not only as Defender of the Faith (a title, let us remember, granted to him by the Pope in happier times), but also 'in earth Supreme Head under Christ of the Church of England'. The Injunctions which Cromwell is to carry out as Lord Privy Seal and the King's Vice-regent are to be observed 'upon pain of deprivation, sequestration or such other coercion as the King's Highness, or his Vice-regent for the time being, shall be seen convenient'. Carte blanche, in other words.

And the attack on the cults and practices of the medieval Church is as menacing as the penalties for disobedience. The faithful are 'not to repose their trust and affiance in any other works devised by men's phantasies besides Scripture, as in wandering to pilgrimages, offering of money, candles, or tapers to images or relics, or kissing or licking the same, saying over a number of beads, not understood or minded on, or in such-like superstition; for the doing whereof, ye not only have no promise of reward in Scripture, but contrariwise, great threats and maledictions of God, as things tending to idolatry and superstition, which of all other offences God Almighty doth most detest and abhor' (Item 6).

The clergy are expected to jump to it: 'such feigned images as ye know of in any of your cures to be so abused with pilgrimages or offerings of anything made thereunto, ye shall, for avoiding that most detestable sin of idolatry, forthwith take down and delay, and shall suffer from henceforth no candles, tapers, or images of wax to be set before any image or picture but only the light that commonly goeth across the church by the rood-loft ...' (Item 7). And they must eat humble pie in public for any past misdoings: 'if ye have heretofore declared to your parishioners anything to the extolling or setting forth of pilgrimages, feigned relics, or images, or any such superstition, ye shall now openly afore the same recant and reprove the same, shewing them (as the truth is) that ye did the same upon no ground of Scripture, but as one being led and seduced by a common error and abuse crept into the church, through the sufferance and avarice of such as felt profit by the same' (Item 10).

When they had their brief days in the sun again, under Mary Tudor, the upholders of the old religion were not slow to give as good as they had got. At her accession, John Christopherson returned from exile in Louvain to become Master of Trinity College, Cambridge, and Mary's confessor. In his *Exhortation to all menne to take hede and beware of rebellion* (July 1554), he made a passionate attack on the iconoclasts:

'... they commaunded images to be plucked downe in every churche, which put us in memorye of the holy lyves of confessours, martyrs, and virgins: yea and they were not so contented, but they would have the image of our saviour Jesus Christ likewise spitefully to be hurled downe, and eyther with fire to be burned, or with instrumentes broken all in peces. And some sinfull wretches were there, that digged up, and overthrewe the crosses in highe ways, whiche were sette up, partly to make men that passed by, remember Christes death and passion, and partly to shewe them the right way, that knew not the same. Who I pray you would thinke, that these folks bare any good affection to our saviour Christ, which could neither abide his image, nor the holsome signe of hys crosse?'[2]

Note that the prime thrust of Christopherson's attack is on the image smashers' hardness of heart, their want of feeling, their lack of passion for the Passion. This is not the place to record all the to-ing and fro-ing in those terrifying years between the rise and fall of Thomas Cromwell and Thomas Cranmer and the death of Mary Tudor. Our only purpose here is to evoke something of the ferocity and anguish on both sides: the furious derision of the reformers at the superstitions of the unlettered and the desolation of the people whose most precious rites had been so rudely snatched from them. The condescension of posterity hasn't helped. Modern historians, Protestant or secular (which often comes to much the same thing), have often endorsed the picture of the 'primitive' and 'superstitious' practices of the peasants which was current in the propaganda of the reformers. By contrast, Eamon Duffy has sturdily defended much of late medieval piety: 'such ideas were built into the structure of the liturgy, and formed the focus for some of its most solemn and popularly accessible moments.'[3] All religion, after all, depends on the exercise of the imagination. Whether the images and symbols are visual or only verbal is a secondary question. In any case, modern semiology and structuralism (and post-structuralism, too) revolve around the interpretation of concepts which are expressed in symbolic terms. To reject the language of symbols is a crippling failure of the imagination in philosophy as it is in religion.

At all events, the repressive actions of Henry, Cromwell, Cranmer and their agents are not in question. Nor is the heartfelt antagonism of the thousands of defenders of the old faith in all classes who took part in the Pilgrimage of Grace and the other risings in Lincolnshire and the West Country. Hundreds of them were burned or hanged, drawn and quartered, along with the other martyrs who were to die at the stake for their beliefs throughout the rest of the sixteenth century.

We are familiar with the arguments in favour of the Dissolution, or at least the arguments palliating its excesses. The abbeys were too rich and too unpopular, the monks too idle or too corrupt. In many monasteries, there were only a handful of them left. Some of the younger monks and nuns were only too glad to be released from their vows. Anyway, the monastic ideal was past its sell-by date. Whatever their faults, Cromwell and his commissioners were agents of modernity.

Such arguments are not without truth, but they make no allowance for the violence done to people's belief, as well as often to their bodies. The mindset that replaced the old faith was a harsher one. In a larger sense, the disenchantment of the world put on a spurt. Hilary Mantel's trilogy revolving around Thomas Cromwell is a marvellous work of fiction, but by telling the whole story from

Cromwell's angle she cannot help making us see him in a softer light and mitigating his hard edges, which were very hard indeed for those on the receiving end.

And what of all the hospitals and infirmaries, maintained by the monastic orders, hundreds of them all over England and Europe, offering care and refuge to the sick and abandoned? The First Sentimental Revolution had seen an explosion of hospitals in England, throughout the twelfth and thirteenth centuries. What they lacked in standards of medical care they often made up for in terms of psychological support, as well as physical maintenance. All monasteries and most large houses possessed a special herb garden and an inmate who knew something about simple cures. A medieval hospital was generally a large, airy hall with tiled floors, rows of clean white beds and an altar at one end, not unlike a big ward in a modern hospital, minus the altar. They had up to a hundred beds, straw pallets to start with, but made of wood from the twelfth century onwards. As we have seen, rough calculations put the number of these hospitals in England at 800. After the Dissolution, only a handful of such institutions remained, although in London the City authorities had established several new hospitals with trained staff. But outside London, there were scarcely any general hospitals until the eighteenth century. Even in the capital, the City authorities were at their wits' end after the Dissolution, addressing a petition to the King complaining of 'the miserable people lying in the street, offending every clean person passing by with their filthy and nasty savours', and requesting to be allowed to take over the revenues of the rich City churches to build new facilities 'for the avoiding of the great infection and inconveniences that be like to happen to your citizens'. The King did not bother to reply. As the plutocrats' mansions rose on the sites of the old abbeys, the poor and sick suffered on a huge scale. Philanthropy never properly revived until the middle of the eighteenth century and the Age of Enlightenment.[4]

For our present purposes, I want only to concentrate on the extremity of the passions stirred, the unwillingness to tolerate, let alone to forgive, and the unyielding hardness of the language. The pervading sternness applied especially to the shedding of superfluous tears, notably at funerals. Tears don't feature much in Cranmer's Book of Common Prayer. On the contrary, we are invited to give hearty thanks to almighty God that 'it hath pleased thee to deliver this our brother out of the miseries of this world'.

The chantries established to pray for the souls of the departed had been sold off at a handsome return under the Chantries Act of 1547. The brasses and obit inscriptions calling for prayers for the dead were ripped up from gravestones and sold by the hundredweight as a consequence of the Act. As Duffy says, 'the removal of the images and petitions of the dead was an act of oblivion ...They, like the Mass and the saints, were now as they had never been before, part of a superseded past. The imaginative power of the cult of the dead in late medieval England had lain in part precisely in its continuity, as generation after generation inscribed its names and imposed its features upon the palimpsest of the parish memory.'[5]

As far as humanly possible, funerals were now to be brief, dry-eyed formalities. In the 1550s, Matthew Parker, soon to be Archbishop of Canterbury, preached the funeral sermon for the German reformer Martin Bucer. He declared bluntly that to mourn for the dead was to show a lack of faith in the Resurrection. It was not only 'unseemly and wicked' but also 'womanish', 'childish' and 'beastly' 'to use any howling or blubbering' for the departed, as the heathen did.[6] Calvin, too, attacked fake tears. You could not judge someone's penitence by how much he blubbed. 'We have taught the sinner not to look on his compunction or on his tears, but to fix both eyes solely on the mercy of God.' At one of their stormy interviews, John Knox reproached Mary, Queen of Scots, for bursting into tears: 'I never delighted in the weeping of any of God's creatures; yea, I can scarcely well abide the tears of my own boys, when my own hands correct them, much less can I rejoice in your majesty's weeping.'[7] Cranmer himself thought that if you had to weep at all, you ought to do so in private.

THE DOWSING ROD

By the early forties of the seventeenth century, this new hardness had crystallized into an even more adamantine rhetoric. To the thoroughgoing Puritans, the compromises of Anglicanism were as intolerable as the idolatry of the Papists. They looked back on the Dissolution of the Monasteries with huge satisfaction, seeing them as but a preliminary to the realization of God's reign on earth. And why should they not be optimistic? So many of these hard-faced men came from families which had done brilliantly out of the Dissolution, not least the Cromwells and the odious Riches who became Earls of Warwick. Oliver was the great-grandson of Thomas Cromwell's sister Katharine, who had married a Welsh innkeeper called Williams, and who scooped up some lush estates around Huntingdon Abbey (the Cromwells, including Oliver, often referred to themselves as 'Cromwell alias Williams'). Even the firebrand John Lambert, Cromwell's number 2 and prime author of Britain's only written, republican constitution, had had a great-grandfather who was quids in with Henry VIII and acquired a large slice of the Bolton Abbey estates. The legendary avarice of the abbots was at least rivalled by the land hunger of those who turfed them out.

The iconoclasm of the 1640s had a cheerful, unrestrained brutality about it which made the process of the Dissolution a century earlier seem almost genteel in retrospect. Across the rest of Europe, the wars of religion were raging, causing suffering on a horrendous scale. The wars between the English, Scots and Irish were on a more modest scale, but they were ghastly enough. And so was the systematic desecration of thousands of English parish churches, many of them standing beside the ruins of the already desecrated abbeys.

It is in just these years that the adjective 'maudlin' first appears. The OED's first finding is dated 1631. I cannot think of a more significant addition to the lexicon of anti-sentimentality. 'Maudlin' is soon being applied to the tears of drunks and Irishmen, especially of their blubbering at their over-the-top wakes, as well as to women and anyone who over-indulges his emotions. Yet the tears of St Mary Magdalen, from whom the adjective derives, are no medieval accretion, no bogus encrustation of the True Faith. On the contrary, the originating episode lies at the heart of the Passion narrative. For many people, John 20. 11–16, is among the most moving passages in the entire Bible: 'But Mary stood without at the sepulchre weeping: and as she wept, she stooped down, and looked into the sepulchre, and seeth two angels in white sitting, the one at the head, and the other at the feet, where the body of Jesus had lain. And they say unto her, Woman, why weepest thou? She saith unto them, Because they have taken away my Lord, and I know not where they have laid him.' Then she turns away and sees Jesus standing there but does not recognize him and thinks he's the gardener, and He says, 'Woman, why weepest thou?' To appropriate the tears of the Magdalen for a sneering pejorative is among the most stony-hearted aspects of this new stony age.

Not the least chilling innovation was the new lack of charity towards the poor. The Anglican settlement of Elizabeth's reign had at least brought in a nationwide system of poor relief. The decay of the former poor law administration began during the Civil War, and not entirely by a neglect which might have been understandable in the chaotic and desperate circumstances of the appalling 'war without an enemy'. This was a deliberate policy. Now paupers were regarded as the architects of their own misfortunes. A pamphleteer of 1646 wrote that the general rule was to whip all wandering vagrants. In 1649, Parliament passed an Act to form a company with power to apprehend vagrants, to offer them a choice between work and whipping, and to set to compulsory work all other persons without means of maintenance, including children. The last blow dealt by the Puritan Revolution to the 'labouring poor' was the Settlement and Removal Act of 1662, which restricted relief to those who could show a certificate to prove they had been settled in a parish for 40 days. No certificate, no relief – a standing temptation to parishes to winkle out as many paupers as they could, at the same time rendering it almost impossible for a poor man to move to seek work and so forfeit his precious certificate. In *The*

Wealth of Nations a century later, Adam Smith devotes half a dozen pages to the problem, concluding: 'There is scarce a poor man in England of forty years of age, I will venture to say, who has not in some part of his life felt himself most cruelly oppressed by this ill-contrived law of settlements.'[8] The spectacle of the wretched homeless shuffling from parish to parish with their bundle of possessions on their back became a scandalously common sight in the England of the late seventeenth and eighteenth centuries. Thus charity for the poor withered on the ground, at the same time as the religious symbols of charity and compassion were being forcibly removed from the churches which had for centuries offered them comfort and refuge.[9]

This huge shift in mental attitudes has provoked some of the classic twentieth-century works in the history of ideas. In their different ways, Max Weber's *The Protestant Ethic and the Spirit of Capitalism* (1905), R. H. Tawney's *Religion and the Rise of Capitalism* (1926) and C. B. Macpherson's *The Political Theory of Possessive Individualism* (1962) all finger the Reformation as the moulder of a new world view. Without the intervening apparatus of saints and pardoners and chantries, man faces God directly and so becomes the maker of his own destiny, what is soon to be called 'a self-made man'. There are no more intercessors; it's no use asking the Virgin to pray for you; *ora pro nobis* inscriptions are to be ripped off every tombstone. Man is on his own. He can no longer earn his salvation by good works, let alone by purchasing indulgences or grovelling before bogus relics. It is his duty to strive for success in this world, and only by achieving it can he show that he may be among those who are to be saved, but only by God's grace. As Weber puts it, 'Waste of time is thus and in principle the deadliest of sins ... every hour lost is lost to labour for the Glory of God.'[10] Or as Benjamin Franklin first said so memorably, 'Time is money' – a thought that would have been incomprehensible to the Middle Ages. And a man's work was his 'calling' – in German, *Beruf* has the same semi-religious overtone. If he does well, 'God blesseth his trade', the old Puritans used to say. Or as that legendary Baptist minister, in Texas, I think, declared, 'the Good Lord loves a successful man'. By contrast, the man who fails to make an effort and slides back into sloth, drunkenness, fornication, etc., is damned. Failure in life ceases to be a misfortune deserving of sympathy. To be a loser is to lose your soul as well as everything else. I over-simplify the argument, but not by much. Weber concludes: 'This thankfulness for one's own perfection by the grace of God penetrated the attitude toward life of the Puritan middle class, and played its part in developing that formalistic, hard, correct character which was peculiar to the men of that heroic age of capitalism.'[11] More recent historians have questioned the sweeping claims of the Weber/Tawney/Macpherson approach, but the general thesis still seems pretty compelling. You have only to read Calvin a little to encounter this chilling austerity. Even today, you can catch pungent echoes of it in the diatribes of right-wing Tory MPs against slackers and freeloaders.

The physical hardness of the image-smashers matched the mental hardness of their attitudes. One witness, Bishop Joseph Hall of Norwich, described the dismantling of his cathedral in 1643 when troops reinforced by local zealots followed Parliament's ordinance against superstition and idolatry with a terrifying gusto:

'Lord what work was here! What clattering of glasses! What beating down of walls! What tearing up of monuments! What pulling down of seats! What wresting out of irons and brass from the windows! What defacing of arms! What demolishing of curious stonework! What tooting and piping upon organ pipes! And what a hideous triumph in the market-place before all the country when all the mangled organ pipes, vestments, both capes and surplices, together with the leaden cross which had newly been sawn down from the Green-yard pulpit and the service books and singing books that could be carried to the fire in the public market-place were heaped together.'

This eloquent lament comes from *Bishop Hall's Hard Measure, written by himself upon his Impeachment of High Crimes and Misdemeanours for defending the Church of England.* For it was the Church of England that was in the firing line now, as the Catholics had been a century earlier. As a young man, Hall had been a nimble satirist, and he had not lost his waspish wit when as a bishop he was brought before the House of Lords to answer a charge of high treason, and then forfeited his estates and was sent to the Tower for a spell. His only offence? To declare that the errors of the Catholic Church did not disqualify her claim to be the true Catholic Church. In other words, though he himself leaned towards Calvinism, he leaned even more towards toleration, which in that era was the unforgivable sin. Sir Thomas Browne, the author of Urn Burial, who attended Hall on his deathbed, described him as 'a person of singular humility, patience and piety'.

Though the image-breaking went on all over England, the Puritan epicentre of East Anglia was just about the hottest spot. And the hottest zealot of them all was William Dowsing, also known as Smasher Dowsing. He was a Suffolk farmer before he became a convinced Puritan and was appointed by the Earl of Manchester as Commissioner for the Destruction of Monuments of Idolatry and Superstition. Over a period of 15 months in 1643 and 1644, he visited 250 churches in Cambridgeshire and Suffolk and carried out his orders à l'outrance.

John Barwick, Fellow of St John's College, Cambridge, and later after the Restoration Dean of St Paul's, describes Dowsing at work in Cambridge:

> 'one who calls himself John Dowsing [sic], by virtue of a pretended Commission goes about the country like a Bedlam breaking glasse windows, having battered and beaten downe all our painted glasse, not only in our Chapples, but (contrary to Order) in our publique Schooles, Colledge Halls, Librayes and Chambers, mistaking perhaps the liberall Arts for Saints ... and having (against an Order) defaced and digged up the floors of our Chappels, many of which had lien so for two or three hundred yeares together, not regarding the dust of our founders and predecessors, who likely were buried there; compelled us by armed Souldiers to pay forty shillings a Colledge for not mending what he had spoyled and defaced, or forthwith to go to prison.'[12]

Headless figures of St Margaret of Antioch, Fingringhoe, Essex and the Coronation of the Virgin, West Front, Wells Cathedral

Thus even the dead were not to be suffered to rest in peace. If all this may sound like the exaggerations of a querulous academic, we have only to consult the unique diary that Smasher left recording his labours. Here's how his extraordinary journal begins:

'SUDBURY, Suffolk. *Peter's* Parish. Jan. the 9th 1643. We brake down a picture of God the Father, 2 Crucifix's and Pictures of Christ, about an hundred in all; and gave orders to take down a Cross off the Steeple; and diverse Angels, 20 at least, on the Roof of the Church.

'SUDBURY, *Gregory* Parish. Jan, the 9th. We brake down 10 mighty great angels in Glass, in all 80.

'All Hallows, Jan. the 9th. We brake about 20 superstitious Pictures; and took up 30 brazen superstitious Inscriptions *Ora pro nobis*, and pray for the soul, &c.

'At HAVERHILL Jan. the 6th, 1643. We brake down about an hundred superstitious pictures; and seven Fryars hugging a nun and the Picture of God and Christ, diverse other very superstitious; and 200 had been broken down before I came. We took away two popish inscriptions *ora pro nobis*; and we beat down a great stoneing Cross on the top of the Church.'[13]

And so on for months, through dozens of mostly peaceful and unresisting Suffolk villages. Note how the *ora pro nobis* inscriptions are regarded as just as offensive as the crucifixes and the painted and graven images. The dead are to be firmly cut off from the living.

CHILLING WITH MICHELANGELO

The Reformation in northern and eastern Europe begins at much the same time as another major shift in cultural history, what came to be known as the High Renaissance, concentrated in but not confined to Italy. Martin Luther (1483–1564) and Michelangelo (1475–1564) were more or less contemporaries. At first blush, these two developments at opposite ends of the same continent might seem quite separate, their coincidence in time literally a coincidence. One movement, after all, is notoriously concerned with the breaking of graven images, the other specializing in creating ever more splendid graven (and painted) images. The Reformation is obsessive in seeing the world from a religious perspective. The Renaissance, by contrast, on the whole takes a step back from religion and turns its attention to classical philosophy, literature and art, in particular to great thinkers like Aristotle whose works had not been directly available in the high Middle Ages.

And yet. What the two movements do have in common is a decisive rejection of the crowded, intimate clutter of medieval culture – its saints, its relics, its myths, its pilgrimages and penitences – and a purposeful moving towards something cleaner, straighter, more spacious, nobler, at the same time something undeniably cooler, more distant from the messy, smelly realities of life. I don't deny that it is hard to pin down the exact nature of these similarities, as it is the nature of their differences. But we might gain a few hints from that supreme master of the High Renaissance, Michelangelo Buonarroti, as decisive and dynamic a thinker as he was an artist.

The painter and essayist Francisco de Holanda (1517–85) was, despite his name, born in Lisbon and became court painter to the

Kings of Portugal. In his early twenties, he had studied in Rome in 1538 and frequented the salon of Vittoria Colonna, the widowed Marchioness of Pescara. She was a popular poet with a wide circle of friends, and she introduced him to the great artists of the day, Parmigianino, Giambologna and, most importantly, Michelangelo, who now in his early sixties had become rather besotted with the 46-year-old Vittoria, drew her and addressed sonnets to her. It was Michelangelo who introduced Francisco to the theory and practice of classicism.

In his three dialogues on painting, Francisco records his conversations with Michelangelo on the subject. Some scholars have questioned how far these reports are verbatim, or merely reconstructions of the sort of thing Michelangelo might have said, like Thucydides' reconstruction of the speeches of Pericles. But they ring pretty true to me, as the kind of views that were being expressed in the Colonna circle, and the remarks attributed to Michelangelo have the downright, abrasive tone of the letters that he indubitably wrote. Hearing that Francisco would love to hear Michelangelo's views on painting, Vittoria sends a message to him to drop by the chapel of San Silvestro, where they are chatting and which, as it happens, he is walking past. When he arrives, she quizzes him directly, smiling as she speaks: 'I very much wish to know, as we are dealing with this subject, what you think of the painting of Flanders, and whom it will satisfy, because it appears to me more devout than the Italian style.'[14]

The great man does not disappoint: 'The painting of Flanders, Madam, will generally satisfy any devout person more than the painting of Italy, which will never cause him to drop a single tear, but that of Flanders will cause him to shed many; this is not owing to the vigour and goodness of the painting, but to the goodness of such devout person; women will like it, especially very old ones, or very young ones. It will please likewise friars and nuns, and also some noble persons who have no ear for true harmony.'[15]

So Flemish painting only brings tears to the eyes of silly old women and soppy young girls and monks and nuns and a few pea-brained toffs. What's wrong with Flemish painting, though, in technical artistic terms? Michelangelo doesn't pull his punches. It's the plodding realism of these northern philistines:

'They paint in Flanders only to deceive the external eye, things that gladden you and of which you cannot speak ill, and saints and prophets. Their painting is of stuffs, bricks and mortar, the grass of the fields, the shadows of trees, and bridges and rivers, which they call landscapes, and little figures here and there; and all this, although it may appear good to some eyes, is in truth done without reasonableness or art, without symmetry or proportion, without care in selecting or rejecting, and finally without any substance or verve.'[16] The sneer and contempt scorch off the page across 500 years. There's no *selection*, no arrangement, no composition. Flemish art just bungs everything in: 'it tries to do everything at once (each of which alone would suffice for a great work) so that it does not do anything really well.'[17] By contrast, Michelangelo does not hesitate to tell us that 'Only works which are done in Italy can be called true painting, and therefore we call good painting Italian ... good painting is nothing else but a copy of the perfections of God and a reminder of His painting. Finally, good painting is a music and a melody which only intellect can appreciate, and with great difficulty.'[18] In other words, great art is not for the masses.

In *The Waning of the Middle Ages*, Johan Huizinga applauds Michelangelo wholeheartedly: 'What he condemns in Flemish art are exactly the essential traits of the declining Middle Ages: the violent sentimentality, the tendency to see each thing as an independent entity, to get lost in the multiplicity of concepts. To this the spirit of the Renaissance is opposed.'[19] 'The triumph of the Renaissance was to consist in replacing this meticulous realism by breadth and simplicity.'[20]

No more tears, no more fuss and mess. Only a noble and grand simplicity. In the eyes of convinced classicists, even the most skilled late-medieval artists overcooked the emoting. The Burgundian sculptor Claus Sluter, for example. In his celebrated *Well of Moses* at Dijon, carried out for the Duke of Burgundy, the figures of the prophets are far too extravagant for Huizinga's taste: 'the gestures of the hands and feet by which the attention is directed to the texts are so emphatic, and there is an expression of such poignant grief on the faces, that the whole is in danger of losing the *ataraxia* which marks great sculpture. It appeals too directly to the spectator. Compared with the figures of Michelangelo, those of Sluter are too expressive, too personal.'[21]

What would Huizinga (or Michelangelo) have said if he had lived to see the images of grieving widows and children in the rubble of Ukraine or Gaza? What would he have made of the war photographs of Don McCullin? John Constable's praise of the landscapes of Thomas Gainsborough would probably have annoyed him, too: 'The stillness of noon, the depths of twilight and the dews and pearls of morn are all to be found in the canvases of this most benevolent and kindly man. On looking at them, we find tears in our eyes and know not what brings them.'[22]

This absence of *ataraxia* – calmness, tranquillity, undisturbedness – is at the heart of the classicist's indictment of medieval art. How far we are here from the modern mindset. For us, it is just about the highest praise for a film or documentary or memoir to be labelled 'disturbing'. The word is first found in English in the form 'ataraxie', significantly in John Florio's famous translation of the *Essays* of Montaigne (1603): 'Ataraxie is the condition of a quiet and settled life.'[23] In the great ancient schools of philosophy – the Epicureans, the Pyrrhonists, the Stoics – the tranquillity of the undisturbed mind was the thing to aim for. That was the modern version of Stoicism that Montaigne transmitted to the literati of Europe. The ideal of *ataraxia* surfed back into the modern consciousness on the back of the classical revival and has never quite gone away. Today there is even a frequently prescribed anti-anxiety drug called Atarax (aka Hydroxyzine).

In its essence, the culture of the High Renaissance aims for the calm sublime. It is uncomfortable with the poetry of everyday life, the hot, smelly details that you find in Shakespeare and Dickens and Joyce. Renaissance art typically proceeds by extracting from and refining reality, rather than by directly reflecting, let alone wallowing in it. At its best, it produces work that we can only gasp at. Yet even after we have admired Michelangelo at his greatest — in the Medici Chapel in Florence, in the Sistine Chapel in Rome — we have to ask, is *ataraxia* enough? Is this calm sublimity the be-all and end-all of art? Is there not something to be said for the unrestrained agonies of the mourning figures in Grünewald's *Crucifixion*, the horrific plague-scarred deadness of his Jesus on the Cross? And Claus Sluter? The famous alabaster mourners, the *pleurants*, who surround his Tomb of Philip the Bold, are shrouded in a grief which is almost palpable. Michelangelo does not seek to make us weep. Sluter does. Can weeping too not be part and parcel of great art?

By contrast, we see the apotheosis of the new dispensation in the Anglican churches of the late seventeenth century, with their clean straight lines and uncluttered interiors. Inigo Jones was the pioneer. He allegedly promised his patron the Earl of Bedford that his new church of St Paul's Covent Garden (1631–5) would be 'the handsomest barn in England'. And so it is, but it's a chilly daunting sort of place, not exactly a refuge for the broken-hearted. Wren's City churches, above all St Paul's Cathedral, combined Classicism and Protestantism in this unadorned style of worship which was imitated all over the English-speaking world. In these bare temples, the prayers of the faithful are aimed at a distant God without any comforting intercessors. Over the years, monuments do pile up in the aisles and transepts, but they are monuments not to saints and martyrs, but to strictly secular heroes, admirals and explorers and even merchants, and the scenes recorded on their tablets are of sieges and naval battles, not, Heaven now forfend, of scenes from the Bible. The Quakers go a step further: the church becomes merely a meeting house, no longer a space that has any claim to be thought of as sacred. It is a colder, barer world, in which tears still fall, but they fall on stony ground.

THREE

The Second Sentimental Revolution

THE MAN WHO INVENTED ME TOO

Then abruptly everything changes again. What I shall call the Second Sentimental Revolution begins just as suddenly as the First, if not more so. It even has a precise starting date. On 6 November 1740, only 30 years after the last stones were laid on St Paul's Cathedral, down the road in Fleet Street a semi-educated, middle-aged jobbing printer published his first novel. Or you could say the first novel in English. For nothing like Samuel Richardson's *Pamela: or Virtue Rewarded* had ever been seen before. It is from *Pamela* that we can date the emergence of the modern European novel, its preoccupations, its passions and its peculiar techniques of seeing the world. *Pamela* is not just a diverting tale or 'romance'; it delves into character to a depth never previously attempted in fiction.

As he was to do with all his other works, Richardson set the type and printed the book on his own presses (something few if any other authors can claim, though Virginia Woolf did lend a hand at the Hogarth Press). This tubby little man had no illusions about his own appearance. He describes himself to Lady Bradshaigh, a female admirer who had not yet met him, so that she could recognize him in the street: 'Short; rather plump than emaciated, notwithstanding his complaints: about five foot five inches: fair wig; lightish cloth coat, all black besides ... looking directly fore-right, as passers-by would imagine, but observing all that stirs on either hand of him without moving his short neck; hardly ever turning back: of a light-brown complexion; teeth not yet failing; smoothish faced, and ruddy cheeked: at sometimes looking to be about sixty-five, at other times much younger.' He was in fact just over 60 at the time.¹

Samuel Richardson by Joseph Highmore, c. 1747

He might be modest about his physique, but for his potential as a writer this chirpy little cock robin had the highest ambitions, with an unbending determination to protect and promote his work and his reputation. And he achieved both. All over Europe, Richardson became celebrated as 'the absolute master of the human heart'. He was not by any means the first person to write stories in the form of letters between the characters rather than by a third-person narrator. But he carried the epistolary technique to a new pitch of intensity: the letter writers live in the moment as they explore their emotions and lay them bare. As the author himself explains in the preface to his masterpiece *Clarissa*: 'much more lively and affecting ... must be the Style of those who write in the height of a *present* distress; the mind tortured by the pangs of uncertainty (the Events then hidden in the womb of Fate); than the dry, narrative, unanimated Style of a person relating difficulties and dangers surmounted, can be; the relator perfectly at ease; and if himself unmoved by his own Story, not likely greatly to affect the Reader!'[2] Even his memorable villain, Robert Lovelace, tells us with his fetching self-awareness: 'I love to write to the moment.'[3]

The plot of *Pamela* is simple enough. Pamela Andrews is a pious but spirited 15-year-old servant girl, the daughter of impoverished labourers, though her father had once been a schoolteacher. She works for Lady B on her Bedfordshire estate. When Lady B dies, she is devastated: 'God, whose Graciousness to us we have so often experienced at a Pinch, put it into my good Lady's Heart, on her Death-bed, just an Hour before she expir'd, to recommend to my young Master all her Servants, one by one; and when it came to my Turn to be recommended, for I was sobbing and crying at her Pillow, she could only say, My dear Son! – and so broke off a little, and then recovering – Remember my poor *Pamela*! – And these were some of her last Words! O how my Eyes run! – Don't wonder to see the Paper so blotted!'[4]

Pamela Fainting by Joseph Highmore, 1743–4

So begins Pamela's first letter to her parents, and with it the whole of the European literature of sentiment. She continues to weep throughout her ordeals, as Lady B's son and heir ruthlessly pursues her and tries every trick he can think of to seduce her, often using rough language and shameless brutality, for example, when she resists his advances in the summerhouse: 'You foolish slut, cease your blubbering!'[5] But Pamela is well able to speak up for herself, and she expresses herself with freshness and vigour in her letters to her parents, as Mr B discovers when he steals them: 'I ... am quite overcome with your charming manner of Writing, so free, so easy and so much above your Sex; and all put together, makes me, as I tell you, love you to extravagance.'[6] The reader, too, comes to love Pamela's candid, saucy voice – in a way that perhaps in the modern era only A. P. Herbert's Topsy and Helen Fielding's Bridget Jones give us an echo of. Pamela has an unshakable sense of her worth as a human being; there is an echo of the philosophy of John Locke in her dialogue with the ghastly Mrs Jewkes who has been deputed by Mr B to prevent her from running off: 'And pray, said I, walking on, how came I to be his Property? What Right has he in me, but such as a Thief may plead to stolen Goods? – Why, was ever the like heard, says she! – This is downright Rebellion, I protest! Well, well, Lambkin, (which the Foolish often calls me) if I was in his Place, he should not have his Property in you long questionable. Why, what would you do, said I, if you was he? Not stand shill-I, shall-I, as he does, but put you and himself both out of your pain.' At which Pamela calls her a Jezebel, and Mrs Jewkes gives her a nasty slap.[7] Mr B himself has even less patience with Pamela's 'piteous Lamentations for the Loss of her fantastical Innocence, which the romantick Idiot makes such a work about'.[8] Yet in the end he cannot help being enchanted even by her floods of tears. While Pamela is sobbing as if her heart would break, he prowls about the room cataloguing her beauties.[9] Soon this spoilt playboy is seriously in love and offers her a lavish settlement to become his official mistress, which she of course rejects. At the same time, Pamela discovers that, much against her will, she too is in love. In her later letters which turn into a sort of diary, she muses and confesses: 'I must own to you, that I shall never be able to think of any body in the World but him! – Presumption, you will say, and so it is. But Love is not a voluntier Thing – *Love*, did I say! – But, come, I hope not! – At least it is not, I hope, gone so far, as to make me *very* uneasy; for I know not *how* it came nor when it begun; but creep, creep it has, like a Thief upon me; and before I knew what was the Matter, it look'd like Love.'[10] It is a fate that she recognizes she can no longer escape: 'I am in for it now, over Head and Ears, I doubt, and can't help loving him, 'tis a Folly to deny it.'[11] Despite his carousing with his crass, hard-drinking cronies and the ferocious and prolonged opposition of his stuck-up sister, Lady Davers, Mr B marries Pamela – and even Lady Davers comes round in the end: 'Her Ladyship sat down, and leaned her Head against my Bosom, and made my Neck wet with her Tears, holding me by my Hands; and I wept for Company.'[12] The rake is reformed – not totally, though, for in Richardson's less compelling sequel, he strays and has to be tugged back into line by his now formidable spouse.

The whole novel is explicitly designed to improve public morality. On the title page we are told that the book is 'Now first published in order to cultivate the principles of Virtue and Religion in the Minds of the YOUTH OF BOTH SEXES'. Note the phrase in capital letters. From the first, Richardson sets his face against any sexual double standard. 'You must see,' he wrote to Lady Bradshaigh, 'that the tendency of all I have written is to exalt the sex.'[13] And in his third and last novel, *The History of Sir Charles Grandison*, he gives us a male hero who is just as unremittingly virtuous as, though rather less lively than, Pamela and Clarissa. He told a friend that *Pamela* would 'catch young and airy Minds, and when Passions run high in them, to shew how they may be directed to laudable Meanings and Purposes, in order to decry such Novels and Romances, as have a Tendency to inflame and corrupt'.[14] But, of course, the novel, like all Richardson's fiction, is anything but a po-faced sermon. As Janet Todd points out in *Sensibility: An Introduction*, 'Despite his insistence on instruction and Christian expression in fiction, Richardson, like his readers, well knew the power of the novel to escape from stated aims and pious intentions.'[15] Or, as Terry Eagleton puts it in his remarkable essay, *The Rape of Clarissa*, 'like Clarissa, his pen exceeds his intentions'.[16]

The impact of *Pamela* was immediate, explosive and enduring. There were five editions in less than a year, and it was soon being translated into all the major European languages. In Eagleton's words, in no time *Pamela* had become less a novel than a password or badge of allegiance. Fashionable ladies displayed their copies in public places and even twirled fans painted with its best-loved scenes. The book became a play, an opera, even a waxwork. It was translated into French by the Abbé Prévost, author of the scarcely less influential *Manon Lescaut*. Voltaire wrote a play upon the theme, *Nanine, ou le Préjugé vaincu*. Carlo Goldoni produced an Italian translation, which he later converted into the libretto for an *opera buffa*, *La buona figliuola*, said to be the most popular in the genre of the whole eighteenth century, the music by Niccolò Piccinni. The same composer and librettist, mirroring Richardson himself, produced a sequel, *La buona figliuola maritata*. Joseph Highmore painted a series of 12 canvases of scenes from the novel (these splendid works are now distributed between the Tate, the Fitzwilliam and the National Gallery of Victoria).

In Germany, Richardson's novel was a prime influence on the creators of the modern German literature that was still in its infancy. Klopstock, Wieland and Goethe were all fans. Goethe was ready to acknowledge Richardson's influence on his own tear-jerking bestseller *Die Leiden des Jungen Werthers*. Richardson's German translator, Christian Gellert, went into rhapsodies in his poem 'On Richardson's Portrait':

The works which he created Time never will destroy,
They are Nature, Taste, Religion.
Homer is immortal, among Christians
The British Richardson is more immortal still.[17]

In Jakob Lenz's play *Die Soldaten*, the Countess de la Roche describes *Pamela* as 'the most dangerous book ever written that a person of the lower orders could read', because it failed to teach them the class distinctions that ruled the world. Well might the nineteenth-century literary critic Erich Schmidt assert that 'Richardson belongs as much to the history of the German as of the English novel.'[18]

Perhaps Richardson's greatest fan in England was his friend Dr Samuel Johnson. He regarded Richardson as the creator of 'characters of nature, where a man must dive into the recesses of the human heart'.[19] Boswell was bewildered by Johnson's enthusiasm:

'It always appeared to me that he estimated the compositions of Richardson too highly, and that he had an unreasonable prejudice against Fielding. In comparing those two writers, he used this expression: "that there was as great a difference between them as between a man who knew how a watch was made and a man who could tell the time by looking on the dial plate".'[20]

Nothing could exceed Johnson's repeated scorn for Fielding: 'Fielding being mentioned, Johnson exclaimed, "he was a blockhead", and upon my expressing my astonishment at so strange an assertion, he said, "What I mean by his being a blockhead is that he was a barren rascal". BOSWELL: "Will you not allow, Sir, that he draws very natural pictures of human life". JOHNSON: "Why, Sir, it is of very low life. Richardson used to say, that had he not known who Fielding was, he should have believed he was an ostler. Sir, there is more knowledge of the heart in one letter of Richardson's than in all Tom Jones. I indeed never read Joseph Andrews."'

A young man called Thomas Erskine put in here: 'Surely, Sir, Richardson is very tedious.' To which Johnson replied tartly: 'Why, Sir, if you were to read Richardson for the story, your impatience would be so much fretted that you would hang yourself. But you must read him for the sentiment, and consider the story as only giving occasion to the sentiment.'[21]

Here we come to one of the great cleavages in the history of literary taste, one which resonates to this day, and in which most of the time Henry Fielding has had the upper hand. For Fielding was himself contemptuous of *Pamela*, and lost no time in dashing off a short, sprightly spoof of the book, entitled *Shamela* (it was his first venture into prose fiction). In *Shamela*, from the start the heroine is an upwardly mobile scheming minx. Not surprisingly,

Richardson never forgave Fielding, whom he had previously counted as a friend.

Fielding followed up *Shamela* with *Joseph Andrews*, a picaresque tale, which further refracts Richardson's bestseller, for the handsome footman of the title is supposedly Pamela's brother (the two books are occasionally published together). The novel follows the fairly conventional lines dating back to Cervantes and Don Quixote: there are rakes, reformed and unformed, eccentric parsons, highwaymen on the high road and long-lost siblings, interspersed with what were to become Fielding's trademark digressions on philosophy and art. What *Joseph Andrews* conspicuously lacks is anything resembling moral tension. The narrative bowls along in a mildly diverting way, never fully engaging our attention or sympathy, or causing us a moment's anxiety about the fate of the characters. Thus it is, in an oblique, unintended way, another anti-*Pamela*.

But Fielding was not alone. For the revulsion *against Pamela* was as immediate and explosive as the enthusiasm. From the start, the Second Sentimental Revolution was vigorously contested. It was said at the time that the world was divided into two different parties, Pamelists and Anti-Pamelists, as though this fierce literary quarrel rivalled, or even eclipsed, the political tussle that was to bring down Walpole's ministry in the early weeks of 1742. In the same month as *Shamela* there was published *Pamela Censured*, in which the attack took a different tack, censuring Richardson for his smutty passages and urging him to delete the sexually explicit encounters and dubious puns. Then there were the spurious continuations, such as *Pamela's Conduct in High Life*, allegedly written by 'a Gentleman more conversant in High Life than the vain Author of Pamela'. This follow-up effort reveals, quite early on, that Pamela's parents are in fact of genteel descent – a common twist in the adaptations of the book on the Continent, where it was thought that audiences would be unable to stomach Pamela's low birth. Many of the Anti-Pamelists would have agreed with Lovelace that it set a dangerous example to the staff to choose a common serving wench as heroine: 'such lessons do most of the dramatic performances I have seen give, where servants are introduced as characters essential to the play, or to act very significant or long parts in it (which, of itself, I think a fault); such lessons, I say, do they give to the footmen's gallery, that I have not wondered we have so few modest or good menservants among those who often attend their masters or mistresses to plays.'[22] Another bogus sequel, *The Life of Pamela*, denounces the vulgar style of the heroine, and argues that Richardson did not know what he was talking about: his writing 'plainly betrays the Mechanick ... knowing nothing of the Behaviour and Conversation of the Nobility' — an accusation that was to be made against another great lower-middle-class novelist, Charles Dickens, when he ventured to portray the aristocracy. In his numerous later revisions of the text, Richardson did indeed take some account of these snobbish criticisms, not least in his own sequel.

But what he did not modify, let alone erase, was the moral passion which illuminates Pamela's troubled progress and which held its contemporary readers spellbound. The intense and prolonged self-examination of the principal characters is an extraordinary reprise of the same phenomenon in the First Sentimental Revolution, in which, as we have seen, the heroes and heroines of the great romances of Béroul and Chrétien explore their doubts and fears in passages (though of verse, not of correspondence) which may run into hundreds of lines. It is just this obsessive dwelling on the ramifications of one's inner feelings that makes the breezy Henry Fielding so uneasy and sets his teeth on edge, as it did many readers of the old school who preferred the hard-nosed comedy of the Restoration and found the new sentimentality mawkish and unhealthy.

It is only now that the new *mentalité* becomes conscious of itself. The word 'sentimental' in the sense we mean it is first found in a letter to Richardson of 1749 from Lady Bradshaigh. She asks him: 'What, in your opinion, is the meaning of the word *sentimental* ... so much in vogue among the polite ... Everything clever and agreeable is comprehended in that word ... I am frequently astonished to hear such a one is a *sentimental* man; we were a *sentimental* party; I have been taking a *sentimental* walk.'[23] Here in the innocence of its debut 'sentimentality' is taken at face value: as the expression of genuine feelings which may enhance our understanding and enjoyment of life. There is no hint of the pejorative sense that we shall soon encounter: of sentimentality as fake, affected, excessive.

The emotional intensity that Richardson deploys in *Pamela* is precisely the quality that inspired his foremost admirer in France, Denis Diderot, to write his *Éloge de Richardson* in 1762. What Diderot admires is Richardson's ability to keep the reader totally involved, to give us the sense of *being there*: 'This author does not send blood flowing down the walls, he does not transport you to distant lands, he does not expose you to being eaten by savages, he does not confine himself within the secret haunts of debauchery. The world we live in is his scene of action, his drama is anchored in truth, his people are as real as it is possible to be, his characters are taken from the world of society, his events belong to the customs of all civilized nations; the passions he portrays are those I feel within me; the same things arouse them, and I recognize their force in myself; the problems and afflictions of his people are of the same kind as those which constantly hang over me; he shows me the general course of life as I experience it.'

Diderot insists that Richardson 'constantly reminds you of the important things in life. *The more you read him, the more pleasure you take in him.* He it is who lights the depths of the cavern with his torch; he it is who teaches you to detect the cunning, dishonest motives concealed and hidden from our sight beneath other, honest motives, which are always the first to show themselves.'

One of Diderot's reasons for writing the *Éloge* was to criticize Prévost's translations, especially of *Clarissa*, for, as we would say, 'bowdlerizing' the original (Dr Thomas Bowdler and his sanitized renderings of Shakespeare still lay 50 years in the future): 'If you have only read Richardson's works in your elegant French translation, and think you know them, you are wrong. You do not know Lovelace; you do not know the unhappy Clarissa; you do not know Miss Howe, her dear, tender Miss Howe, because you have not seen her with her hair dishevelled, lying across her friend's coffin, wringing her hands, lifting her tear-stained eyes to heaven, filling the Harlowes' home with her shrill cries and casting imprecations upon the whole of this cruel family. *You know nothing of the effect of these things, which your shallow taste would suppress*, because you have not heard the mournful sound of the bells of the parish church, carried on the wind to the Harlowes' house, and awakening the remorse which lay dormant in these stony hearts; because you have not seen them start up at the sound of the hearse bearing the corpse of their victim.'

Diderot emphasizes that Richardson's moral intensity achieves its effects by the accumulation of details at crucial moments (often physical, even sordid details of the sort which the classical drama excludes on principle). This is indeed one of Richardson's defences when he is accused of intolerable prolixity. *Pamela* is 500 pages long. His masterpiece, *Clarissa*, published seven years later, is three times as long, nearly twice the length of Tolstoy's *War and Peace*, which was to become the exemplar of the mega-novel. Richardson in part admits the justice of the accusation. 'I am a poor pruner,' he confesses.[24] He tells us in the Postscript to *Clarissa* that some readers had complained that the story moved too slowly, particularly in the first and second volumes which are chiefly taken up with the altercations between Clarissa and the various members of her family. He responds with a careful defence of his technique on the grounds of realism:

'But is it not true that those altercations are the foundation of the whole, and therefore a necessary part of the work? The letters and conversations where the story makes the slowest progress, are presumed to be *characteristic*. They give occasion likewise to suggest many interesting *personalities*, in which a good deal of the instruction essential to a work of this nature is conveyed ... To all which we may add, that there was frequently a necessity to be very circumstantial and minute, in order to preserve and maintain that air of probability, which is necessary to be maintained in a story designed to represent real life; and which is rendered extremely busy and active by the plots and contrivances formed and carried on by one of the principal characters.'[25]

The reader needs to see exactly how the fiendish Lovelace deploys and disguises his army of spies, brothel-keepers and rogues for hire to ensnare and deceive poor Clarissa. Yes, the epistolary technique does spin out proceedings. Letters are by their nature a fragmentary, unreliable form of communication. In *Clarissa*, as Terry Eagleton points out in *The Rape of Clarissa*, 'Letters, the most intimate sign of the subject, are waylaid, forged, stolen, lost, copied, cited, censored, parodied, misread, rewritten, submitted to mocking commentary, woven into other texts which alter their meaning, exploited for ends unforeseen by their authors.'[26]

Yet letters are also so immediate, so brimming with feeling. How moved we still are to come across an old letter from a soldier at the front to his mother or sweetheart, both writer and recipient totally unknown to us, the ink and paper long faded, but the sentiments as fresh as the day they were scribbled down in some sodden foxhole.

We must not imagine either Clarissa herself as some kind of humourless, pious character, always in tears or on her knees. On the contrary, she is a lively, feisty girl of 18, who is fed up with her peevish elder sister Arabella with her jealousy, her foul temper and her 'plump, high-fed face'. Her brother James is just as bad: 'How happy might I have been with any other brother in the world but Mr James Harlowe and with any other sister but *his* sister!'[27] She is exasperated, too, by her meek mother who is under the thumb of her father who she does continue to be fond of, despite his temper also being soured by 'the torture of a gouty paroxysm'. She is driven to distraction when the whole crew gang up on her to persuade her to marry Mr Selmes, the wealthy creep whom she can't stand.

Not that she is blind to the faults of the mercurial rake Robert Lovelace, who pursues her throughout the book and who has become anathema to the Harlowe family after he injures James in a squalid fracas. From the first, Clarissa can see what a poseur Lovelace is: 'You cannot imagine how saucily the man looked; as if, in short, he was disappointed that he had not made a more sensible impression upon me; and when he recollected himself (as he did immediately), what a visible struggle it cost him to change his haughty airs for more placid ones!'[28] She notices, too, how rude he is to his own servants while sucking up to the staff in other houses to curry favour.²⁹ Lovelace develops into one of the great bad hats of European literature, whether he is breaking up Mr Smith's glove and soap shop in Covent Garden³⁰ – a scene reminiscent of and no less vivid than the Bullingdon bloods on the razzle in Evelyn Waugh's *Decline and Fall* – or schmoozing the local ladies at Colonel Ambrose's reception by a mixture of adept flattery and shocking indecencies. Watching him in action at Colonel Ambrose's, Anna Howe, who regards all men with equal contempt, has to concede that 'Nothing can touch him for half an hour together.'³¹

After fruitlessly trying to persuade Clarissa to become his mistress and repeatedly imprisoning her under the guard of a bunch of his old whores, he finally date-rapes her, first by putting a drug in her tea, then giving her beer when she asks for water. After he has done with her, he is now and then overcome with a stagey sort of remorse, but quickly recovers his *bienséance* and tells his cronies not to make such a big deal of the whole thing: 'When all's done, Miss Clarissa Harlowe has but run the fate of a thousand others of her sex – only that they did not set such a romantic value upon what they call their *honour*; that's all.'³² He laughs off even the resort to the drugs: 'Then, as to the worst part of my treatment of this lady – How many men are there, who as well as I have sought, by intoxicating liquors, first to inebriate, then to subdue? What signifies what the *potations* were, when the same end was in view?'³³ In no time, he is organizing another orgy with his mates and a few of the whores who have been assisting in his dirty work: 'I am really sick at heart for a frolic ...'³⁴

Yet Lovelace is depicted with such dash that early readers of the book could not help falling a little in love with him. 'Little did I think at the time', Richardson complained to Lady Bradshaigh, 'that those Qualities ... would have given Women of Virtue and Honour such a liking to Lovelace, as I have found to be the case with many.' Laurence Lerner detects a hint of simulation in the author's astonishment: 'Deep down in Richardson, there must have been an identification ... with Lovelace, the kind of identification on which such a dramatic genius necessarily draws.'³⁵ Lerner, like Eagleton, detects a good deal of proto-feminism in the book, though Richardson always publicly protests his belief in paternal authority, but only if wisely exercised. 'If ever there was a case where we should trust the tale and not the artist, it is *Clarissa*.'[36] Or, as Eagleton concludes, 'there is also a more radical current flowing through Richardson, which can be traced all the way through from eighteenth-century women's writing, resurfaces explosively in the "female Gothic", finds its major articulation in the Brontës and passes on to the women's writing of our own time'.[37] Lerner goes further, in identifying Anna Howe and Charlotte Grandison as carrying 'the seed of the modern feminist attack on love. Incipient in Anna and Charlotte are Kate Millett and Shulamith Firestone.'[38] If that assertion sounds over the top, just listen to Anna on men: 'But I, who think our sex inferior in nothing to the other but in want of opportunities, of which the narrow-minded mortals industriously seek to deprive us, lest we should surpass them as much as in what they chiefly value themselves upon, as we do in all the graces of a fine imagination ...'[39]

To our post-modern eyes, the complaints of Anna and Clarissa seem so familiar as to be stating the obvious. Every day, the media report cases of the brutal abduction and rape of a bewildered, unwilling young girl, often under the age of consent, sometimes followed by forcible imprisonment. A variety of date-rape drugs, including, of course, alcohol, are often deployed. Clarissa's imprisonment in Mrs Sinclair's genteel Soho brothel cannot but remind us of the goings-on at Jeffrey Epstein's island paradise, or of the treatment that aspiring film actresses could expect if they answered the summons to Harvey Weinstein's hotel suite, or any young woman who went for a job interview at Harrods when Mohamed Al-Fayed owned the store. The modern response to *Clarissa, or the History of a Young Lady* would be short, and anything but sweet: Me Too! What Chaucer first described so piercingly in *Troilus and Criseyde*, nearly four centuries later Richardson has brought to a pitch even more passionate and unforgettable.

We must not imagine that because Richardson does not describe the actual rape itself – it is a deliberate, and resonant, absence in the text — that he is therefore squeamish. On the contrary, his thickness of description piles on the horror. To look for such overwhelming evocations of disgust in our own time we would need to resort to the deplorable pages of Céline or Michel Houellebecq. Even they would need to salute Richardson's description of 'Mrs Sinclair', the brothel-keeper's assumed respectable name, on her deathbed:

'Her misfortune has not at all sunk but rather, as I thought, increased her flesh, rage and violence perhaps swelling her muscly features. Behold her then, spreading the whole tumbled bed with her huge quaggy carcass: her mill-post arms held up, her broad hands clenched with violence; her big eyes goggling and flaming-red as we may suppose those of a salamander; her matted grizzly hair made irreverent by her wickedness (her clouted head-dress being half off) spread about her fat ears and brawny neck; her livid lips arched, and working violently; her broad chin in convulsive motion; her wide mouth by reason of the contraction of her forehead (which seemed to be half-lost in its own frightful furrows) splitting her face, as it were, into two parts; and her huge tongue hideously rolling in it; heaving, puffing as if for breath, her bellows-shaped and various-coloured breasts ascending by turns to her chin and descending out of sight with the violence of her gasping.'[40]

How extraordinary in retrospect seem the responses, not of Richardson's original readers but of those twentieth-century critics who could not see what all the fuss was about, and who proudly confess that they find all his novels unreadable. F. R. Leavis, for example, while conceding that *Clarissa* is 'a really impressive book', asserts that 'it's no use pretending that Richardson can ever be made a current classic again',[41] and firmly excludes him from *The Great Tradition* (1948), while Leavis's wife, the no less formidable Q. D. Leavis, dismisses *Clarissa* as 'of almost entirely historical interest'.[42] John Mullan in his *Sentiment and Sensibility* (1988) declares that 'If Richardson's writings have become in some ways alien or inaccessible to us, one reason is that their moral didacticism and their indulgence in cameos of lachrymose emotion together invite a practice of reading now forgotten. The preoccupations of these narratives have become foreign, or even embarrassing.'[43] Lawrence Stone, in his highly influential The Family, Sex and Marriage (1977), claims that 'one has to steel oneself to read such boring, moralistic and sentimental contemporary bestsellers as Richardson's *Pamela*, or the archetype of the new trend, Henry Mackenzie's *The Man of Feeling* of 1770, in which there is an outburst of weeping (by either sex) on average every ten-and-a-half pages'.[44]

Another strand of twentieth-century criticism, especially prevalent in the 1960s, is to echo Lovelace in declaring that all this fuss about a mere rape is ludicrously overdone. In *The Rape of Clarissa*, Eagleton describes, barely able to believe it, how the deconstructionist William Beatty Warner finds 'Lovelace the hero and Clarissa the villain, without allowing a little matter like rape to modify his judgment. "By winning our laughter and giving us pleasure, Lovelace helps to undo the matrix of truth and value through which Clarissa would have us see, know and judge."'[45]

V. S. Pritchett, normally a sensible critic, insists that Clarissa 'represents that extreme of puritanism which desires to be raped'.[46] Dorothy van Ghent, in her essay on the novel, remarks that, considered in the abstract, 'the deflowering of a young lady' represents 'a singularly thin and unrewarding piece of action ... and one which scarcely seems to deserve the universal uproar which it provokes in the book.'[47] She is predictably scornful of the scene of Clarissa's dying: 'The scene in the death room is an astonishing one. The room is crowded with people, all pressing round the dying woman to obtain her blessing. The mourning is as public as possible; every sigh, every groan, every tear is recorded. One is given to understand that nothing could be a greater social good than Clarissa's death, nothing could be more enjoyable than to watch her in her death throes (she performs them charmingly), nothing a greater privilege than to be present at this festival of death and to weep and sniffle in the common orgy.'[48] But surely even a twentieth-century American academic must at some time in her life have been part of a sorrowing family grouped in a hospital room and shedding the odd stifled tear. Or perhaps they don't do that sort of thing any more.

How weird Professor van Ghent's reaction would have seemed to Lady Bradshaigh who wrote to Richardson after reading *Clarissa*: 'I verily believe I have shed a pint of tears, and my heart is still bursting, tho' they cease not to flow at this moment, nor will, I fear for some time ... When alone, in agonies would I lay down the book, take it up again, walk about the room, let fall a flood of tears, wipe my eyes, read again, perhaps not three lines, throw away the book, crying out, excuse me, good Mr Richardson, I cannot go on.'[49]

Those reactions from the 1960s seem to come from another age. This flaunted callousness belongs to a renaissance of stony-heartedness, which we shall come to in its proper place, but which needs to be mentioned here, if only to show the continued power of Richardson's great novel to provoke and mystify across centuries. What also needs to be said here, and with some force, is that any modern reader who embarks on *Pamela* or *Clarissa* with an open mind and a ready sympathy may find herself (or even himself) in for an experience which is both startling and, in my own experience, uniquely satisfying. To come clean and speak personally, I found myself wholeheartedly engaged from start to finish. By contrast, even my favourite novels by Jane Austen, George Eliot and Henry James seem a little dry and distanced; this is even more true of the French realists, Stendhal, Balzac and Flaubert. Much of what Diderot said in praise of Richardson seems to me unquestionably correct. Ultimately, as another early Richardson enthusiast, Johann Wolfgang von Goethe, said: 'Feeling is everything.'

LOVE DIVINE, ALL LOVES EXCELLING

Just as in the First Sentimental Revolution, romance and religion get into their stride almost simultaneously. Once again, the zeitgeist blows through all the deepest chambers of the human heart. Only a few months before Samuel Richardson settled down to write *Pamela*, the Revd John Wesley was sitting, rather reluctantly he tells us, at a Moravian service in Aldersgate in the City of London in the evening of 24 May 1738, when 'I felt my heart strangely warmed. I felt I did trust in Christ, Christ alone, for salvation, and an assurance was given me that he had taken away my sins, even mine, and saved me from the law of sin and death.' His brother Charles had reported having had an identical experience only three days earlier, in a house round the corner in Little Britain, next to St Bartholomew's Hospital. It was this sensation of personal salvation that constituted the evangelical conversion of both brothers. Methodists today still celebrate 24 May as 'Aldersgate Day', and there is a bronze monument on the site of the Moravian meeting house next to the Museum of London. Is there anywhere else in the world a memorial to a mere heart-warming moment? Well, yes, there is, because there's a more modest plaque commemorating the heart-warming moments of both brothers, round the corner in Postman's Park, very near the site of Charles's conversion experience.

The brothers had long been pious believers since their Oxford days, nearly 20 years earlier. Their relentless schedule of prayer, fasting and visiting the sick and needy had caused them to be mocked as 'Method-ists' by their impious fellows. They had happily embraced the label, just as Tories and Whigs had adopted their insulting nicknames a few decades earlier. But what really started Methodism as we know it was Aldersgate Day: the movement of the heart, the assurance of salvation and the unrestrained display of religious emotion that the Wesleys and their followers became famous for. 'Methodism' seems something of a misnomer, in fact, for a faith so unmethodical, at its best so springy and instinctive.

And what tears they could shed in the practice of that faith and in spreading it to millions all over the world! George Whitefield, a friend of the brothers since Oxford, came to be regarded as the greatest preacher of the age, and the greatest public weeper. A contemporary reported that 'I hardly ever knew him go through a sermon without weeping, more or less, and I truly believe his were the tears of sincerity ... sometimes he exceedingly wept, stamped loudly and passionately, and was frequently so overcome, that for a few seconds, you would suspect he never could recover.' His audiences on both sides of the Atlantic might number 10,000 or more. And he used to comment on their tears. During one sermon, preached in a field, in which he retold the story of Abraham and

Isaac, he told his huge audience, 'I see your hearts affected. I see your eyes weep.' The tears were a sign of God's presence with them. Some of his earliest sermons were given to outdoor gatherings of miners at Kingswood colliery, Bristol. 'My bowels have long since yearned towards the poor colliers, who are very numerous, and as sheep having no shepherd.' He noted that 'the first discovery of their being affected, was, to see the white gutters made by their tears, which plentifully fell down their black cheeks, as they came out of their coal pits'.[50]

What a contrast these exuberant services, whether held out in the fields or in crowded halls, made with the bland and dignified proceedings of the Church of England. Methodist meetings were lifted to even greater exhilaration by their passionate singing of hymns. The earlier Protestant churches had sanctioned only the singing of metrical psalms, such as the Old Hundredth, 'All people that on earth do dwell', a version of Psalm 100. Although these could often be resonant and impressive, by their nature they drew only on the Old Testament, and did not mention Jesus. The 16-year-old Isaac Watts complained about this to his father, who was the Elder of a Dissenting congregation, and his father told him to do something about it. The result was the first hymns focused on the saving mission of Jesus, many of them still sung today, such as 'When I Survey the Wondrous Cross'. In the next generation, Methodist hymn-writers, above all Charles Wesley, turned this trickle of new hymns into a torrent, unparalleled since the outpourings of the troubadours. Charles is reckoned to have written somewhere between 5,000 and 10,000 hymns for all occasions, including such enduring favourites as 'Christ the Lord Is Risen Today', 'Hark! The Herald Angels Sing', 'Jesu, Lover of My Soul', 'Lo! He Comes with Clouds Descending' and perhaps greatest of all, 'Love Divine, All Loves Excelling'.

It is not too much to say that the hymns of Charles Wesley are the true love poetry of the mid-eighteenth century. They burn with a passion which is curiously absent from the secular poets of the Augustan Age, or perhaps not curiously, for they were writing to classical models which favoured serenity and *ataraxia*.

The sentimentally charged worship of the Methodists provoked instant fury from the anti-sentimentalists, just as quickly as had the sentimental fiction of the 1740s. As early as 1744, Edmund Gibson, Bishop of Hereford, issued the sort of tirade which was to become familiar over the succeeding decades, as the Methodists conquered more and more hearts, especially among the poorer classes in the new industrial districts. Gibson lambasted their disobedience to the Church hierarchy, their indifference to orthodox doctrine, their nomadic preaching which encouraged 'the rabble' to meet outdoors and make trouble. How much better was 'regular attendance on the publick offices of religion' than 'those sudden Agonies, Roarings and Screamings, Tremblings, Droppings-down, Ravings and Madnesses'.[51] This revulsion against 'Enthusiasm' was still going hot and strong in the nineteenth century. Witness the character of the Revd Melchisedech Howler in *Dombey and Son*, Stiggins in *The Pickwick Papers* and Mr Chadband in *Bleak House*, the Methodist banker Bulstrode in *Middlemarch* with his murky past, oily hypocrites every one. The distrust even persisted into the twentieth century, by which time Methodism had become rather depressingly respectable. E. P. Thompson in *The Making of the English Working Class* (1963) is particularly severe. Methodism was 'almost diabolic in its penetration into the very sources of human personality, directed towards the repression of emotional and spiritual energies ... The box-like blackening chapels stood in the industrial districts like great traps for the human psyche.' In Thompson's view, 'it is difficult not to see in Methodism these years a ritualized form of psychic masturbation'.[52] For militant socialists like Thompson, what was wrong with Methodism was the opposite of the indictment of orthodox Anglican divines. Far from stirring up trouble among the lower orders, Methodism kept them too quiet. 'These Sabbath orgasms of feeling made more possible the single-minded weekday direction of these energies to the consummation of productive labour.'[53] Religion was 'the opium of the masses', in Marx's famous phrase, echoed four years later by that restless Anglican clergyman the Revd Charles Kingsley, in his letter to Chartists (1848): 'We have used the Bible as if it was a constable's handbook – an opium dose for keeping beasts of burden patient while they are being overloaded.'

The connections between sacred and secular sentimentality were anything but coincidental. The Puritan traditions of self-examination and of diary-keeping are echoed in the psychological depths of Richardson's novels and in their epistolary technique, not to mention their proclaimed (if not exactly fulfilled) moral purpose. Both the preachers and the heroines are vulnerable souls and acutely conscious of being vulnerable. Accordingly, they are equally liable to burst into tears. Their lachrymosity is part of being morally alive. Janet Todd catches these correspondences perfectly: 'The hymns of Methodism, like Charles Wesley's "Jesu, Lover of My Soul", are a kind of sentimental dramatic poetry reaching out to the singers and taking them into the religious theatre.'[54] Todd emphasizes that many of Wesley's hymns are less confessions or songs of praise than efforts to align the emotions of the singers and teach the feeling heart the correct response. They are written not for the regular church services (in which they still play such a part today) but for the emotional happenings of field meetings: 'His hymns tell of sudden, extreme transitions from despair to ecstasy and they express emotions in the broken speech typical of sentimental literature.'[55] Jesus and the Man of Feeling become the same sort of kindly friend and comforter. John Wesley himself reissued a sentimental novel, Henry Brooke's *The Fool of Quality*, as an illustration of Methodism, or 'the religion of the heart'.[56] Just as the secular love poems of the troubadours had in the thirteenth century morphed into verses in praise of the Virgin, so in the eighteenth century the hymns of the Methodists brought Christianity back to the adoration of Jesus; religion became personalized again.

THE CONTINENTAL VERSION

The craze for the English novel of sentiment almost immediately spread to the Continent, as we have seen, inspiring translations, imitations and adaptations of every kind. Naturally, the leading writers in France and Germany felt drawn to try their own hand, for a mixture of patriotic and commercial reasons. And they, too, were richly rewarded, none more so than the two greatest lions of the day, Jean-Jacques Rousseau and Johann Wolfgang von Goethe. The bestsellers they turned out in amazingly quick time deserve a little closer attention, to reveal some interesting contrasts with the English originals they had themselves lapped up.

For all their many dissimilarities, what Rousseau and Goethe did have in common was that they could launch themselves into virtually any artistic genre and make a huge commercial success of it. Among much else, Rousseau composed an opera, a huge treatise on education, virtuoso exercises in political theory and a constitution for Corsica. Goethe was a brilliant lyric poet from the start, then a playwright and theatre director at Weimar, before he wrote his first novel. What the two men of genius did with the sentimental novel was something new. Both were professed admirers of Richardson, and they copied his epistolary technique, but the result could scarcely be more different.

Rousseau was a master of blithe self-contradiction. Having denounced 'effeminate', sentimental novels, he himself produced the most sentimental, effeminate novel ever written – and one of the most successful. The *comédie larmoyante*, the convention that light literature should bring tears rather than laughter, was nearly a century old when Rousseau brought out *Julie* in 1761, a year before *Émile*, his seminal work on education. It leaves its predecessors trailing far behind in its relentless lachrymosity.

Julie, her tutor and later lover, Saint-Preux, her best friend, Claire, and their friend the English milord with the improbable name of Lord Bomston are all in tears from start to finish. They weep when they meet, they weep when they say goodbye, they weep when they are happy, they weep when they are sad, they weep when they have sex, they weep even more when they don't have sex. All the characters are intrinsically good by nature. Even Julie's father, the crotchety Baron whose snobbishness prevents her from marrying the humbly born Saint-Preux, turns out at the end to be a loveable old codger. It is only the *convenances* and *bienséances* of society that make them unhappy. The one man who does not weep is the imperturbable M. de Wolmar, who eventually marries Julie. He, too, believes that 'all characters are good and healthy in themselves; there are no errors in nature'.[57] According to Wolmar, every criminal would have followed the path of virtue, if only he had been better directed. By the end, even M. de Wolmar is in tears, too. No book has ever tugged more shamelessly at the heartstrings. As Saint-Preux warbles to Edward Bomston: 'O sentiment, sentiment! Sweet life of the soul, what heart of iron have you not touched! From what unfortunate mortal have you never torn tears?'[58]

The Niagara of tears that Julie squeezed from its readers all over Europe cannot disguise the reality that the book is a deliberate, if not cynical, attempt to catch the popular market, unique only in its unbridled effusiveness, but also borrowing shamelessly from earlier successful models, most obviously *Clarissa* (long as *Julie* is, *Clarissa* is three times as long). The interminable laments of all the characters borrow from classical French drama, too. I lost count of the echoes of Racine, especially from *Phèdre* and *Bérénice*. Anthony Powell observed that 'an immense self-pity is an almost essential ingredient of all bestsellers'. There is scarcely a page of *Julie* that is not drenched in the stuff. The style, too, is quite unlike that of the finer passages of the *Confessions* or the *Reveries*, which are genuinely lyrical or poignant. With *Julie*, it is as though Philip Roth had knocked out a vast romantic saga in the style of Barbara Cartland.

Nor is Rousseau blind to the defects of the book. As so often, he is almost post-modern in his readiness to subvert himself. In a puckish preface, he anticipates all the criticisms that might be made of the book. There's not a single evil deed or bad man in it, he says. It's full of exclamations, and overflowing with verbosity and sentiment. Nobody's going to like it, certainly not the libertines or the society ladies. Also, it's full of commonplaces and flat language, because the people in it are not witty academicians or philosophers but provincial folk – solitaries, young people, almost children – with a romantic imagination. In fact, he tells us, it's a girly sort of book, the kind of effeminate novel for which previously he had nothing but scorn. So, this vast hymn to nature and the natural goodness of man is admitted by the author to be a deeply artificial production, conceived with Rousseau's usual amazing fertility and energy (he seems to have written it in not much more than a year) but with no ambition to reflect the real world.

Just as the political reformation that Rousseau envisages demands a completely artificial remoulding of society from top to bottom, so *Julie* makes no effort to confront the world as it is but prefers to conjure an imaginary universe of unblemished sentiment and virtue. It is a bleached-out fantasy in which all the men and women are good but unlucky. Compare its interminable vapourings with Rousseau's *Confessions*, that salty, venomous, deceitful, salacious but also gloriously vivid and occasionally warm and touching masterpiece. When Rousseau speaks kindly there of some ill-used abbé or wretched prostitute, you feel he means it.

Rousseau's success with the public was not matched by the reactions of his old, mostly now former friends. Part of the purpose of Diderot's *Éloge de Richardson* was to praise Richardson for all the qualities which he thought the recently published *Julie* conspicuously lacked. Voltaire denounced *Julie* as 'stupid, bourgeois, impudent, boring' and thought that the novel would be a success 'to the shame of this country'. He even went so far as to write an attack on it entitled *Quatre Lettres sur La Nouvelle Héloïse*, which he had published under the name of his friend, the literary hack the Marquis de Ximénès, known to posterity only for having coined the phrase 'la perfide Albion'.

Equally commercial motives cannot be denied in the case of *Werther*. *Götz von Berlingen*, Goethe's barnstorming first play, was aimed at the patriotic German public. By contrast, his novel *The Sorrows of Young Werther* was for young people everywhere. In tone and technique it owes a lot to *La Nouvelle Héloïse* and *Clarissa*. The copious weepings, the unbridled privileging of personal feeling, the letters format – all these are characteristic of the eighteenth-century novels of sensibility. Werther differs only in two respects. The letters all come from one person, young Werther, and the novel is drenched in the possibility of suicide as the only noble way out of an intolerable situation.

Werther is the 'I', whose hankerings, recollections and opinions fill the 100-odd pages of this novella, which overwhelmed the European reading public because they already thought as

Werther does. He worships Nature as they do, loves the simple life as everyone up to Marie Antoinette claimed to do, he is at his happiest picking peas in the inn's garden and shelling them while reading his Homer. And, of course, he simply adores Ossian, who replaces Homer in his heart, to the extent that he reads six pages of his translations of Ossian to his beloved Lotte, who bursts into tears, the only possible reaction. The latter part of the story, rather awkwardly, has to be told, 'by the Editor to the Reader', because Werther has already shot himself with pistols belonging to Lotte's husband Albert. Werther's mind has been on killing himself for much of the novel, because the situation is hopeless from the start, as Lotte is already engaged to Albert.

Copycat suicides have been dubbed the Werther Effect, but Goethe's biographers tend to dismiss it as only a persistent rumour that young men actually killed themselves in droves after reading the book. Quite a few, though, did go around spouting Ossian and dressed in the Werther uniform of blue frock coat, buff vest and pants. Goethe himself went on a walking tour with three friends in this kit, with the addition of grey bowler hats. This must be a debut for the bowler, normally identified as a nineteenth-century innovation. When Napoleon met Goethe at Erfurt in 1808, he claimed to have read *Werther* seven times, though this is the kind of boast dictators make – Mussolini claimed to have read all hundred volumes of Giuseppe Mazzini's collected works.

There was, however, one attested case of suicide painfully close to Goethe. On 16 January 1778, Christel von Lassberg, daughter of a court official in Weimar, while embroiled in an unhappy love affair, jumped from a pontoon bridge into the icy waters of the River Ilm and drowned. A copy of *Werther* was found in her pocket – or was that only a rumour, too? The biographers don't seem quite sure. At all events, Goethe was summoned from a nearby pond where he was skating with the Duke (how cold the river must have been), and he immediately commissioned a memorial to the unlucky girl near the bridge which he crossed every day on his way into Weimar from his Garden House. He wielded a pickaxe and shovel himself and told Charlotte von Stein that they worked deep into the night: 'in the end I continued alone until the hour when she had died; that's the kind of evening it was. Orion stood so beautifully in the sky ... There is something dangerously attractive and inviting about this grief, like the water itself, and the reflection of the stars of heaven that shines from both.' This is pure Goethe: he alone digs on, watching Nature, watching himself, appropriating Christel's feelings if not her fate.

At the same time, he was undeniably under pressure. Had he inspired a terrible example? Was he in a similar case to W. B. Yeats:

> Did that play of mine send out
> Certain men the English shot?
> Did words of mine put too great strain
> On that woman's reeling brain?

Only a couple of weeks before Christel's death, Goethe had put on at the Weimar court theatre a farce he had written, called *The Triumph of Sentimentalism*, with himself playing a King who has gone mad with the craze for Nature and Sentiment and who fills the arbour in his garden with soppy books like *La Nouvelle Héloïse* and *Werther* itself. Everything about the King is fake and ridiculous. This rather mediocre piece made some viewers uncomfortable. Wasn't Goethe heartless to make fun of the silly folk whom he himself had misled three years earlier? People at the time found Goethe's behaviour decidedly creepy. Emilie von Berlepsch, the author and campaigner for women's rights (she became an admirer of Mary Wollstonecraft), wrote to Herder: 'Tell me something about this strange new play Goethe has written! Presumably a satire on the unfortunate girls and young men he used to make dizzy with his writings, and now he's laughing at them. An odd person! ... I find him quite distasteful with his everlasting vacillation between wit and feeling, weakness and power. And it's proving more and more difficult to get a clear idea of him from the things I happen to know about him.'[59]

Safranski is inclined to acquit his subject: 'Goethe's ridicule of Werther-like sentimentalism could surprise only those who hadn't read *Werther* closely. For the novel presents Werther as a young man who has read too much of such literature, and whose feelings come more from books than life.'

But will this quite do as a let-off? There is so much of Goethe in the character of Werther: the Nature worship, the simple-lifery, the enthusiasm for physical activity, the craze for Ossian (egged on by Herder) and above all the importance of the Ego and of one's feelings. It's not Werther, after all, but Goethe's Faust who says 'Gefühl ist alles' (admittedly he is chatting up Gretchen at the time). Yes, it was, as Boyle says, a novel about a fashion, but Goethe himself was swept up in this fashion. He admitted: 'I myself was in this case and know best what anguish I suffered in it and what exertion it cost me to escape from it.' We are reminded of Flaubert saying of his controversial masterpiece, 'Madame Bovary, c'est moi.' But the difference is huge. From first to last, Flaubert mercilessly mocks Emma's fantasies and pretensions. When she finally takes poison, she is ending a life which she herself is responsible for ruining. No such mercilessness is visible in *Werther*.

The question remains just how far Goethe ever did escape from the Werther mindset. He rewrote, or more often added to, the novel several times, in 1782, 1783, 1785 and 1786, each time trying to meet the charge that the novel commended suicide. He makes Werther's love appear a little more pathological and self-destructive and Lotte's feelings for him a good deal more doubtful. But he can't destroy the underlying emotional pull of the book, and he doesn't really try to.

When looking back over Goethe's in-and-out tactics on the Werther question, we are strongly reminded of Rousseau's disingenuous preface to *Julie*. It is hard to avoid the feeling that both books are drenched in bad faith, written to secure a fast buck but endowed with the author's brilliant page-turning facility. There is none of the moral intensity of *Clarissa*, none of Richardson's marvellous realism in the depiction of character and incident.

THE DAWN OF TOLERATION

But where does it all come from? How does England, and then the whole of Europe, suddenly become awash with sentiment? How does this tubby jobbing printer come to embark on an entirely new form of fiction? And how is there already a reading public eager to lap up the heroine's tears and blot the book's pages with their own?

We must briefly turn back to review the bitter history of the previous century and the religious strife which repeatedly erupted into both civil and foreign wars. Nothing in England quite equalled the horrific massacre and then expulsion of the French Protestants in the reign of Louis XIV. Nor did England suffer the appalling miseries of the Thirty Years' War which impoverished and depopulated the German-speaking lands. But our island story during those years was ghastly enough. After the repeated burning and hanging of heretics under Mary and Elizabeth (yesterday's heretics turning into today's enforcers of orthodoxy), the regime ricocheted from parliamentary monarchy to absolute monarchy under Charles I, then to a shape-shifting republic under Cromwell, then to the restoration of a parliamentary monarchy. The second of the four Stuart monarchs was executed, the fourth forced to abdicate and flee into exile, he and his descendants perpetuating the civil conflict into the middle of the next century. Throughout the period, England was a byword for instability and intolerance. During the 86 years of the Stuart era, every single variety of the Christian faith was harassed and persecuted at one time or another, not excluding the Church of England, which had been founded with the aim of uniting the nation under a single national church.

As early as 1641, Cromwell and Sir Henry Vane proposed the abolition of the Anglican bishops in the Root and Branch Bill. This objective was finally achieved in 1646, after the First Civil War. Then, under the Cromwellian protectorate, the State grabbed direct control over the nation's worship: a commission of 'Triers' was set up to judge whether local ministers were obeying the new rules. The Triers were backed up by a nationwide network of 'Ejectors' to chuck out the offenders, for such offences as using the old prayer book, following Popish practices, or 'writing, preaching or otherwise publishing any disaffection to the present government'.[60] Any lingering illusion that Cromwell seriously believed in religious tolerance cannot survive close attention to what he actually did when in power. Contemporaries had no hesitation in comparing Oliver with his great-great-great-uncle Thomas Cromwell. Later Whig historians tried to conscript Oliver into a rosy narrative of the gradual emergence of religious liberty. He just doesn't fit. The same Whig historians have also tried to represent these conflicts as episodes in a heroic struggle for the emergence of parliamentary democracy, and/or as a 'War of the Three Kingdoms' which was to morph into the sunlit uplands of our United Kingdom. But these formulations, too, make an uncomfortable fit with the facts. These were brutal clashes which set families against families and county against county, and left millions in despair who wanted no part of 'this war without an enemy'. It was not so much a story of spasmodic progress towards modern democracy as of repeated *restorations* of constitutional monarchy and of the nation finally subsiding into civil peace out of sheer exhaustion.

William of Orange landed at Brixham on 5 November 1688. James II fled to France on 23 December. The following February, a special Convention Parliament declared that James had 'vacated' the throne, and installed William and his wife, James's daughter Mary, as joint monarchs. James tried to recoup by landing in Ireland, but was eventually defeated at the Battle of the Boyne in July 1690. Parliament hastened to agree the new settlement in the Bill of Rights. A crucial underpinning was provided by the Toleration Act of May 1689, which permitted most Dissenters to worship publicly; the proclaimed aim was 'to unite their Majesties' Protestant subjects in interest and affection'. By December 1689, the Glorious Revolution was a fact.

Among the exiles returning from the Continent in William's train was the philosopher John Locke, who had fled to the Netherlands six years earlier under suspicion of involvement in the Rye House Plot to assassinate Charles II and his brother James. Locke now proceeded to publish in quick succession the works which he had composed during his years abroad, and for which he is now best known: the *Essay Concerning Human Understanding*, *Two Treatises of Government* and the *Letters on Toleration*. The reputation of these founding documents of liberalism grew slowly, but the *Letters on Toleration* were of immediate relevance as a rationale for the new dispensation. The first of them was licensed for publication on 3 October 1689, less than two months after Samuel Richardson was born on 19 August.

It is hard for us now to grasp what a decisive break with the old mindset Locke's *Letters on Toleration* represent. It had been the long-standing orthodoxy that the State had the right to dictate and regulate the form of national worship, and to punish backsliders, apostates and heretics. This religious dictatorship was dignified by the name of Erastianism, and it was set in stone by the brilliant rhetoric of Thomas Hobbes in *Leviathan*. In his own life, Hobbes had to come to terms with three distinct and opposing forms of such dictatorship: the personal rule of Charles I, the Cromwellian Republic and the Restoration of Charles II. He seems to have accommodated himself cheerfully enough to each of these dispensations, without apparently pausing to ponder whether there might not be something amiss with a system subject to such rapid and violent upheavals.

Locke had no hesitation in identifying what was wrong: 'This Narrowness of Spirit on all Sides, has undoubtedly been the principal Occasion of our Miseries and Confusions.' And the antidote was equally plain: 'Absolute Liberty, just and true Liberty, equal and impartial Liberty, is the Thing that we stand in Need of.' This was no outlandish dream. On the contrary, he begins, 'Since you are pleased to enquire, what are my Thoughts about the mutual Toleration of Christians in their different professions of Religion, I must needs answer you freely, That I esteem that Toleration to be the chief characteristic Mark of the true Church ... The Toleration of those that differ from others in matters of Religion, is so agreeable to the Gospel of Jesus Christ, and to the genuine Reason of Mankind, that it seems monstrous for Men to be so blind as not to perceive the Necessity and Advantage of it in so clear a light.' How, in God's name, could it be right to burn with fire and faggot those who differ on 'nice and intricate matters' of doctrine? These things cannot possibly be the business of the State: 'The Care of Souls cannot belong to the civil Magistrate, because his Power consists only in outward force: but true and saving Religion consists in the inward Persuasion of the Mind, without which nothing can be acceptable to God ... all the Power of civil Government relates only to Mens civil Interests; is confined to the care of the Things of this World, and hath nothing to do with the World to come.' And it's not the business of Parliament either: 'Nor can any such Power be vested in the Magistrate by the *Consent of the People*; because no Man can so far abandon the Care of his own Salvation, as blindly to leave it to the Choice of any other, whether Prince or Subject, to prescribe to him what Faith or Worship he shall embrace.'

Locke's toleration is not boundless. He excludes Roman Catholics on the grounds that their Church is no respecter of either civil or religious liberty, and atheists because he thinks they are liable to stir up trouble (though one suspects that he might have softened that exclusion on further reflection, but he had enough controversy on his hands already).

But the direction of travel is clear. From now on, civility begins to trump theology. Men ought not to be persecuted by the State for their religious opinions. And after 1689, that happened less and less. Already in the second half of the seventeenth century the 'Latitudinarian' or 'Broad Church' approach had been gathering strength. Freedom of thought, whether endorsed by philosophers or just practised by ordinary people, becomes taken for granted. The furious pamphleteering of the previous century dwindles into a hectic memory. People settle down to the innocent pastime of making money. Historians of the period talk of 'the commercialization of English society in the eighteenth century', just as they do of 'the commercialization of English society in the thirteenth century', even about 'the birth of a consumer society'.[61]

And after Marlborough's wars were over, there was peace, too. In 1734, six years before *Pamela* sees the light of day, Sir Robert Walpole makes his great boast to Queen Caroline: 'Madam, there are fifty thousand men slain this year in Europe, and not one Englishman.'

Above all, the general climate of toleration clears social and mental space for the comfortable classes to recognize the poor as their fellow human beings, to take an interest in their misfortunes, and to begin to develop institutions to help them. This is the historic contribution of the Second Sentimental Revolution.

THE THREE SCOTTISH SYMPATHIZERS

This new society of merchants and markets needed only a new social philosophy to replace the old religious authoritarianism. And at the dawn of our crucial year of 1740, it got one: *A Treatise of Human Nature* by the young Scottish philosopher David Hume, still in his late twenties. Hume famously complained at the time that his *Treatise* 'fell dead-born from the press'. Yet this extraordinary book was to inspire subsequent great philosophers and scientists from Kant to Einstein. For our present purposes, what we can take from it is the supreme role that Hume allots in human intercourse to the passions, and in particular to the quality of 'sympathy'.

For Hobbes, the passions had been dangerous, feral things, primal appetites which could be and must be curbed only by an arbitrary power, 'the Leviathan', as he called the State; only a monster could chain another monster. Reason had to be master, otherwise life would continue to be as 'nasty, brutish and short' as it had been in the state of nature. In total contrast, Hume denies 'the supposed pre-eminence of reason above passion'. He contradicts those philosophers down the ages who have insisted on the 'blindness, inconsistency and deceitfulness' of the passions. There is no such conflict between passion and reason. On the contrary, it is the passions that are our drivers, and so they should be: 'Reason is, and ought only to be the slave of the passions, and can never pretend to any other office than to serve and obey them.'[62] It is the passions that lead us to communicate, to socialize: 'The passions are so contagious, that they pass with the greatest facility from one person to another, and produce correspondent movements in all human breasts.'[63] These movements of feeling from one person to another constitute the principle of sympathy. Human beings are naturally sociable. This idea was not new, of course: Aristotle: 'by nature, man is a social animal.' But nobody before Hume made the idea work so hard.

And it is this idea of sympathy that runs through the Second Sentimental Revolution, reaching its fullest expression 20 years later in The Theory of Moral Sentiments, by another Scottish philosopher and devoted friend and admirer of Hume's, Adam Smith. Though Smith started off at the University of Glasgow, he got a scholarship to Balliol College, Oxford, where he had a miserable time, sharing Edward Gibbon's low opinion of the place: 'in the University of Oxford, the greater part of the public professors have, for these many years, given up altogether even the pretence of teaching.' Smith is said to have complained that the University officials once caught him reading a copy of Hume's Treatise and confiscated the book. The theory of sympathy, nevertheless, remains the highest contribution of the Scottish Enlightenment to the world, and Smith and Hume share the credit.

The Theory of Moral Sentiments arose originally out of Smith's lectures on ethics in Glasgow. That is no disadvantage, because he tells us quite a bit about the other philosophers he has been lecturing on, and about how his opinions differ from theirs. The book is just as meticulous and thoughtful as The Wealth of Nations, though not nearly so famous and not quite so enjoyable to read. But its many merits have not prevented it from being misunderstood by those who have not read it or have not progressed much further than the opening chapter, 'Of Sympathy', and the first sentence: 'How selfish soever man may be supposed, there are evidently some principles in his nature, which interest him in the fortune of others, and render their happiness necessary to him, though he derives nothing from it, except the pleasure of seeing it. Of this kind is pity or compassion.'[64]

At first blush then, it seems as if we are in for a treatise on Sympathy, in the rather limp sense in which we sign off a letter of condolence 'with deepest sympathy'. This leads on to the quite understandable inference that there is some kind of contradiction between Adam Smith's two great works. This inference has had a long innings in the nineteenth and twentieth centuries, especially in Germany, where much ink has been spilt on das Adam-Smithproblem. It looks as if Smith first wrote one big book about being nice to each other, then another big book, twice as long, about looking after number one. Isn't there an insuperable conflict between other-love and self-love, between sympathy and self-interest?

In reality, the problem is not so hard to resolve, especially if you read *The Theory of Moral Sentiments* before *The Wealth of Nations*, as most of Smith's eighteenth-century readers would have done, because it was published 17 years earlier and it was a bestseller.

What the earlier book sets out to establish is that our moral world is based on our imagination of what other people think is admirable or deplorable. This has to be an effort of the imagination. 'As we have no immediate experience of what other men feel, we can form no idea of the manner in which they are affected, but by conceiving what we ourselves should feel in the like situation.'[65] We cannot see inside other minds, a problem that continues to vex philosophers with nothing better to think about.

What if we differ, perhaps violently, from our neighbours on some question? Where can we find a reliable alternative guide on how to behave or not to behave? Smith says that we can imagine 'an impartial spectator', someone who is level-headed and well-informed about the case. What would he or she think? Would he or she be horrified or tolerant or even approving? Approbation (and disapprobation) is the name of Smith's game. He insists from the outset that this is ultimately and originally a matter of feeling, of our gut reaction. That is where our moral sentiments come from, not from rational thought, or social utility, or some mysterious indwelling 'moral sense', or from God who supposedly implanted it. Smith derived this idea from his hero and friend David Hume, but he carries the line of thought much further, to denounce all the alternative explanations offered by Plato and Aristotle, by Epictetus and the Stoics, by Hobbes and even by his immediate Scots predecessors such as Francis Hutcheson. The Christian casuists are just as far off the mark, Smith says, because 'they attempted, to no purpose, to direct by precise rules, what it belongs to feeling and sentiment only to judge of'.[66] For Smith, as for Goethe: '*Gefühl ist alles*' ('Feeling is everything').

We can and do work up fancy arguments to justify our moral feelings for or against, let's say, homosexuality or alcohol, but ultimately our feelings will be shaped by our feelings of revulsion or approval, and those feelings will in turn be shaped by the sea we and our contemporaries are swimming in. As David Raphael sums up in his little book on Smith: 'Sympathy and imagination in the *Moral Sentiments* are the cement of human society in forming socializing attitudes.'[67] They generate approbation and disapprobation, and induce conformity to social norms both in behaviour and in attitude.

Sympathy and imagination create a social bond. It's different from the social bonds of mutual dependence that are described in *The Wealth of Nations* as resulting from the division of labour and the workings of the market. But the two sorts of bond are not inconsistent with one another. They may overlap and dovetail, according to context. I may dispose of my extra rubbish by taking it to the recycling centre myself (self-love and good citizenship), or the dustman may take it if I give him a few quid (market forces), or I may take my housebound elderly neighbour's rubbish as well as my own (altruism). All of these actions have their place in the great scheme of waste disposal. I may buy Wimbledon tickets from a tout and give one of the tickets to a friend. Altruism mingles with market forces. There's no contradiction. Do I approve of the ticket tout as a useful middleman for the efficient distribution of tickets, or do I deplore his existence as a knavish profiteer? There's something to be said for both views. My position may depend on whether I am a committee member of the Lawn Tennis Association or a desperate tennis fan.

Smith insists that our moral feelings of admiration or disgust are just that: feelings, not rational deductions from some overarching philosophical system. When we put those feelings together into an ethical code, we are constructing what Smith calls 'an imaginary machine', or as academics say today: 'a model'. To get a sharper sense of what Smith is up to, it may help to refer to his earlier 'History of Astronomy' essay – a pioneer document in the history and philosophy of science. What Smith says there is that when we are uncomfortable with a scientific orthodoxy that no longer seems to fit the facts of observation – Ptolemy's account of the cosmos, for example, or, centuries later, the system of Copernicus – we grope around for a new 'paradigm', as Thomas Kuhn calls it in *The Structure of Scientific Revolutions* (1962). We quickly come to think of the new paradigm as the last word, when it is only the latest word, the best that our imaginations can devise to fit the facts as we presently know them. Smith brilliantly hazards that even Newton's system may one day be superseded: 'Even we, while we have been endeavouring to represent all philosophical systems as mere inventions of the imagination . . . have insensibly been drawn in to make use of language expressing the connecting principles of this one, as if they were the real chains which Nature makes use of to bind together her several operations.' No wonder that Newton's system had gained 'the general and complete approbation of mankind' and that it was now considered 'not as an attempt to connect in the imagination the phaenomena of the Heavens, but as the greatest discovery that ever was made by man, the discovery of an immense chain of the most important and sublime truths'.[68]

Smith is an outstanding figure in the chain of thinkers who have taught us that scientific truth is provisional – not relative, but provisional. A hypothesis is valid so long as – and only so long as – it stands up to the most rigorous tests that are available to us. Much the same line of thinking is set out by Karl Popper in his *Logic of Scientific Discovery*:[69] science progresses by a series of falsifiable hypotheses. If a thesis cannot be falsified, then it cannot be counted as part of scientific knowledge – Popper offers Freud and Marx as ripe examples of pseudo-scientific thinkers who fail this test.

Similarly, in constructing our moral codes, we may find that the old shibboleths no longer fit the world as we see it today. We are no longer disgusted by homosexuality or abortion as we once were, and so we construct a new moral code to fit our feelings. 'The general rules of morality are . . . ultimately founded upon experience of what, in particular instances, our moral faculties, our natural sense of merit and propriety, approve or disapprove of. We do not originally approve or condemn certain actions, because, upon examination, they appear to be agreeable or inconsistent with a certain general rule.'[70]

The Theory of Moral Sentiments went into numerous editions and drew warm praise from the great men of the day. Edmund Burke described it as 'one of the most beautiful fabrics of moral theory, that has perhaps ever appeared'. He was convinced of the 'Solidity and Truth' of Smith's theory, because it was based on 'the whole of Human Nature'.[71] The appeal to what Burke often called 'prejudice' rather than abstract theory was very much in line with Burke's own psychological approach to political thought.

Perhaps the most memorable reaction from an early reader came not from a reviewer but from a poet. Robert Burns had been reading a copy of the first edition, perhaps belonging to his father. There's a quatrain in 'To a Louse' which is a vivid paraphrase of Smith's argument:

O wad some Pow'er the giftie gie us
To see oursels as others see us!
It wad frae monie a blunder free us
An' foolish notion.

The third friend in this trio of Scottish Sympathizers has not achieved the enduring fame of Adam Smith and David Hume, but in his day Henry Mackenzie was just as celebrated, as was his short novel *The Man of Feeling*, which, I think, represents the high point of sentimental fiction, although it does not begin to touch a masterpiece like *Clarissa*. Robert Burns was as warm an enthusiast for the novel as he had been for Adam Smith's book, describing *The Man of Feeling* as 'a book I prize next to the Bible', and he carried his copy around with him constantly, until it fell to pieces.[72]

Harley, the Man of Feeling of the title, journeys through a cruel and heartless world, meeting a card sharp, a sour old philosopher, several prostitutes and various other unfortunate casualties of life. Wherever he can, he bestows generous gifts on these victims and even more generous tears. Hearing the story of a young woman who has been sent mad by a thwarted love affair, he gives it 'the tribute of some tears'. She responds: 'I would weep, too, but my brain is dry, and it burns, it burns, it burns!' She is wearing a ring given to her by her dead lover and she holds out her hand to Harley and he presses it with both of his, and bathes it with his tears, then gives the asylum keeper a couple of guineas for her care and leaves, still weeping. Thomas Dixon in *Weeping Britannia* chooses this episode to illustrate Harley's lachrymosity, but he could have chosen plenty of others.[73]

The reader is expected to shed his or her own tears in sympathy, as it were in unison with Harley. *The Monthly Review* declared at the time that 'the Reader, who weeps not over some of the scenes it describes, has no sensibility of mind'.[74] Reading the book at the age of 14, Lady Louisa Stuart 'had a secret dread I should not cry enough to gain the credit of proper sensibility'.[75] But within Mackenzie's lifetime (he lived until 1831), the novel had become a laughingstock. Lady Louisa recalls the reaction when a country-house party, 50 years later, in 1826, chose to have the book read aloud: 'I, who was the reader, had not seen it for many years. The rest did not know it at all. I am afraid I perceived a sad change in it, or myself, which was worse, and the effect altogether failed. Nobody cried, and at some passages, the touches that I used to think so exquisite – oh dear! They laughed. I thought we never should get over Harley's walking down to breakfast with his shoe-buckles in his hand. Yet I remember so well its first publication, my mother and sisters crying over it, dwelling on it with rapture.'[76]

And the satirists were just as quick to deride *The Man of Feeling* as they had been to parody *Pamela*. Both James Gillray and Thomas Rowlandson used the title for a drawing. Rowlandson's print (1788) shows a plump parson feeling up the voluminous skirts of a young woman with his other hand on her breast. In fact, Rowlandson used the title twice more, for other prints of parsons seducing damsels. The Royal Collection's copy of this one was probably bought by George IV when he was Prince of Wales. Gillray's more ambitious coloured print (1800) of the subject shows the notoriously amorous William V, hereditary Prince of Orange, in a dressmaker's shop with each of his hands feeling up the skirts of two outraged young women.

The Man of Feeling by Thomas Rowlandson, 1788

The modern reaction to Mackenzie's novella is no less derisive. In Sentiment and Sociability (1988), John Mullan describes The Monthly Review as 'advocating a reaction which seems ludicrous now'.[77] Writing in 1930, Aldous Huxley found The Man of Feeling 'not merely vulgar but positively ludicrous ... vulgar to the point of ridiculousness'.[78] As we have seen, Lawrence Stone lumps it together with Pamela as 'boring, moralistic and sentimental' and virtually unreadable.

Yet, whatever its faults, The Man of Feeling remains a work of great literary interest, especially in its techniques which are unmistakably and deliberately what we would call modernist. The story starts nowhere in particular and hops from one fragmentary episode to another. In fact, the whole thing is apparently dumped in our lap by accident. The narrator is out shooting with a curate who offers him this torn bundle of papers which he has been using as wadding for his gun. When the narrator has leisure to read this stuff, he 'found it a bundle of little episodes together without art and of no importance on the whole, with something of nature and little else in them'.[79] This, of course, is the art that conceals art, the self-deprecating soft sell, the wilful indirection that leads us on and continues to beguile us as the narrative wanders all over the place. Here and there we are brought up short by a sharp political comment: for example, on the human costs of landscaping à la Capability Brown, then the height of fashion: '"Alack a-day!" said she, "It was the schoolhouse indeed; but to be sure, Sir, the squire has pulled it down, because it stood in the way of his prospects." "What! how! prospects! pulled down!" cried Harley. – "Yes, to be sure, Sir; and the green where the children used to play, he has ploughed up, because, he said, they hurt his fence on the other side of it." – "Curses on his narrow heart," cried Harley, "that could violate a right so sacred! Heaven blast the wretch!"'[80] Just as sharp, in fact, as the footnote in *Das Kapital* where Marx quotes the lament of Lord Leicester when he was complimented on the completion of the landscaping at Holkham Hall: 'It is a melancholy thing to stand alone in one's country. I look around and not a house is to be seen but mine. I am the Giant of Giant Castle, and have eat up all my neighbours. My nearest neighbour is the King of Denmark.'[81]

Or, again, Harley digresses to deplore the greed of the British in India and the havoc they have caused: 'what title have the subjects of another kingdom to establish an empire in India? to give laws to a country where the inhabitants received them on the terms of friendly commerce? You say they are happier under our regulations than the tyranny of their own petty princes. I must doubt it, from the conduct of those by whom these regulations have been made. They have drained the treasuries of Nabobs, who must fill them by oppressing the industry of their subjects.'[82] But this digression is saved from sinking into a political sermon by the ironic headline that Mackenzie gives to the chapter: 'The Man of Feeling talks of what he does not Understand – an Incident.'

The reality is that Mackenzie is a sophisticated literary craftsman. And far from being a limp-wristed poetaster, he was a tough

Edinburgh lawyer. Another of his Edinburgh friends, the great judge Henry Cockburn, recorded retrospectively (by which time Mackenzie was himself popularly known as 'The Man of Feeling'): 'Strangers used to fancy that he must be a pensive sentimental Harley; whereas he was far better − a hard-headed practical man, as full of worldly wisdom as most of his fictitious characters are devoid of it; and this without in the least impairing the affectionate softness of his heart.'[83] These were in fact all practical men. Smith was a senior customs officer and political adviser. And Richardson came to be official printer of the Journals of the House of Commons, and was eventually Master of the Stationers' Company in 1754−5.

Nobody could have been a sterner critic than Mackenzie himself of futile soppiness.

A decade after *The Man of Feeling* had wowed the nation, he declared in *The Lounger* (one of the several journals he ran): 'In the enthusiasm of sentiment there is much the same danger as in the enthusiasm of religion, of substituting certain impulses and feeling of what may be called a visionary kind, in the place of real practical duties, which in morals, as in theology, we might not improperly denominate good works. In morals, as in religion, there are not wanting instances of refined sentimentalists, who are contented with talking of virtues which they never practice ... That creation of refined and subtile feeling, reared by the authors of the works to which I allude, has an ill effect, not only on our ideas of virtue, but also on our estimate of happiness ... It inspires a certain childish pride of our own superior delicacy, and an unfortunate contempt of the plain worth, the ordinary but useful occupations and ideas of those around us.'[84] Remarks which remind us of the famous closing words of George Eliot's *Middlemarch*: 'the growing good of the world is partly dependent on unhistoric acts; and that things are not so ill with you and me as they might have been, is half owing to the number who lived faithfully a hidden life, and rest in unvisited tombs.'

Mackenzie can be taken at face value here. He is undoubtedly criticizing the adverse tendencies of his own writings. But he is also saying something more, something very much in the spirit of Adam Smith: he is urging that these tender sympathies should be *converted* into practical action. What critics of sentimental literature, then and now, fail to acknowledge or simply don't notice that, as a matter of historical fact, this is what happens, and often on a staggering scale. This is what happened in the First Sentimental Revolution, the great age of building hospitals and asylums and cathedrals. And this is what happens in the Second Sentimental Revolution too. The change in *mentalité* is a necessary prelude to the mobilization of political and social reform in every imaginable field. Sentimentality doesn't only shift minds. In the long run, often slowly and painfully, it shifts social and political systems.

I can no longer hold back from quoting again the resonant lines of William Blake, which form the epigraph to this book:

> But vain the Sword and vain the Bow,
> They never can work War's overthrow.
> The Hermit's Prayer and the Widow's tear
> Alone can free the World from fear.
> For a Tear is an Intellectual Thing,
> And a Sigh is the Sword of an Angel King,
> And the bitter Groan of the Martyr's woe
> Is an Arrow from the Almighty's Bow.

Radical writers, then and now, have refused to see any link between the cult of sensibility and the achievement of social reform. They insist that sensibility, in Janet Todd's words, 'did not mount a general attack on the social problems of an unequal and unfree society and it did not encourage political response'.[85] In fact, it often reinforced the legitimacy of the ruling class (when it showed a benign face) and of the status quo. John Mullan argues: 'It was by the restriction of sociability to a private space, the curbing of any ambition to generalize society, that sentimentalism achieved its fashionable status.'[86] In her trailblazing *A Vindication of the Rights of Woman* (1792), Mary Wollstonecraft declares that women will make progress only by being tough and rational: 'soft phrases, susceptibility of heart, delicacy of sentiment, and refinement of taste, are almost synonymous with epithets of weakness ... those beings who are only the objects of pity ... will soon become objects of contempt.'[87] Wollstonecraft had herself written a fairly routine sentimental novel, *Mary, A Fiction* (1788), but she could see no connection between these sterile self-indulgences and the serious business of reform.

But there *was* a connection. The process might be slow, halting and fiercely contested; the time lag between sympathy and social action might seem intolerably long for the campaigners, let alone the victims. But in the end, shared sensibility generated the momentum for collective political action. *Pace* Jeremy Bentham, rational calculation alone could not create the climate of compassion.

As we have seen, Lawrence Stone finds *Pamela* and *The Man of Feeling* as nauseously sentimental as does any other modern critic. But he concedes, handsomely and forcefully, that 'behind the flow of tears lies a new attitude towards man's inhumanity to man. Between 1770 and 1820, it was fashionable to express emotional anguish concerning cruelty, a distress which finally opened the way to remedial legislation and institutional reform.'[88]

In his classic work *The Family, Sex and Marriage*, Stone describes how the reformers deployed newspapers, sermons, novels, cartoons and prints to influence the wider public and then mobilized the public through mass petitions to put pressure on Parliament. This led in time to such momentous changes as the abolition of the slave trade, the suppression of cruel sports, prison reform and new approaches to the treatment of the mentally ill. 'The movement was a genuinely moral one involving the upsurge of new attitudes and emotions, which acquired an enormous stimulus thanks to the development in the mid-eighteenth century of a new ideal type, namely the Man of Sentiment, or the Man of Feeling ...'[89]

There had been reforming societies before, of course, but they had tended to be of a rather different nature. Richard Mount, my six-times-great-grandfather, was a prosperous stationer on Tower Hill and Master of the Stationers' Company 30 years before Samuel Richardson. When he died after falling off his horse on London Bridge in 1722, his funeral tribute described him as 'a hearty friend to the Societies of Reformation of Manners and Suppression of Vice', who did greatly 'lament the growing wickedness of the Time and Place in which he lived' (he was born in 1652).[90]

These societies had spread across the country in the first years of William and Mary's reign. They were designed to stamp out profanity, robbery, drunkenness, adultery, homosexuality and lewd and disorderly conduct of all sorts. Their supporters hired vigilantes or became enforcers themselves. They deployed spies and *provocateurs* to arrest and prosecute droves of men for sodomy and adultery. Quite a few were hanged. A string of laws to ban gin-drinking and brothel-keeping were introduced. These repressive campaigns, the backwash of the Puritan spirit, encountered considerable local resistance, and they eventually fizzled out as the eighteenth century wore on.

But they are worth mentioning to show how entirely different were the new movements for compassionate reform. There was a sea change, and it coincided with the flowering of the literature of sensibility. In the literature, we have concentrated on three seminal events: 1740, the year of Richardson's *Pamela*; 1759, the year of Adam Smith's *The Theory of Moral Sentiments*; and 1771, the year of Mackenzie's *The Man of Feeling*. In the real world, we can pick out a dozen or more social advances in those years and in the following decades which turned out to be of lasting significance for the people's flourishing.

What we cannot help noticing is that each of these advances was inspired, promoted and carried through by a single individual or by a small group of friends. They were all private citizens, holding no great office and of no particular social prominence: a retired sea captain, a satirical artist, a small farmer in Bedfordshire, a Quaker mother of 11 children from Norfolk, an ex-Army major, a former master of slave ships, a failed teacher-turned-governess, a tea merchant from York. It was these oddly assorted, often reputed to be 'difficult' or quirky characters, who turned the sentimental revolution of the mind into social reality. With relentless perseverance, they 'compassionated' others and gathered the funds and the public momentum to turn their personal hare-brained scheme into a revered national institution.

MOVERS, SHAKERS AND QUAKERS

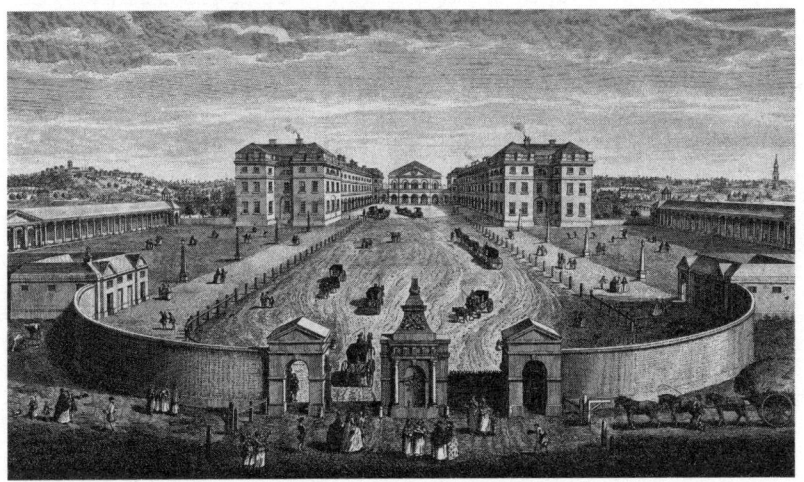

The Foundling Hospital by L. P. Boitard, 1753

Captain Thomas Coram is usually described as a retired sea captain, which he was, but he was much more. He ran a shipyard in Massachusetts for ten years, he promoted the founding of colonies in what are now Maine and Georgia, he devised a successful scheme for resettling unemployed artisans in Nova Scotia. During his years in America, he agitated for a scheme to educate Native American girls. The idea of educating Native Americans was audacious enough, but educating *squaws*!

Female education was also at the forefront of this gruff, awkward livewire's most favoured project of all, at which he laboured for 20 years: *A Hospital for the Maintenance and Education of Exposed and Deserted Children*, known to posterity as the London Foundling Hospital.

On his return from America, Coram had been horrified by the poverty in London which existed side by side with the unimaginable opulence. On his daily trudge from Rotherhithe to the City, he would pass the bodies of dead babies abandoned on the roadside and small children dying of starvation on the streets. At first, his campaign to do something for them met indifference or positive hostility. Caring for these little bastards would only encourage immorality. It was a full decade before he attracted the patronage of Queen Caroline and the nobility began to flock to his cause. When the hospital opened with a Royal Charter in temporary quarters in Hatton Garden in 1742, the infants could be dropped off with no questions asked, accompanied only by an identifying note, trinket or token. Some of these poignant markers are still on display at the Foundling Museum in Coram's Fields.

Among the earliest supporters of the project was Coram's friend the artist William Hogarth. His magnificent portrait of the bluff old salt is also on view in the museum. He designed the letterhead for the Hospital, too. Childless himself, he and his wife fostered several foundlings, and he encouraged the other great artists of the day – Reynolds, Gainsborough, Highmore and Richard Wilson – to adorn the walls with their pictures. Handel composed a special choral piece, the Foundling Hospital Anthem, and held performances of *The Messiah* in the chapel every year.

The Foundling Hospital was not the first of its kind, even in the British Isles. Foundling hospitals had been started in Dublin in 1704 and in Cork in 1737, both funded by government rather than private subs. In continental capitals, they were a long-standing feature. The Hospital of the Innocents in Florence, with its marvellous palazzo by Brunelleschi and medallions of babies by Andrea della Robbia, dates back to 1419. But in Britain this was something new, an embodiment of softening hearts towards society's rejects, recalling the words from Isaiah that Handel included in *The Messiah*: 'He is despised and rejected of men.'

In the same year that the Foundling Hospital was receiving its Royal Charter, seven gentlemen met in the Feathers Tavern in Cheapside to subscribe to the building of 'an intended new infirmary'. Less than two months later, the London Infirmary opened in a house on Featherstone Street, Moorfields (just off the present-day Old Street roundabout). It had a staff of one surgeon, one physician and an apothecary, charged no fees and was funded entirely from subscriptions of well-wishers. The Infirmary moved several times to other premises nearby, before settling on Whitechapel Mount, where in 1757 a new hospital opened with 300 beds. From the start, medical students had been studying under the professional staff, but it was not until 1785 that the London Hospital Medical College was founded, the first ever purpose-built medical school inside a hospital. The London also became a specialist institution for the training of nurses, led by the redoubtable Eva Luckes, who was addressed by Florence Nightingale (herself a Governor of the Hospital) as 'O Matron of Matrons.' In 1990, 250 years after its founding, it became the Royal London.

The London was by no means the first new hospital to be built in the capital in the eighteenth century. There was the Westminster in 1719, St George's at Hyde Park Corner in 1733, the Middlesex in Windmill Street in 1745. Perhaps the most memorable founding was that of Guy's in 1725. Like Samuel Richardson, Thomas Guy was a successful printer. He had made his first fortune publishing mostly bibles and prayer books, then multiplied it by selling at the right time in the South Sea Bubble, turning £50,000 of South Sea stock into over £250,000 (approximately £400 million at today's prices). His last will and testament endowed a hospital for 400 'poor persons who may be adjudged or called incurable and as such not proper objects to be received into or continued in the present hospital of St Thomas' (a medieval foundation). As a governor of Tommy's, Guy had witnessed at first hand the rejection of these patients. To further the new hospital's vocation as a refuge for the rejected, he also stipulated that there should be a proportion of lunatics in each intake. Guy got the project going in 1721, but died in 1724, just before it opened its doors.

The eighteenth century saw the biggest increase in the number of new hospitals built since the last great wave, back in the thirteenth century, which we have already seen something of. We should notice three features of this remarkable renaissance: the new emphasis on professional medical and nursing education, the welcome given to the most untreatable and impoverished patients, and the absence of fees.

The absence of fees was a key feature of another of Hogarth's initiatives; education and support for his struggling fellow artists. He had started the St Martin's Lane Academy himself in 1735. And its success and the success of the trailblazing exhibitions of new pictures at the Foundling Hospital, organized by the Dilettanti Society, led soon after Hogarth's death to the creation of the Royal Academy of Art itself in 1768. It immediately attracted all the great painters of the day as well as royal patronage. Though the Academy's premises were to move several times, from Somerset House to a wing of the newly completed National Gallery before settling in Burlington House, a constant key feature from the start was the Academy Schools, which provided three years of art education free of charge. Among the artists who passed through the Schools, many of them from modest backgrounds, were Turner, Soane, Lawrence, Constable and Rowlandson. The schools also provided a template for the founding of other such academies, mostly in the early nineteenth century, in other disciplines such as music, design, architecture and needlework. Here were the beginnings of a cultural state in England (and parallel new institutions mushroomed in Scotland, too).

Another of Hogarth's causes that lived on after him until the present day was the prevention of cruelty to animals. He loved animals and painted his self-portrait with his pug dog Trump. In 1751, he published a series of four prints entitled *The Four Stages of Cruelty*, which, in modern parlance, went viral. In the first of the four, he shows the villainous yob Tom Nero sticking an arrow up a dog's rectum. Other louts are torturing cats, dogs and cockerels. In the second, Tom Nero is a hackney coach-driver. His coach has overturned, and he is beating the wretched fallen horse with his whip. In the third, he is depicted as a murderer with his dead woman victim lying on the ground beside him. The fourth, entitled 'The Reward of Cruelty', shows Tom's withering corpse being dissected by surgeons, the hangman's rope still around his neck. Hogarth was delighted with the results of his work. He told a City bookseller: 'there is no part of my works of which I am so proud, and in which I now feel so happy, as in the series of *The Four Stages of Cruelty*, because I believe the publication of them has checked the diabolical spirit of barbarity to the brute creation which, I am sorry to say, was once so prevalent in this country.'[91]

The Four Stages of Cruelty: Stage One: boys being cruel to small animals by William Hogarth, 1751

The new revulsion against cruelty to animals began to show itself especially in the growth of literature produced specifically for children. The prolific publisher John Newbery (1713–67), 'the Father of Children's Literature', produced a raft of books in which 'wanton cruelty is reprehensible, particularly to young animals and, above, all, young birds. Most reprehensible of all is cruelty to a mother bird, by the taking or destruction of eggs.'[92] This theme is everywhere in the fables of a regular Newbery author, Edward Augustus Kendall, such as *The Swallow*, *The Crested Wren*, *The Canary Bird*, *The Sparrow*.[93] In fact, the new valuation of childhood goes hand in hand with this new sensitivity to the suffering of animals. Another pioneering campaigner for what we would call animal rights was Jeremy Bentham, except that Bentham notoriously dismissed talk of rights as 'nonsense on stilts'. He claimed that he was arguing from strictly scientific grounds; that is, it was clearly proven that animals could feel pain. Adam Smith, and Hume, too, would have retorted, yes, but the obligation on us not to cause them pain can be derived only from our feelings of sympathy, and not from reason alone.

It only remained for Blake's *Auguries of Innocence* to immortalize the principle (though these famous lines were not first published until long after Blake's death):

> A robin redbreast in a cage
> Puts all heaven in a rage.
> A dove-house fill'd with doves and pigeons
> Shudders hell through all its regions
> A dog starved at his master's gate
> Predicts the ruin of the State.
> A horse misused upon the road
> Calls to heaven for human blood.
> Each outcry of the hunted hare
> A fibre from the brain does tear.

All the same, it was to be a long time before the new sensibilities were enshrined in legislation. Colonel Richard Martin

– dubbed 'Humanity Dick' by George IV – did manage to get the Cruel Treatment of Cattle Act passed in 1822, but he was much mocked for his sympathies, and caricatured with donkey's ears. The Society for the Prevention of Cruelty to Animals did not come into existence until 1824 (Royal from 1840). And it was 1835 before the Cruelty to Animals Act banned the baiting of bulls, dogs, bears or badgers. It also banned dogfighting and cockfighting, but both continued underground for decades afterwards. As we know, hare coursing and hunting foxes with hounds were not banned until 2005.

The compassionate energies of people like Billy Hogarth and Humanity Dick and the gentlemen who founded the London Hospital could blossom in all sorts of unexpected directions. Another institution which survives to this day is the Royal Humane Society, founded in 1774 with the rather bizarre title of the Society for the Recovery of Persons Apparently Drowned. Impressed by the possibilities of artificial respiration, two physicians each brought 15 friends to a meeting at the Chapter-House, St Paul's Churchyard, where the Society was founded. They set up branches all over the country, most frequently in ports and coastal towns where the risks of drowning were obviously gravest. By the end of the nineteenth century, the Society had more than 280 depots complete with life-saving apparatus – comparable with the widespread provision of defibrillators at public places today. It widened its remit to distributing money and medals to heroes who saved or tried to save people from other potentially fatal accidents, such as suffocating in mines and blast furnaces. Today the Society honours all life-saving acts of bravery. For example, the Leader of the Liberal Democrats, Sir Ed Davey, received a bravery award in 1995 for rescuing a woman who had fallen onto the line in the face of an oncoming train at Clapham Junction.

Among early beneficiaries of the Royal Humane Society was Mary Wollstonecraft, after she threw herself into the Thames in a second suicide attempt after being deserted by her faithless lover, Gilbert Imlay. She went first to Battersea Bridge, but thought it too public, so paid six shillings to be rowed upstream to Putney. It was night and pouring with rain. Obsessively methodical as ever, Mary walked up and down for half an hour to make her clothes sodden-heavy. Then she paid the halfpenny toll to gain access to the wooden bridge and jumped off the central arch. She floated downstream, unconscious, her lungs full of water.

Amazingly, she was rescued by a fishing boat and carried to an inn at Fulham. There she was restored by a medical man from the Royal Humane Society. What a lot this tells us, both about the rise of these new charitable institutions like the Foundling Hospital and about the numbers of desperate young women who made it worthwhile for the RHS medicos to be on call. And how cruel that Wollstonecraft should have come to seek the same fate as the unfortunates she was fighting for.

Even the prisoners banged up in Britain's foul and insanitary gaols, often for years on trivial charges without hope of release, found a champion in these years. John Howard was a modest landowner from a Calvinist family in Cardington, Bedfordshire, and he had just been appointed High Sheriff of the county. Among his duties he was keeper of the county gaol. Most sheriffs delegated this task to the under-sheriff, but Howard was a dutiful man. On visiting the gaol, he discovered that prisoners who had been acquitted or whose cases were stuck in the legal system were dragged back to prison until they paid the gaoler's fees. This led him to visit gaols in neighbouring counties, where he came across all sorts of squalor and cruelty. He soon allied with other penal reformers and gave evidence to the House of Commons in support of a Bill requiring acquitted prisoners to be set free and their fees to be paid by the county; he was then called to the Bar of the House to be thanked for his humanity and zeal. All this within a few months of taking up the cause.

Far from letting this instant acclaim go to his head, he spent the next three years visiting more than 200 prisons, not to mention dozens more in France, the Netherlands and Germany. Single-handedly, he invented the tradition of regular prison inspection and the submission of detailed reports on conditions of hygiene and welfare. He recommended new purpose-built prisons, well-lit and ventilated with proper sanitation, a healthy diet, opportunities for exercise and rehab. It was not so much that all his recommendations were beyond challenge. His great successor, the Quaker Elizabeth Fry, an altogether more attractive character, disagreed with his view that prisoners should always have single cells; she believed in the therapeutic value of prisoners associating with one another; she also campaigned for the separation of women prisoners and their protection from sexual abuse – so many of these early reforms have a special emphasis on improving the treatment of women. What mattered and what led to the formation of the Howard League for Penal Reform nearly a century later was that conditions in prisons should be kept under constant review. The practice of incarcerating one's fellow human beings imposed a moral duty of care on society. Even convicted felons could not be excluded from the reach of sympathy.

Howard himself was a stern and rather unappealing man. When he rebuilt his tenants' cottages and arranged their children's education, he insisted that they attend divine service and abstain from pubs and prize fights. Before marrying his second wife, he secured a pre-nup from her which stipulated 'that to prevent altercations about little matters which he had observed to be the chief grounds of uneasiness in families, he should always decide'. He was a teetotaller and vegetarian, and was so obsessive about not wasting a minute of God's time that he rose at 3 a.m. and when conversing sat with a watch on his knee, so that he could stop the interview at the exact time he had fixed. But he was unflinching, immune to personal vanity and dedicated to the welfare of society's victims. What he had above all, in addition to sympathy, was System. Even the great systematic Jeremy Bentham took his hat off to Howard: 'his book is a model for method and for the sort of style which is competent for his subject, He carries his plan with him in his head. He is set down at the door of a prison, makes enquiries under a certain number of heads which exhaust the subject, does his business and drives off again to another. His thoughts, his conversation, his writings are confined to this one subject.' Here we have the basis of the modern tradition of rigorous sociological enquiry leading to radical action, which was to culminate in the Beveridge Report. It is this chilly monomaniac whom thousands of prisoners to this day have to thank for the fact that their plight is never quite forgotten.

An altogether more charming but equally indefatigable reformer was Major John Cartwright. In 1776, two years after John Howard took up prison visiting, Cartwright published a pamphlet with the snappy title of *Take Your Choice!*. This is the first substantial call for universal manhood suffrage in Britain. The year is better known for another resounding call: Thomas Jefferson's Declaration of American Independence. It is not well known, though, that Major Cartwright had also beaten Jefferson to that punch. Two years earlier, he had published *American Independence: The Glory and Interest of Great Britain*, a radical squib which argued that the colonists had the right to choose their own rulers and tax themselves and, furthermore, that American independence would actually benefit British trade.

He was an unlikely radical, John Cartwright. Born in 1740, he had joined the Royal Navy and served with distinction in the Seven Years' War, at Cherbourg and Quiberon Bay among other engagements. But he declined to serve in American waters in Lord Howe's expeditionary force to subdue the colonists in 1775. He left the Navy and joined his local militia in Nottinghamshire, and was known for the rest of his life as Major Cartwright. He could, I suppose, be said to be the first British casualty of the American War of Independence.

But he was a cheerful, good-humoured fellow who bore no grudges. From that moment on, he devoted himself to the single cause of reforming Parliament. Over and over again he repeated the same six points of *Take Your Choice!*: the vote for all adult males, annual parliamentary elections, equal-sized electoral constituencies, the secret ballot, no property qualifications for candidates and the payment of MPs – all the things we now take for granted, except number two. With only minor modifications, these continued to be the demands of the various organizations he founded or joined: the Society for Constitutional Information, the better-known London Corresponding Society and the Hampden Clubs. Seventy years later, the Chartists were still echoing Cartwright's same six points (and acknowledging their debt to the major) – some of which finally struggled into law in the great reform acts of 1832, 1867, 1884 and 1918.

He didn't just support the rights of British voters: he supported the Spanish opposition to Napoleon, opposed the international slave trade and stuck up for Greek independence. He was still active after the end of the Napoleonic Wars; he only just escaped the carnage at Peterloo in 1819. He was convicted of sedition in 1821 at the age of 81, and just before his death a couple of years later he exchanged touching greetings with ex-President Jefferson. Unlike many reformers, he was obviously a lovely man, brimful of sympathy but with plenty of common sense – just the type that would have appealed to our Scottish sympathizers.

Cartwright was in the thick of the anti-slavery campaign. Quakers made up most of the Committee, but, because they were not eligible to sit in Parliament, Anglican evangelists had to lead the campaign inside the House, notably William Wilberforce, Thomas Clarkson and Granville Sharp. This necessity for Anglican leadership in Parliament should not obscure the fact that, like all the campaigns for humanitarian and democratic reform, this one was led by Dissenters of one sort or another. In these years, the Church of England gained, and has never quite lost, a reputation for complacency in the face of injustice, despite such mavericks as Beilby Porteus, Bishop of Chester, who also in 1783 called on the C of E to cut its ties with the slave trade and improve the condition of Afro-Caribbean slaves.

But the most remarkable Anglican clergyman to take a leading part in the campaign was the altogether amazing John Newton. To describe him in this way is to overlook the extraordinary story of his first 40 years. He went to sea at the age of 11, served on numerous slave ships, himself briefly became the slave of a princess of Sierra Leone, where he was maltreated as brutally as any African slave, was rescued, but undaunted returned to the slave trade, becoming the captain of several slave ships. Even after retiring from the sea, he continued to invest in the slave trade. Halfway through all this, he experienced a conversion to evangelical Christianity, but went on slaving nonetheless. Eventually, by now in his forties, he really did see the light and managed to become an Anglican curate at Olney, Bucks, with the poet William Cowper, and collaborated with Cowper on *Olney Hymns*. Two of Newton's hymns are the best beloved in the hymnal, 'Glorious Things of Thee Are Spoken', still sung lustily to Haydn's tune (which does double duty for 'Deutschland Über Alles') and, above all, 'Amazing Grace', which remains the most piercing evocation of what it is to be converted:

> Amazing Grace! How sweet the sound
> That saved a wretch like me!
> I once was lost, but now am found
> Was blind, but now I see.

Newton was over 60 and had been retired from the slave trade for years before he eventually described its horrors in *Thoughts upon the African Slave Trade* (1788): 'It will always be a subject of humiliating reflection to me, that I was once an active instrument in a business at which my heart now shudders.' He sent a copy to all MPs, many of whom were still at least passive instruments in that business. He lived just long enough to see the slave trade in the British Empire abolished by the Act of 1807. Slavery itself was abolished by the Act of 1833. The whole painful process had taken almost as long as the emancipation of Roman Catholics, which was stuttering forward during these years, in face of the stubborn resistance of George III. Under the 1833 Act, Parliament voted no less than £20 million to compensate the slave owners, a sum equivalent to 40 per cent of total government spending at the time. As the Caribbean sugar and cotton trade was declining, it was reckoned that many slave owners were delighted to take the money and run.

In 1808, just after the Abolition Act was passed, Thomas Clarkson published a fascinating list of 'forerunners and coadjutors' of the abolitionist movement, ranging from Elizabeth I and Charles V, through Alexander Pope, Montesquieu, Rousseau, Burke, Adam Smith, John Wesley, Laurence Sterne and numerous Quakers. I mention this list, not to quarrel with Clarkson's choices (there are plenty more names he could have mentioned), but to point out for how long slavery had been a glaring abomination to anyone of the slightest moral sense, and how hard it had been to shift the forces of greed and self-interest that had allowed the 'peculiar institution' to continue. Once more, we see how only the active enlistment of *sympathy* by campaigning groups began to undermine the status quo and generate the momentum for change.

We must not forget one last group of the despised and rejected, a group which even some Quakers were initially reluctant to help: the mentally ill, or 'the wrongheads', as they were cruelly dismissed. At a Society of Friends meeting in York in 1792, the wholesale tea merchant William Tuke proposed to set up an institution for 'those who labored under the most afflictive dispensation – the loss of reason'. Outside his own family, Tuke's initiative met with a frosty response from the other Quakers, who felt that such matters were none of their business. But he persisted, and after raising the cash through the sale of annuities he bought 11 acres where he built a spacious airy 'Retreat', which opened its doors in 1796. Though Tuke superintended the new sanatorium himself, he gave both doctors and patients free rein: no more chains or bleeding; plenty of fresh air and exercise and warm baths. Patients were encouraged to take up activities like sewing and knitting. Derided at first, the Retreat soon became famous worldwide as a model for the more humane treatment of mental illness. Tuke also strenuously opposed the inhumanity of the East India Company and supported the African Institution which sought to create a refuge for freed slaves in Sierra Leone.

Tuke was not the only pioneer of humane treatment in that era. In France at the same time, there was the famous Philippe Pinel. And down in Lincolnshire, there was Dr Francis Willis who had bought Greatford Hall, near Bourne, which he, too, developed as a private rural sanatorium with plenty of fresh air and exercise for the inmates who were also encouraged to do manual labour to help their recovery. In 1796, a visitor recalled: 'As the unprepared traveller approached the town, he was astonished to find almost all the surrounding ploughmen, gardeners, threshers, thatchers and other labourers attired in black coats, white waistcoats, black silk breeches and stockings, and the head of each bewigged, well powdered, neat and arranged. These were the doctor's patients with dress, neatness of person, and exercise being a principal feature of his admirable treatment system where health and cheerfulness conjoined to aid recovery of every person attached to that most valuable asylum.'

Dr Willis had already secured a national reputation as the physician who in 1788 had cured George III of the first attack of his mysterious malady by a mixture of traditional restraints, kindness and therapeutic activities such as the talking cure and the King's favourite pastime of taking his watches apart and putting them back together again. Dr Willis and his sons, who also treated the King less successfully in his later attacks, have received a poor press from Whig historians. But in his recent biography, Andrew Roberts argues persuasively that in fact the Willises employed recognizably modern methods and resorted to the straitjacket only when the King turned violent. Like Tuke and his nicely turned-out patients with their ploughs and pitchforks, Willis treated the mentally afflicted, up to and including the King, as fellow human beings who could be gently shepherded back into normal life.

Among the various reformers and reforming groups we have mentioned, the high proportion of Quakers and other Dissenters repeatedly stands out. In their position outside the frameworks of Church and State, excluded from most public office, they paradoxically enjoyed the uncovenanted benefit of experiencing an instinctive fellow feeling for other outsiders, not excluding felons, lunatics and slaves. At their best, the Dissenting reformers were the walking embodiment of the principle of sympathy (at their worst, they could be prudish busybodies). We cannot help noticing, too, how often these initiatives seem to emerge at meetings of friends/Friends in taverns and coffee houses. The social instinct warms the spirit of reform into life.

FOUR

Manliness Rules OK

REACTING INTO REACTION

From the start 'sentimentalism was always on the defensive', as Janet Todd puts it.[1] The cult of tears and sensibility was never going to enjoy an uncontested run in a nation which was firing up to be an aggressive imperial and industrial power. From the moment *Pamela* hit the bookstalls in 1740, there had been no shortage of hard-boiled critics to pillory the new sentimental literature mercilessly. If no book in English literary history was more frequently imitated than *Pamela*, none was more often spoofed and parodied. By the 1780s the parallel streams of sloppy imitations and mordant take-offs had combined to discredit the genre. Works such as *The Curse of Sentiment* (1787) and *The Illusions of Sentiment* (1788) began to appear. Younger sentimentalist writers claimed not to be writing sentimental novels at all, although their heroines, and their heroes, too, were still wiping away the tears. The most famous practitioners began to warn their readers of the danger of taking their work too seriously. We have seen how emphatic Henry Mackenzie was in denouncing tears without practical follow-up. The older Goethe, while still cherishing his profits from *Werther*, prefixed verses to later editions, which included the line, 'Be a man and do not follow me.'[2] And, of course, he had rubbished the whole idea in *The Triumph of Sentimentalism*.

In her novel *Mary, A Fiction* (1788), Mary Wollstonecraft had praised sensibility as 'the most exquisite feeling of which the human soul is susceptible; when it pervades us, we feel happy ... It is this quickness, this delicacy of feeling, which enables us to relish the sublime touches of the poet, and the painter; it is this which expands the soul ... [and makes it] disposed to be virtuous.'[3] Only four years later, in her masterpiece *A Vindication of the Rights of Woman* (1792), she insists on severe rationality as the necessary basis of reform: 'soft phrases, susceptibility of heart, delicacy of sentiment, and refinement of taste, are almost synonymous with epithets of weakness ... those being who are only the objects of pity ... will soon become objects of contempt.'[4] She now agreed with the man who was soon to become her husband, William Godwin, that 'it is to the improvement of reason ... that we are to look for the improvement of our social condition'.[5] What had happened in between was, of course, the outbreak of the French Revolution. If sensibility was already on its last legs, the events of 1789 onwards killed it off.

No upheaval in history has generated more instant jubilation among its fans. Major John Cartwright wrote that in seeing 'many millions of my fellow creatures suddenly redeemed from a cruel servitude ... my heart leaped with joy, and the tear of ecstatic gratitude to the Disposer of events glistened in my eye.'[6] A fortnight after the Fall of the Bastille, Charles James Fox wrote. 'How much the greatest event it is that ever happened in the world! And how much the best!'[7] Most memorable of all, William Wordsworth, looking back 20 years later as a disillusioned conservative, conveyed the feelings of exhilaration and enchantment, of being carried out of the workaday world – an enchantment enhanced in Wordsworth's case by the months he spent in Blois in 1791 with Annette Vallon, during which their daughter Caroline was conceived. His enchantment was sustained even through the six weeks he spent in Paris the following year at the time of the September Massacres:

> Bliss was it in that dawn to be alive,
> But to be young was very heaven! – Oh times,
> In which the meagre, stale, forbidding ways
> Of custom, law, and statute, took at once
> The attraction of a country in romance.

The poem conveys brilliantly how the enthusiasm swept up both the macho militants, 'the playfellows of fancy, who had made / All powers of swiftness, subtility and strength / Their ministers' and the softer sentimental types, those 'too, who of gentle mood ... Had fitted their own thoughts, schemers more mild'.

We must remember that soberer spirits, too, were caught up in the excitement, not excluding the British Prime Minister. In his heart, William Pitt had always been a friend to political reform, though he had been frustrated in the 1780s by a crabbed House of Commons. With Parliament in recess, he was able to avoid giving any considered reaction until February 1790, when he was guardedly optimistic: 'the present convulsions of France must, sooner or later, terminate in general harmony and regular order; and though the fortunate arrangements of such a situation might make her more formidable, it might also render her less obnoxious as a neighbour ... Whenever the situation of France should become restored, it would prove freedom rightly understood; freedom resulting from good order and good government; and thus circumstanced France would stand forward as one of the most brilliant Powers in Europe; she would enjoy just that kind of liberty which I venerate.'[8] Even two years on, by which time the new regime was clearly on the warpath, he still hoped that Britain at least might preserve her neutrality. In his Budget speech of 17 February 1792, Pitt declared that 'there never was a time in the history of this country when, from the situation of Europe, we might reasonably expect fifteen years of peace, than we might at the present moment'.

The disillusion came with a sickening thump that reverberated far into the nineteenth century. Burke's warnings, issued in the early days of the Revolution (his *Reflections* was published in November 1790, nearly three years before the executions of Louis XVI and Marie-Antoinette), came to seem not only prescient but also to describe an inevitable sequence of causes leading from the initial ideals to the worst excesses of the Terror. And the culprit, nailed in the frame and lambasted by conservative critics for decades, was the cult of sensibility. At first sight, the linkage might seem bizarre.

As Dixon asks, 'How did the literature of sensibility get connected with Robespierre's bloody regime? How could consuming soppy novels and saccharine paintings be supposed to lead to the mass killing of aristocrats and the tearing down of all the traditions of Church and state?'[9]

But there was a clear connection between the rhapsodies of Jean-Jacques Rousseau and the rhetoric of Maximilien Robespierre, between the so-called Father of the Revolution and its avenging executioner. At the height of the Terror, Robespierre was still speaking the language of *La Nouvelle Héloïse*. In a speech to the National Assembly, he declared that all 'feeling and pure souls' experienced virtue as a 'natural passion': that 'tender, irresistible, imperious passion, torment and delight of magnanimous hearts, that profound horror of tyranny, that compassionate zeal for the oppressed, which extended to a sublime and sacred love of humanity'.[10] All this amid the rumbling of the tumbrils and the swish of the guillotine. When coolly considered, everything about the cult of sensibility at its most unbridled seemed to pose a danger to the social fabric: the false theatrics, the privileging of passion over reason, the sloppy compassion swamping common sense and restraint.

By the time Thomas Carlyle came to write his *History of the French Revolution*, published in the year of Queen Victoria's accession, he took it for granted that the ideology of the Revolution had arisen from no other cause: 'out of that putrescent rubbish, of Scepticism, Sensualism, Sentimentalism, hollow Machiavelism, such a faith has verily arisen ... A whole People, awakening as it were to consciousness in deep misery, believes that it is within reach of a fraternal Heaven-on-Earth.'[11] 'Sentimentalism, so useful for weeping over romances and on pathetic occasions will avail nothing ... Is not sentimentalism twin sister to Cant, if not one and the same with it?'[12] 'The rose-pink vapour of sentimentalism' could never forge the bonds required to hold a human society together. That required stern and strong leadership, ready to face reality and demand sacrifice.

Even those radicals who stuck with the Revolution and believed, or hoped, that a relatively tranquil reformed social order would eventually emerge wanted to see the process purged of its sentimental excesses. Mary Wollstonecraft had seen the King being taken to his trial on 26 December 1792, and she had wept at the pitiful spectacle. She abhorred Robespierre and the Jacobins. Yet she still believed fervently that 'Europe ought to be grateful for a change that, by altering the political system of the most improved quarter of the globe, must ultimately lead to universal freedom, virtue and happiness.'

Yes, 'Europe will probably be, for some years to come in a state of anarchy', but 'out of this chaotic mass a fairer government is rising than has ever shed the sweets of social life on the world'.[13] At the same time she readily agreed with her new husband that sensibility was 'a moonstruck madness' and the result of the upper classes having too much time on their hands, species of 'folly begotten upon fastidious indolence'.[14]

Samuel Taylor Coleridge was more thoroughly disillusioned by the Revolution, and he aimed several sharp kicks at the cult of sensibility on his journey to conservatism. The self-indulgent lady reader, he claims, 'sips a beverage sweetened with human blood, even while she is weeping over the refined sorrows of Werther and Clementina. Sensibility is not Benevolence. Nay, by making us tremblingly alive to trifling misfortunes, it frequently prevents it and induces an effeminate and cowardly selfishness.'[15] Coleridge insists on the new quality which is to replace the played-out sentimentality: what he calls 'a mannerly manliness of taste'.[16] By 'mannerly' he seems to mean not lurching over into what we would call male chauvinism or macho behaviour, but an attitude which is courageous, bold and stoical in its outlook on the world.

This manliness had come to seem essential to a Britain now engaged in a gruelling war abroad and alarmed by revolutionary rumbles at home. Would the two threats coalesce into one, as Napoleon's all-conquering regime turned its attention to planning an invasion of Britain? Biographies of Napoleon tend to insist, no doubt rightly, that so long as Britain retained command of the Channel, the invasion was never plausible, but seen from the potential receiving end it looked all too likely.

Between 1803 and 1805, there was, after all, a new army of 200,000 men, L'armée des côtes de l'Océan or L'armée de l'Angleterre, massed at camps in Boulogne and elsewhere near the Channel coast. The British media were particularly spooked by Napoleon's plans for a fleet of troop-carrying balloons, though Sophie Blanchard, wife of the pioneer balloonist, who had caught Napoleon's eye to become the first ever female air marshal (and also the first woman to be killed in an aviation accident when she set off fireworks and her balloon caught fire during an air show at the Tivoli Garden in Paris), told the Emperor that the winds were not right. At all events, the whole invasion was called off, even before Britain's control of the seas had been confirmed at Trafalgar. But the fear lingered.

Already the British government had been stampeded into panic measures, notably the two 'Gagging Acts' of 1795: the Seditious Meetings Act, which restricted the size of public meetings, and the Treason Act, which punished any plot against the King, the government or the constitution with transportation, if not execution. Law-abiding radicals like Major Cartwright and the other members of the London Corresponding Society suddenly found themselves tarred as criminals liable to be banged up in the Tower of London. The trials of some of them in November 1794 proved an embarrassment for the government. The jury flung out the charges in minutes. But the efforts to repress dissent continued unabated even after Waterloo, with two more similar gagging acts brought in by Lord Liverpool's government in 1817, and the even more notorious Six Acts of 1819, prompted by the Peterloo Massacre. The Six Acts in turn provoked the Cato Street Conspiracy of 1820, the most violent plot to overthrow the government since the Gunpowder Plot, but one that was penetrated and provoked by government spies from the start. A further round of executions and transportations followed.

The system of repression was formidable. Government spies were everywhere. The peacetime army after Waterloo still numbered 150,000 – twice the size of the army today with a far smaller population. With no foreign enemies to worry about, thousands of troops could be ordered up at short notice to quell any disturbance, usually from near at hand. The eighteenth century had seen Ireland turned into a huge military camp, with 270 barrack sites constructed across the island. Now the same thing happened in London. The barracks familiar to us today – Knightsbridge, Regent's Park and so on – mostly date from this period. Daniel Defoe had noted long ago that Britain had more prisons than any other nation in Europe. Now further Bastilles were added. London also had the highest rate of executions in Europe, although this dropped markedly with the opening of the Australian penal settlements in 1788.

In this feverish climate, 'manliness' seemed, not a mere lifestyle choice, some whimsical offshoot of the cult of Beau Brummell, but a pressing national necessity. In the background of the novels of Jane Austen, you can hear the yeomanry drilling and the troops massing for embarkation, both lots often officered by her brothers and cousins.

WOMEN CAN BE MANLY, TOO
We must not think that manliness was to be thought of as an exclusively gendered quality. High-spirited women in the tradition of Anna Howe in *Clarissa* would have been scornful of any such assumption. None more so than the republican historian Catharine Macaulay (1731–91), much admired by Pitt and Condorcet and fellow historians such as Lecky.

In her *Vindication*, Mary Wollstonecraft denounces the patronizing twaddle of Rousseau and Burke on the subject of women, and gives a rousing defence of Macaulay as a model: 'Catherine Macaulay was an example of intellectual acquirements supposed to be incompatible with the weakness of her sex. In her writing, indeed, no sex appears, for it is like the sense it conveys, strong and clear.'

Wollstonecraft bangs home the point: 'I will not call hers a masculine understanding, because I admit not of such an arrogant assumption of reason; but I contend that it was a sound one, and that her judgment, the matured fruit of profound thinking, was a proof that a woman can acquire judgment, in the full extent of the word.'[17]

This was not, of course, the first occasion on which women's intelligence had been declared the equal, if not the superior, of men's. Back in 1405, the proto-feminist poet Christine de Pizan, in her famous work *The Book of the City of Ladies*, had asserted that, 'Although women may have weaker and less agile bodies than men which prevent them from doing certain tasks, their minds are in fact sharper and more receptive when they do apply themselves.'[18]

There was, however, work to be done, to make all this clear to the world, not least to those generations of women whom society had degraded into simpering flirts, obsessed with bonnets and shopping: 'It is time to effect a revolution in female manners – time to restore to them their lost dignity – and make them, as part of the human species, labour by reforming themselves to reform the world.'[19] In this immense undertaking there could be no gendered virtues, not even modesty. 'For man and woman, truth, if I understand the meaning of the word, must be the same.'[20] It was time for women to grow up and 'leave the go-cart' (then a sort of Zimmer frame on castors, to teach children how to walk, not a miniature racing car, as today). It was crucial to teach both sexes that there could be no reasonable grounds for excluding 'woman' from the definition of 'man'.

Mary Wollstonecraft by John Opie, 1797

Today, much of what she wrote is the conventional wisdom, not just of those who would call themselves feminists. It was not the conventional wisdom then. And though the occasions for much of her outrage have diminished, there are a vision and a resonance in *A Vindication of the Rights of Woman* that have not faded, and an agenda that is, even now, far from finished. Woman was no longer to be 'the toy of man, his rattle'.[21] 'Let woman share the rights and she will emulate the virtues of man, for she must grow more perfect when emancipated.'[22] There at last on her final page is the word 'emancipated', for which generations of women were to fight and to chain themselves to distinguished railings that they might finally snap the chains that had confined them for so many centuries. I have not seen the word applied to women before, as opposed to slaves or prisoners, and nor has the *Oxford English Dictionary*.

Although it was to be a long time before the legal and social barriers to emancipation were to be finally dismantled, for many women in the early nineteenth century the emancipation of the mind had already happened. 'Feminism', another term not yet used in the modern sense, was already an *intellectual* presence, nowhere more so than in the minds of the great English women novelists of the nineteenth century.

All of Jane Austen's works, from the Juvenilia parodies to *Persuasion* and the unfinished *Sanditon* are fiercely engaged in the sentimentalism debate, as Janet Todd points out. Austen mercilessly takes apart any sign of pretension, silliness, soppiness or snobbery, in fact every form of affectation. Which is partly why she immediately attracted the attention of sophisticated men and women of the world, who loved her acute observation and dry wit. Sir Walter Scott, in his notice of *Emma* in the *Quarterly Review* of 1816, declares that, although the novel 'remained fettered by many peculiarities derived from the original style of romantic fiction', it proclaims 'a knowledge of the human heart, with the power and resolution to bring that knowledge to the service of honour and virtue', unlike those 'ephemeral productions which supply the regular demand of watering places and circulating libraries'.

Nearly ten years after Austen's death, in his diary Scott gave a far more generous appreciation of her work: 'That young lady has a talent for describing the involvements and feelings and characters of ordinary life, which is to me the most wonderful I have ever met with. The Big Bow-Wow strain I can do myself like any now going; but the exquisite touch which renders ordinary commonplace things and characters interesting from the truth of the description and the sentiment is denied to me.'[23] No matter, as Claire Tomalin points out, that the young lady was long dead and had been 40 when he first reviewed her. She was now, in Sir Walter's eyes, one of the boys.

Yet it was precisely those qualities that Scott admired so much which, a quarter of a century later, Charlotte Brontë was to find somewhat limiting. In a letter about *Emma* in 1850, she wrote: Austen 'ruffles her reader by nothing vehement, disturbs him by nothing profound, the Passions are perfectly unknown to her ... her business is not half so much with the human heart as with the human eyes, mouth, hands and feet.'[24]

This alleged absence of passion, this dry materialism, is disputed, of course, by modern Janeites who would maintain that any such simplistic reading fails to grasp Austen's subtlety and depth. Yet there does seem to be a loss. Austen's novels, entrancing though they are, do lack the intensity, the unpredictable violence, the sense of tragedy that you find in *Clarissa* (in fact, Austen greatly admired Richardson's novels; her nephew wrote in his memoir of her that 'her knowledge of Richardson's works was such as no one is likely again to acquire'; every incident in it [*Sir Charles Grandison*] was familiar to her, and every character like a friend).[25] And as for the charge of materialism, one has only to recall the famous opening words of *Pride and Prejudice*: 'It is a truth universally acknowledged, that a single man in possession of a good fortune, must be in want of a wife.' The erasure of sentimentalism was not all gain. But for our present purposes, all we need to note is that it was Jane's anti-sentimental tenor which secured her such an instant and lasting reputation. Her outlook was unmistakably manly in the new, broad sense.

Charlotte Brontë herself had to confront the difficulties posed by this new imperative. Her explanation of why the three sisters decided to publish under shared pseudonyms is worth quoting at length: 'Averse to personal publicity, we veiled our own names under those of Currer, Ellis and Acton Bell; the ambiguous choice being dictated by a sort of conscientious scruple at assuming Christian names positively masculine, while we did not like to declare ourselves women, because – without at that time suspecting that our mode of writing was not what is called "feminine" – we had a vague impression that authoresses are liable to be looked on with prejudice.'[26]

Compare this with the explanation that George Eliot offered for her pen name in a letter to her publisher William Blackwood in 1857: the male name was created partly to conceal the gender of the author and partly to disguise her irregular position, living with a married man. She assured Blackwood – who was at that time unaware of her true identity – that the pen name was necessary to employ as 'a tub to throw to the whale in case of curious enquiries'. The cases are different, but underlying both explanations is the assumption that the 'tub' will sail better under a male, or at any rate not-female skipper. Both Brontë and Eliot take it for granted that there is nothing characteristically feminine about the way they write; their fear is that male readers might think there was, if they knew it was a woman writing.

Such assumptions – and such fears – would not have come so readily to mind a century earlier, in the heyday of sensibility. It would not have occurred to Catharine Macaulay or Mary Wollstonecraft to take a male pseudonym. The truth is that, despite Wollstonecraft's brilliant pleading, the advent of manliness continued to pose awkward questions for women who wanted to smash the 'separate spheres' and compete or collaborate with men out in the world. For women, the playing field was still potholed, bumpy and anything but level.

But there was no shortage of female heroes to satisfy the public thirst. Out of the prolonged debacle of the Crimean War, botched in its inception and its execution, only Florence

Nightingale emerged with lasting credit. Charles Kingsley might preach the need for 'muscular Christianity' to fortify the British Empire, but it was his niece Mary who made a more practical and durable contribution. She was not only an intrepid traveller but bold enough to challenge the stale imperial shibboleths about the inferiority of African culture. Mary Kingsley is now recognized as a pioneer anthropologist as well as an extraordinarily original writer. At the outbreak of the Second Boer War, she volunteered as a nurse in Cape Town, where she treated Boer prisoners of war and contracted typhoid. When she recognized that she was dying, she asked to be left alone, saying that she did not wish anyone to see her in her weakness. Animals, she said, went away to die alone. She asked only to be buried at sea. And then, finally, there was Nurse Edith Cavell on the eve of her execution: 'Patriotism is not enough. I must have no hatred or bitterness towards anyone.'

The Edith Cavell Monument

Or if you are looking for stoicism, but stoicism infused with passion, look no further than the wildest and greatest of the Brontë sisters:

> No coward soul is mine,
> No trembler in the world's storm-troubled sphere:
> I see Heaven's glories shine,
> And faith shines equal, arming me from Fear.

But the faith that shone for Emily Brontë was not some limp conventional thing but one of her own proud devising:

> Vain are the thousand creeds
> That move men's hearts, unutterably vain,
> Worthless as withered weeds
> Or idlest froth amid the boundless main.

This poem was included in *The Poems of Currer, Ellis and Acton Bell* and published in 1846. The book sold two copies and received two reviews.

THE DRY IMPERIAL EYE

Charlotte Brontë shared the general worship of the Duke of Wellington. In fact, she carried her adoration of the Iron Duke to some lengths. When she visited London in 1850, her great treat was to go to the Chapel Royal to watch the great man pass by. It was not simply his courage and coolness under fire, but his stoicism and common sense that made him the *beau idéal* of the age. He was unique, for he had not only won the war in Europe and defeated the invincible Napoleon, as a young general he had saved the Empire in India. He was the embodiment of Britain's mission in the world, and of manliness.

Now for the first time, that mission took concrete shape in the British Empire. The East India Company was no longer seen as a sleazy bunch of unscrupulous merchants. Purged, in theory anyway, by the reforms of Pitt and Cornwallis, the Honourable Company, too, became a missionary for British values (not Christian values; Christian missions were still banned from India, if not from Africa). Britain had something of unique value to teach the world, and its teachers had to be properly educated for the task. It is in these years that the EIC founds its military academy at Addiscombe in Surrey and its Imperial Service College at Haileybury, Herts. New recruits would set out from the motherland primed, no longer so much to make their fortunes as to spread British civilization.

From 1818 onwards, they would have been prepared for this life's work by reading the hugely successful *History of British India* by the Scottish historian and economist James Mill, who was to become head of the East India Office largely on the strength of this success, though he had never once visited India, and never did.

Despite this lack of first-hand experience, Mill's hostility to the people of India was visceral. Of the Hindus, he wrote, 'under the glosing exterior of the Hindu, lies a general disposition to deceit and perfidy'. Like the Chinese, they were dissembling, cowardly and unfeeling, 'in the highest degree conceited of themselves, and full of affected contempt for others', as well as 'disgustingly unclean in their persons and houses'. The Muslims were little better, in Mill's eyes. The Indologist Max Müller argued that this vicious portrayal of the Indians as an inferior race was 'responsible for some of the greatest misfortunes' that happened to India.

James Mill certainly had a profound and damaging effect on his son, the philosopher John Stuart Mill, who describes his father in his *Autobiography* of 1873: 'For passionate emotions of all sorts, and for everything which has been said or written in exaltation of them, he professed the profoundest contempt. He regarded them as a form of madness. "The intense" was with him a bye-word of scornful disapprobation. He regarded as an aberration of modern times, compared with that of the ancients, the great stress laid upon feeling.'[27] John Stuart Mill tells us that he took a lifetime to recover from the emotional blankness instilled in him. But his experience was not unique, especially among boys who were sent away to boarding school. As early as 1841, Harriet Martineau describes in her novel *The Crofton Boys* an emotion-stifling ambience that was to become familiar for the rest of the century to readers of such books as Thomas Hughes's *Tom Brown's Schooldays* (1857) and Rudyard Kipling's *Stalky & Co.* (1899). The hero, on arriving at Crofton School, is advised by another boy that 'you will find in every school that it is not the way of boys to talk about feelings – about anybody's feelings. That is the reason why they do not mention their sisters or their mothers.'[28] Boys were expected to show 'manly spirit' at all times, and above all never to 'blub' – the new term common from the 1860s – whether when suffering homesickness or after a brutal thrashing. Many boys then and much later, reared by parents and teachers who shared the same bleak stoicism, never recovered, especially if they were torn away from their families in their teens to go out and govern a subcontinent whose languages they barely understood and whose people they understood not at all.

In India, this alienation was intensified by the Cornwallis Code introduced by Lord Cornwallis as Governor-General (1786–94). In the interests of rooting out corruption, the old easy, interracial relations were deliberately frozen. Company officers no longer lived with their native *bibis*, no longer accompanied their men to the cockfight and the nautch dancing. Intimate contact was regarded as pernicious. From 1793, even people of mixed race were banned from government service. In *India Conquered*, Jon Wilson records delicious extracts from the diary of Julia Thomas, whose husband James was appointed judge at Rajahmundry in 1836. They were a well-meaning couple, who set up a school for Indian children. But James was incurably reclusive. When they travelled through his patch, he refused to engage with the locals and kept the door of his palanquin closed, despite his hosts' plea that he show himself to the people he ruled.[29]

Manliness degenerated into standoffishness and a wooden sense of racial superiority. By contrast, company officers were horrified by the ready emotional display of Indians at all levels, and especially by the unmanly tears of the Rajas. My great-great-grandfather Captain John Low, who spent 50 years in the service of the East India Company, was first taken aback by this when he was sent to receive the surrender of the Ruler of the Marathas, the Peshwa Baji Rao II, whose big, dark eyes filled with tears at each of their painful interviews.[30] Lord Ellenborough was similarly discomposed when the 13-year-old Maharaja of Gwalior sobbed throughout Ellenborough's blustering homily. The little boy understood no English and could only have been dimly aware that he was being stripped of all his powers.[31] Again, when the now Colonel Low was expropriating the Nizam of Hyderabad: 'I found the Nizam in a state of considerable excitement; his face was much flushed and his eyes appeared somewhat inflamed', Low reported, as if it was surprising that the Nizam should take on so, when he was being stripped of the richest part of his kingdom.[32] In the last of these grand acts of pillage, when Colonel Outram was dethroning the King of Oudh, the attractive poet Wajid Ali Shah, after a grief-stricken lament that he should be losing the throne which his ancestors had occupied for a hundred years, the King wept and took off his turban and placed it in Outram's hands as a sign of his utter impotence.[33]

The British were invariably scornful of such 'exaggerated display of helplessness', as Sir John Kaye called it in his *History of the Indian Mutiny*. Kaye's sympathies were entirely on the side of the embarrassed British officer: 'No man was more likely than Outram to have been doubly pained, in the midst of all his painful duties, by the unmanly prostration of the King.' But Outram was not to be deterred from doing his duty, 'because an effeminate Prince, when told he was no longer to have the power of inflicting measureless wrongs on his country, burst into tears, said that he was a miserable wretch, and took off his turban instead of taking out his sword'.[34]

Fortitude was the number one quality of the high imperial age. In verse, perhaps its most memorable expression is W. E. Henley's short poem 'Invictus'. Written in 1875 and originally published with no title, it was reprinted in newspapers with various other titles, and given this final title by Sir Arthur

Quiller-Couch when he included it in his *Oxford Book of English Verse* (1900). Never forgotten and now enshrined in the Invictus Games, the poem was written when, after a lifetime of tuberculosis, Henley was recovering in hospital in Edinburgh after having his leg amputated. It ends with the lines, 'I am the master of my fate, I am the captain of my soul', but what he is proudest of is his fortitude:

> In the fell clutch of circumstance,
> I have not winced nor cried aloud.
> Under the bludgeonings of chance
> My head is bloody, but unbowed.

Just before Henley wrote 'Invictus', the expression 'stiff upper lip' appears in print in England for the first time, in Charles Dickens's magazine *All the Year Round*; it is included among 'Popular American Phrases', and its meaning has to be explained: 'to remain firm to a purpose, to keep up one's courage'.[35] The first traceable uses of the phrase occur in *Uncle Tom's Cabin*, when Uncle Tom is twice encouraged to 'keep a stiff upper lip' when he is taken off in leg irons, once by his young friend George and then again by the slave-dealer who has just fettered him.[36] But if ever a catchphrase was born for its age, this was it. In no time 'stiff upper lip' became a watchword, and then a cliché, until it could no longer be invoked without irony, as in P. G. Wodehouse's *Stiff Upper Lip, Jeeves* (1963) and the song sung by Gracie Allen in the Fred Astaire musical *Damsel in Distress* (1937), which listed 'stiff upper lip', 'chin up' and 'muddling through' as the secrets of Britain's success through the ages.

The final appearance of the stiff upper lip, to date anyway, is in the title of the book by Alex Renton (2018), which is an unsparing history of brutality and sexual abuse in English boarding schools.

There is not much irony in the only poem on the theme to rival the popularity of 'Invictus'. Rudyard Kipling's 'If' was voted the nation's favourite poem in a BBC poll of 1996, a century after it was published in 1895. It was Margaret Thatcher's favourite poem, and it perfectly reflects her outlook on the world. The poll seems to have been taken from BBC Radio 4 listeners. The younger age group of BBC Radio 1 might have produced a rather different result.

Kipling's poem explores, with memorable resonance, the ramifications of the stoical outlook: boldness, endurance, modesty, hard work, self-confidence. If you can master all these qualities, 'You'll be a Man, my son!'. But what a lot this Manliness leaves out: pity, affection, grief, remorse, even friendship. In fact, close friendship appears to be a no-no:

> If neither foes nor loving friends can hurt you,
> If all men count with you, but none too much.

That underlying indifference was always at the core of the Stoic's world view, going back to Marcus Aurelius and Epictetus. But it is a chilly recipe for life to tuck into the middle of a children's book, as Kipling did by including 'If' in *Rewards and Fairies* (1910).

Many of those who voted for 'If' were probably not aware that the poem was inspired by Kipling's admiration for the Jameson Raid, a freebooting attack on the South African Republic, designed to seize control of the Transvaal goldfields for Cecil Rhodes and the British South African Company. The occasion for Kipling's other great imperialistic ode was no more savoury. 'The White Man's Burden' (1899) was an exhortation to the United States to annex the Philippines and colonize them, because the natives were not fit to govern themselves. In fact, a version of the poem had originally been written for Queen Victoria's Diamond Jubilee two years earlier, but he substituted for it the less vainglorious 'Recessional', which exhorted the British to remember that their Empire, too, would one day pass away, 'one with Nineveh and Tyre!'.

In all three poems, Kipling emphasizes the personal costs that the British will have to suffer in carrying out their imperial mission and the moral duties they must not forget. But in imperial terms, the cult of manliness always rests on assumptions of the white man's indelible superiority to 'the lesser breeds without the law' and 'your new-caught, sullen peoples, / Half devil and half child'.

We cannot help noticing something else, something decidedly peculiar about the style in which the British commemorated the battles of the Empire in its heyday. The deepest mourning and the finest monuments were reserved for those heroes who had suffered conspicuous deaths in battles that the British had lost. In *Heroic Failure and the British*, Stephanie Barczewski, with all the post-colonial detachment that comes naturally to an American academic, gives a long and stirring list: from that feisty Ulsterman Rollo Gillespie, strutting alone to a hero's death against the Gurkhas at Kalunga (his men had refused to follow him), and Ned Pakenham and Samuel Gibbs falling one after the other in the disaster at New Orleans (the British had over 2,000 casualties, the Americans a mere 22), through the insane Charge of the Light Brigade and the Last Stand at Isandlwana to the death of Gordon at Khartoum before the relief column got there. Where these stories do not end in death, they end in the relief of a starving garrison – at Lucknow (relieved three times during the Mutiny of 1857), at Ladysmith, at Mafeking – who now remembers the word 'mafficking' or the boisterous rejoicing that gave rise to it?

Whether in mourning or pent-up relief, the message was clear: only death or near-starvation could justify the cause. If the British were to convince themselves that their empire was just, benevolent and moral, Barczewski argues, they needed 'to occlude Britain's military might and to shift attention away from extremely lopsided battles that were more akin to slaughter'. For the sake of our self-respect, we had to forget that we had the Maxim gun and they had not.

Gillespie is commemorated by no less than five monuments, at Kalunga itself, in his native Co. Down, in Calcutta and Meerut and in St Paul's Cathedral in the same transept as Pakenham and Gibbs. He is remembered, not for his bloody victories in the West Indies and in India, still less for his massacre of hundreds of unarmed prisoners when quelling the mutiny at Vellore, but simply for the manner of his glorious ultimate sacrifice.

There is, Barczewski admits, nothing exclusively British about this memorial strategy. Americans still honour the dead of the Alamo and Little Big Horn as a distraction from the one-sided massacres that disfigured the westward march of the United States. Barczewski also includes several non-military deaths among her lost causes: that of Sir John Franklin in his vain search for the Northwest Passage, David Livingstone's fruitless missions to the Zambezi, and Scott of the Antarctic's doomed mission to the South Pole. All these deaths were indeed flawed: Franklin's by the large number of people who died looking for him and by the cannibalism to which his desperate companions resorted at the last, Livingstone's by his brutal treatment of so many Africans, and Scott's by his arrogant mistakes. But none of them had set out to subjugate other human beings or to kill anyone. I find it hard not to be a little bit moved by their stories, just as I was moved at the Tate exhibition 'Artist and Empire' by the roomful of huge, not very good canvases depicting last stands and heroic deaths from Wolfe at Quebec to Gordon at Khartoum. But note the difference between Benjamin West's picture of 1770 showing the dying Wolfe surrounded by weeping aides and G. W. Joy's 1893 painting of the stoical Gordon, in which the only figures showing their emotions are the screaming dervishes. In between, the imperial eye has totally dried.

The Death of General Wolfe by Benjamin West, 1770; The Death of General Gordon by G. W. Joy, 1893

All the same, the contrast with the non-imperial battles of the twentieth century does tend to support Barczewski's thesis. After the two world wars, it was the sacrifice not of individuals but of whole regiments, in battles won as well as battles lost, which tended to be commemorated. The thousands of deaths on both sides were scrupulously recorded. There was no need of obfuscation or embellishment, because national survival was seen to be at stake, and after 1916 the whole nation was conscripted into the struggle. So the memorials, whether local or national, tend to be simple and sombre and above all communal. On town and village memorials there are often no distinctions of rank. The names are given by bare alphabetical order.

The conscription to the national cause is a conscription of the imagination. These brave or foolhardy ventures – whether military, scientific or even in Livingstone's case religious – were often financed by private individuals (by Lady Franklin, for example) or by societies, but they were increasingly presented in the media as undertaken for the glory of the nation. In the crudest sense, it has to be a British expedition that gets to the Pole first or discovers the Northwest Passage. In a loftier sense, though, even being first doesn't matter so much (nobody remembers who actually discovered the Northwest Passage while looking for Franklin – it was either Commander Robert McClure or a fur trader called William Kennedy). The ultimate purpose of these exemplary hardships and deaths is to demonstrate the unrivalled manliness of the British race, to proclaim and establish a moral *imperium*. These public parables are designed to tighten the grip of nationhood and to intensify the reach of the State that embodies that nationhood.

And yet as the nineteenth century wore on, there was something increasingly implausible about these high moral claims, an implausibility that was felt at the time, especially in the Boer War when it was not hard to see that the British were not really fighting for any great principle but for grubby commercial gain. The Empire began to be a subject, not only for sharp moral critique but also, fatally, for mockery.

Which is partly why, when the Great War eventually came, it was initially perceived not as a catastrophe but as a curious kind of relief. In retrospect, the enthusiasm of the first war poets seems tragically misplaced, but what is unmistakable is the specific nature of that relief. The war was, or could be, a *cleansing*. This feeling was common to very different sorts of people.

The artist Filippo Tommaso Marinetti had written in the *Manifesto of Futurism* (1909): 'We intend to sing the love of danger, the habit of energy and fearlessness ... We will glorify war – the world's only hygiene – militarism, patriotism, the destructive gesture of freedom-bringers, beautiful ideas worth dying for, and scorn for woman.'

Rupert Brooke said the declaration of war was 'like swimmers into cleanness leaping'. Julian Grenfell's 'Into Battle' describes the experience of battle as a more intense way of living: 'he is dead who will not fight; and who dies fighting has increase. / The fighting man shall from the sun / Take warmth, and life from the glowing earth.' In his wonderfully clear-eyed memoir of Julian's cousins, the Grenfell twins, Francis and Riversdale, who won the VC and the MC respectively, John Buchan describes their dismal pre-war life of polo and pigsticking and occasional dodgy jobs in the City, and their consequent excitement when war came at last. They were so looking forward to transferring their riding skills to real warfare.

Winston Churchill confided to Violet Asquith in 1915 that 'I would not be out of this delicious war for anything', hurriedly adding, 'mind you, don't say I said delicious.' He told Siegfried Sassoon, who had seen what trench warfare was like and won the MC for his heroism, that 'war is the normal occupation of man', adding, again hurriedly, 'war – and gardening'. 'Pacing the room, with a big cigar in the corner of his mouth, he gave me an emphatic vindication of militarism as an instrument of policy and stimulator of glorious individual achievements, not only in the mechanism of warfare but in spheres of social progress.' He told the transfixed Sassoon that the present war had brought about inventive discoveries which would ameliorate the condition of mankind. For example, there had been immense improvements in sanitation (the cleansing theme again).[37] Churchill did not mention the invention of the tank or the aeroplane, or, his own distinctive contribution, the idea of large-scale bombing raids on cities.

There seemed, above all, an *appropriateness* about the call to arms, one which the fake imperatives of imperialism embarrassingly lacked. Rupert Brooke begins one of his most famous poems, 'Now, God be thanked Who has matched us with His hour.' Here at last was an unmistakable test of manliness, one not sought out of imperial greed or personal vainglory, but imposed by inexorable duty and national necessity. In *Son of Oscar Wilde*, Vyvyan Holland (the two sons took their mother's name after Oscar was jailed) wrote of his brother Cyril's determination to expiate their father's shame. Cyril had trained at the RMA Woolwich and was commissioned into the Royal Field Artillery. After three years in India, by the outbreak of war he was a captain. He wrote to Vyvyan that 'first and foremost, I must be a *man*. There was to be no cry of decadent artist, of effeminate aesthete, of weak-kneed degenerate ... I am no wild, passionate, irresponsible hero. I live by thought, not by emotion ... I ask nothing better than to end in honourable battle for my King and country.'[38] He had his wish. On 9 May, near Neuville-Saint-Vaast, Cyril was shot dead by a German sniper. Rupert Brooke had died of septicaemia on 23 April, on a hospital ship moored off the Greek island of Skyros. Julian Grenfell died on 26 May, after being hit by a German shell a fortnight earlier. Two days earlier, Francis was killed in action. Riversdale had already been killed in September 1914, only a month after the outbreak of the war. Their dreams of cavalry charges had faded within weeks to the grim reality of the trenches. Edith Cavell was shot at dawn on 12 October.

After 1915, the ideal of manliness had lost whatever innocence it had once possessed. It might still be a commanding virtue, but as Nurse Cavell might also have said, 'Manliness is not enough.'

FIVE

Mr Popular Sentiment

THE CASE OF CHARLES DICKENS

The Warden was the fourth novel by Anthony Trollope to be published (in 1855) and the first to catch the public eye. It was also to be the first of his enormously popular Barsetshire Chronicles, the tales set in an ancient cathedral close and occupied with the doings of the bishop, clergy and their families. Trollope claimed in his *Autobiography* that he had no previous knowledge of clerical life (although he had spent three unhappy years at Winchester as a schoolboy). He had simply been working for the Post Office and was looking into rural deliveries in Wessex and happened to be wandering round the close at Salisbury one mid-summer evening when the plot of *The Warden* came to him.

It is a strange story, pedestrian yet almost dreamy, in fact just the kind of story that might float into your mind on a summer evening in beautiful surroundings.

The Warden is the Revd Septimus Harding, a sweet old boy who likes nothing better than to play his cello and chant the litany in the Cathedral. In return for being nice to the 12 ancient bedesmen in Hiram's Hospital, he receives the huge salary of £800 a year, paid out of the funds accumulated by property development on the patches of land bequeathed by the original Mr Hiram. By contrast, the decayed pensioners under his care receive a mere one shilling and fourpence a day. This gross inequality comes to the notice of John Bold, a thrusting young surgeon who is in love with Harding's daughter, Eleanor, and she with him. Bold takes up the bedesmen's cause, and enlists the support of his friend Tom Towers, the equally thrusting young lion of The Jupiter (= The Thunderer, then and now the nickname of the London Times, at that period the dominant newspaper with a circulation of 50,000). A ferocious legal and media campaign follows. In the end, the distraught Eleanor persuades John Bold to call off the campaign, but not before Harding, stricken with belated shame, has decided to give up the Wardenship and its whopping income, and go and live in relative poverty with his cello. John Bold and Eleanor are married, and the story ends on a serene diminuendo.

But this account fails to convey the passion with which Trollope insists on the sweet and saintly character of the old Warden and the crass brutish behaviour of his assailants. From the start, the scales are loaded against the campaigners. Bold himself is an interfering busybody: 'It would be well if one so young had a little more diffidence himself, and more trust in the honest purpose of others – if he could be brought to believe that old customs need not necessarily be evil, and that changes may possibly be dangerous.'[1] When the bedesmen's eyes light up at the prospect of getting a hundred pounds a year, they are denounced for their greed. The Jupiter is denounced, too, as a terrifying 'pope who manages his own inquisition, who punishes unbelievers as no most skilful inquisitor of Spain ever dreamt of doing – one who can excommunicate thoroughly, fearfully, radically, put you beyond the pale of men's charity; make you odious to your dearest friends, and turn you into a monster to be pointed at by the finger!'[2] Seldom until the advent of the Leveson Inquiry can the irresponsible cruelty of the press have been so flayed.

Trollope's plot draws on two *causes célèbres* of the day, the St Cross almshouse at Winchester where the Master, the Earl of Guilford, was pulling in £2,000–3,000 a year for doing nothing, and a slightly different case at Rochester, where the Dean and Chapter were accused of enriching themselves at the expense of charities. In his *Autobiography*, Trollope tells us how he was struck by two opposite evils. The first was 'the possession by the Church of certain funds and endowments which had been intended for charitable purposes, but which had been allowed to become incomes for idle Church dignitaries'.[3] But Trollope seems to have been more affected by the opposite evil. 'Though I had been much struck by the injustice above described, I had also often been angered by the undeserved severity of the newspapers towards the recipients of such incomes who could scarcely be considered the chief sinners in the matter.'[4] To keep us on the Warden's side, the book tugs at our heartstrings as fervently as Mr Harding saws at his cello: 'Mr Harding could not well speak now, for the warm tears were running down his cheeks like rain in May, but he held his child close to his heart and squeezed her hand as a lover might, and she kissed his forehead and his wet cheeks, and lay upon his bosom, and comforted him as a woman only can do.'[5]

The Warden is an affecting little novel, but it is also a decidedly odd one. In its barely 200 pages, Trollope finds space for a prolonged parody of Thomas Carlyle, alias Dr Pessimist Anticant, in his most tub-thumping manner. Odder still, he throws in a sketch of the same novel as Charles Dickens might have written it. In a shop window, John Bold sees the first instalment of *The Almshouse* by Mr Popular Sentiment. In Sentiment's version, the Warden becomes an out-and-out villain living in luxury, while the paupers in his care are starving on sixpence-farthing a day. After reading the first instalment, John Bold tosses it aside, thinking that the book 'at least had no direct appliance to Mr Harding, and that the absurdly strong colouring of the picture would disenable the work from doing either good or harm'.[6] But Trollope tells us firmly: 'He was wrong. The artist who paints for the million must use glaring colours, as no one knew better than Mr Sentiment when he described the inhabitants of his almshouse, and the radical reform which has now swept over such establishments has owed more to the twenty numbers of Mr Sentiment's novel, than to all the true complaints which have escaped from the public for the last half-century.'[7]

Here then we have a completely new critique of popular sentimental fiction. No longer is the objection that they are self-indulgent weepies. In that sense, as we have seen, *The Warden* is just as sentimental. The trouble now is not that these books are powerless to affect the injustices they are moaning about. On the contrary, the objection is that this new wave of sentimental twaddle is *too powerful*.

'Of all such reformers Mr Sentiment is the most powerful. It is incredible the number of evil practices he has put down: it is to be feared he will soon lack subjects, and that when he has made the working classes comfortable, and got bitter beer put into proper-sized pint bottles, there will be nothing left for him to do.' His secret is gross oversimplification: 'Mr Sentiment is certainly a very powerful man, and perhaps not the less so that his good poor people are so very good, his hard rich people so very hard, and the genuinely honest so very honest. Namby-pamby these days is not thrown away if it be introduced in the proper quarters.'[8]

In his parody, Trollope reproduces some of the overwhelming firepower of Dickens at his hottest, for example, in his description of the villainous Master of the Almshouse: 'He was a man well stricken in years, but still strong to do evil: he was one who looked cruelly out of a hot, passionate, bloodshot eye; who had a huge red nose with a carbuncle, thick lips and a great double, flabby chin, which swelled out into solid substance, like a turkey-cock's comb, when sudden anger inspired him: he had a hot, furrowed, low brow, from which a few grizzled hairs were not yet rubbed off by the friction of his handkerchief: he wore a loose, unstarched white handkerchief, black loose ill-made clothes, and huge loose shoes, adapted to many corns and various bunions: his husky voice told tales of much daily port wine; and his language was not so decorous as became a clergyman.'[9]

This portrait of an imaginary character in an imaginary novel rather reminds me of the bravura portrait of the dying 'Mrs Sinclair', the brothel-keeper in *Clarissa*. It is also a good deal livelier than Trollope's descriptions of his actual characters in *The Warden*, which are all drawn judiciously, as he always does, with a careful mixture of good and bad in them, but drawn pallidly, a little blandly, in watercolour rather than Dickens's furious impasto. Might one perhaps have enjoyed *The Almshouse*, if it had ever got written, rather more intensely than *The Warden*?

It is hard, too, not to wonder whether mid-Victorian almshouses were all as blissful as Hiram's Hospital, and not to look forward to the scandals we read of in modern care homes, those harrowing tales of abuse and neglect, of callous nurses and greedy proprietors, just as Clarissa's ordeal reminds us of the sexual abuse inflicted by the Lovelaces of our own day? Trollope was always hot on the failings of the Post Office. What would he have made of *Mr Bates and the Post Office*? Would he have been among the few media voices to denounce the hounding of innocent sub-postmasters? Or would his first reaction have been to 'put more trust in the honest purposes' of those who were running the Royal Mail?

I have quoted Trollope's indictment of Dickens at some length, not because it is unique but because it is so vivid and candid. Dickens's other critics sing much the same tune. One's first reaction, in fact, on reviewing his critical heritage, is to marvel that these critiques are so plentiful and so ferocious. As the essayist, G. H. Lewes, George Eliot's partner, one of the fairer of these critics but not the least harsh, put it: 'there probably never was a writer of so vast a popularity whose genius was so little appreciated by the critics.'[10] Dickens might have effortlessly conquered the popular market. By the guardians of high culture, he continued to be received with distaste and even loathing. In fact, it is the very ease which he came to dominate the market for popular fiction that awakened the direst suspicions of the intelligentsia (as it was not yet called).

This hostility mingled political fear with aesthetic distaste. Dickens's novels were *dangerous*. They wrenched political debate out of the secluded calm of Westminster committee rooms and London clubs, and hyped it up to explosive levels. At the same time, Dickens's novels were also *nasty*: 'puppy pie and stewed cat', as James Fitzjames Stephen described *A Tale of Two Cities* in the *Saturday Review*.[11]

Stephen asserts that 'if it had not borne Mr Dickens's name, it would in all probability have hardly met with a single reader ... it would perhaps be hard to imagine a clumsier or more disjointed framework for the display of the tawdry wares which form Mr Dickens's stock-in-trade'. The author's technical tricks are beneath contempt: 'the two main sources of his popularity are his power of working upon the feelings by the coarsest stimulants, and his power of setting common occurrences in a grotesque and unexpected light ... No popularity can disguise the fact that this is the very lowest of low styles of art.'

'The Death of Paul Dombey' from Dombey and Son, Harry Furniss

By profession, Stephen was a lawyer, a grim hanging judge who spent much of his life doling out justice in India. Even today, rock-ribbed conservatives adore his celebrated tract Liberty, Equality, Fraternity (spoiler alert: he didn't much care for any of them). He also happened to be Virginia Woolf's uncle, a fact which may seem irrelevant at this stage, but which may come into play later.

Stephen hated Dickens's novels because he was fearful of them: 'it may be admitted that he can scarcely attract the attention of the more intelligent classes of the community, but he may, and, as we believe, does exercise a very wide and a very pernicious political and social influence.'[12] 'He is a man with a very active fancy, great powers of language, much perception of what is grotesque, and a most lachrymose and melodramatic turn of mind – and this is all.' He 'knows absolutely nothing of law or politics', but does not hesitate to pour contempt on all the great institutions of this country.

Dickens won't last, Stephen tells us: 'It does not appear to us certain that his books will live, nor do we think that his place in literary history will be by the side of such men as Defoe and Fielding ... Fifty years hence, most of his wit will be harder to understand than the allusions in the *Dunciad*; and our grandchildren will wonder what their ancestors could have meant by putting Mr Dickens at the head of the novelists of his day.'[13]

But while it lasted, the Dickens formula for success was toxic. 'Mr Dickens was led by nature as much as by art to mix up a very strong dose of sentiment with his caricature. From first to last, he has tried about as much to make his readers cry as to make them laugh; and there is a very large section of the British public – and especially of the younger, weaker, and more ignorant part of it – which considers these two functions as comprising the whole duty of novelists ... There is a sex in minds as well as in bodies, and Mr Dickens's literary progeny seem to us to be for the most part of the feminine gender, and to betray it by most unceasing flirtations, and by a very tiresome irritability of nerve.'[14]

Dickens's works are so dangerous because they are so damnably available. These cheap editions were now on sale by the million at every railway bookstall: 'the effect of these publications on the whole mind of the community, especially on the minds of the young, the ignorant and the inexperienced can scarcely be imagined.'[15]

Another great Victorian sage, the political and economic essayist Walter Bagehot, was equally apprehensive. Mr Dickens 'is utterly deficient in the faculty of reasoning'. He knows only the common sort of people: 'the delicate refinement and discriminating taste of the idling orders are not in his way; he knows the dry arches of

London Bridge better than Belgravia ... His delineations of middle-class life have in consequence a harshness and meanness which do not belong to that life in reality.' His 'sentimental radicalism' might have been appropriate to the first 20 years of the nineteenth century which had been marked by a 'harsh unfeelingness', but that unfeelingness had now been corrected by 'an extreme, perhaps an excessive sensibility to human suffering'. Bagehot, like Thackeray, was suffering from an early case of compassion fatigue. Restrictions on child labour, the end of slavery, poor law reform – it had all gone quite far enough. Mr Dickens had begun his career by describing removable evils, but 'he has ended by describing the natural evils and inevitable pains of the present state of being in such a manner as must tend to excite discontent and repining'.[16]

Bagehot was a confirmed sceptic about political reform in particular, especially about the extension of the franchise in Disraeli's 1867 Act: 'I am exceedingly afraid of the ignorant multitude of the new constituencies.'[17] These new voters would need to be 'guided by their betters'.[18] There could be no more disastrous guide than the novels of Charles Dickens with their scattershot attacks on all the revered institutions of the Constitution – Parliament, the Law, the Civil Service. Nothing gave Bagehot and Stephen more pain than Dickens's attacks on the Circumlocution Office, which completely caricatured the due process and proper deliberation of the British system of government. It was bad enough giving these hordes the vote, but putting the shilling volumes of Dickens into their hands would give them ideas, too. They would become as greedy as the bedesmen at Hiram's Hospital.

George Henry Lewes, the revered critic most famous for living in sin with George Eliot, had enjoyed many of Dickens's earlier novels like *Oliver Twist*. As even the severer critics did, he paid tribute to the creation of memorable characters like Mrs Gamp and Mr Micawber. And he had corresponded amicably with Dickens himself. But after Dickens's death, he gave a more caustic assessment. His characters were like frogs whose brains had been removed for the purpose of scientific experiment. These brainless frogs would continue to hop and jump as before, but the hops and skips would be 'always the same'. They lacked the complexity and unpredictability of real living creatures. In Dickens's tear-jerkers, 'the pictures will not move the cultivated mind, nor give it the deep content which perfect Art continues to create making the work "a joy for ever"'. He is thinking of something like the *ataraxia*, the serene unmovedness which Johan Huizinga found in Michelangelo and deplored the absence of in the sculpture of Claus Sluter.

This absence of *ataraxia*, this lack of nobility in modern fiction, especially Dickens, was also deplored by John Ruskin in his polemical essay *Fiction Fair and Foul*. He lists with undisguised revulsion the stream of squalid deaths recorded in a single novel, *Bleak House*. By contrast, he insists, 'In the work of the great masters, death is always either heroic, deserved or quiet and natural.'[19] The wretched demoralization of life in the modern city has left the reader craving cheap and frightful sensations, typified by the 'loathsome mass' of the Dickens oeuvre (he excepts only *Oliver Twist*, perhaps because there are no cripples in it, although the murder of Nancy and the death of Bill Sikes could scarcely be more lurid). According to Ruskin, the rot set in with Victor Hugo's *Notre-Dame de Paris* (published back in 1831): 'the effectual head of the whole cretinous school is the renowned novel in which the hunchbacked lover watches the execution of his mistress from the tower of Notre Dame; and its strength passes gradually away into the anatomical preparations, for the general market, of novels like *Poor Miss Finch* [by Dickens's best friend Wilkie Collins, published in 1872], in which the heroine is blind, the hero epileptic, and the obnoxious brother is found dead with his hands dropped off, in the Arctic regions.'[20] Ruskin's hero, Sir Walter Scott, disdains the sentimental deathbed scenes in which Dickens delights: 'he never once withdrew the sacred curtain of the sick chamber, nor permitted the disgrace of wanton tears round the humiliation of strength, or the wreck of beauty.'[21] There are no cripples, hunchbacks, epileptics or half-wits in the Waverley novels. Such miserable specimens were seldom to be met with in the healthy Scottish country air. They are exclusively the spawn of the London slums.

The summing up that Lewes comes to is much the same as Ruskin's: 'Only the cultivated who are made fastidious by cultivation paused to consider the pervading commonness of the works, and remarked that they are wholly without glimpses of a nobler life; and that the writer presents an almost unique example of a mind of singular force in which, so to speak, sensations never passed into ideas. Dickens sees and feels, but the logic of feeling seems the only logic he can manage. Thought is strangely absent from his works.'[22]

So: low, common, thoughtless, lacking in serious aspiration. This kind of assessment of Dickens was still alive 70 years later. In *The Great Tradition*, the primer for a whole generation of literary academics and critics, F. R. Leavis allows of him only that his 'genius was that of a great entertainer and he had for the most part no profounder responsibility as a creative artist than this description suggests ... The adult mind doesn't as a rule find in Dickens a challenge to an unusual and sustained seriousness.' Note the stern headmasterly tone, typical of Leavis, as if dealing with some falling-off in school discipline, rather than with matters of the imagination and the heart. Leavis admits only *Hard Times* as an exception to Dickens's exclusion from *The Great Tradition*. It was to be another 20 years before both Leavis and his redoubtable wife Queenie recanted and devoted nearly 500 pages to celebrating his genius in *Dickens the Novelist*.

The critique of Dickens as sentimental and vulgar, and therefore a bad influence both on literature and politics, lasted for decades, until the more generous assessments of George Orwell and Edmund Wilson more or less smothered it. Oscar Wilde was certainly not the last prominent writer, for example, whose stomach was turned by Little Nell's deathbed. In *Vulgarity in Literature* (1930), Aldous Huxley, too, lays into *The Old Curiosity Shop*: yes, Dickens 'had an overflowing heart, but the trouble was that it overflowed with such curious and even rather repellant secretions ... Mentally drowned and blinded by the sticky overflowings of his heart, Dickens was incapable, when moved, of re-creating, in terms of art, the reality which had moved him, was even, it would seem, unable to perceive that reality ... The history of Little Nell is distressing indeed, but not as Dickens presumably meant it to be distressing; it is distressing in its ineptitude and vulgar sentimentality.'[23]

Lewes was at least right in claiming that no popular English novelist ever got such a roasting from the critics as Mr Popular Sentiment. That roasting was part of the ongoing reaction against sentimentality which we have been describing. But it was also the beginning of a more defined cleavage between high culture and popular culture, a cleavage which we shall see sharpening and widening over the early years of the twentieth century with lasting and fateful consequences. We shall see that cleavage appear in other arts and in other countries. It is in fact a defining feature of modernism. Perhaps it is the defining feature.

UNCLE TOM AND AUNT PHILLIS

What the Dickens critics really hated was the way he took up so many diverse causes, and with so little apparent effort. One after another, the fictional polemics pour from his pen: in Oliver Twist, against the poor laws and the workhouses; in Nicholas Nickleby only a matter of months later, his target is the cruel Yorkshire schools; in Little Dorrit, the injustice of long-term imprisonment for debt; in Pickwick and Bleak House, the law's life-sapping delays; in Hard Times, the inhumanity of the utilitarians. All these tirades left their mark; we still speak today of a scandalously brutal school as a Dotheboys Hall, or of a long-drawn-out legal pile-up as another Jarndyce vs Jarndyce.

But none of Dickens's campaigns had one tenth the impact of a single epic novel by the wife of a New England clergyman. Harriet Beecher Stowe had never written a novel before she started Uncle Tom's Cabin, only sketches and short stories. She was turning 40 at the time, and was pregnant with her seventh child. Her sixth child, Samuel Charles, had just died in infancy of cholera.

The book was published in March 1852, after appearing in 40 weekly instalments in The National Era. It was an instant hit, selling 10,000 copies in the first week, and being translated into all the major European languages. By the outbreak of the Civil War, it had sold four and a half million copies. Mrs Stowe was the most famous author in the world, and her book universally agreed to be the most influential ever written by an American, and, as we have seen, outsold in the nineteenth century only by the Bible. Doubt has already been cast on the story that when she first met President Lincoln in 1862, he said to her, 'so this is the little lady who started this great war'. Harriet herself wrote to her husband only a few hours later only that 'I had a real funny interview with the President.' But the point remains that the anecdote was plausible enough to be widely believed and long remembered.

From the first, the novel aroused fierce and widely differing reactions. Many literary critics dismissed the whole thing as 'a typical sentimental novel', 'Sunday-school fiction', 'full of women's sloppy emotions', a book which would have attracted no attention at all if it had not been for its super-hot theme. In the South, it was denounced as a pack of lies, a vile slander on the Southern way of life. Harriet was sent a package from a Southern address containing the severed ear of a black man with an accompanying card deriding her defence of the 'D—n niggers' (typical of the pieties of the time that the blank should be placed in d—n and not the other word). Calvin Stowe intercepted the package and disposed of the ear before his wife had a chance to see it.

As the serialization proceeded, Stowe was besieged with complaints about the improbability of various incidents in the book, a criticism still to be heard a century later when James Baldwin, in *Notes of a Native Son*, denounced the novel as 'both badly written and wildly improbable'. Stowe had time to add an explanatory postscript to the published version of the book, and later brought out *A Key to Uncle Tom's Cabin* going into more detail. For example, she tells us that the dramatic incident of Eliza escaping with her little boy across the ice floes of the Ohio River actually happened in real life. So did the tragic end of poor drunken old Prue. Just after I had read another complaint of improbability in the novel, about the sudden death of St Clare, the attractive sceptical planter, stabbed by accident in a tavern brawl in which he was not implicated, a friend of mine emailed me to say that she had just been sitting in a café in Kingsland High Street when a little girl sitting at her table had been shot, all but fatally, by a stray bullet from a gunfight between two rival heroin gangs. These terrible things happen. Readers who find such incidents improbable are not only failing to use their imagination, they are failing to read their daily newspapers.

Inattentive critics also laid into Stowe for supporting the plan for free blacks to emigrate to Liberia and found a new country there, those left behind being left to rot in slavery. Stowe was certainly in favour of the Liberian enterprise, and the plan is supported by the free-thinking George in the book. But this solution is clearly rebutted as inadequate by the author in her Concluding Remarks: 'Do you say, "We don't want them here; let them go to Africa?" That the providence of God has provided a refuge in Africa, is, indeed, a great and noticeable fact; but that is no reason why this Church of Christ should throw off that responsibility to this outcast race which her profession demands of her.'[24] And St Clare, who is often presented as the voice of reason in the book, says to his cousin Ophelia, in rebuking the humbug of Northerners who inveigh against slavery: 'You would not have them abused; but you don't want to have anything to do with them yourselves. You would send them to Africa out of your sight and smell, and then send a missionary or two to do up all the self-denial of elevating them compendiously. Isn't that it?'[25]

From the start, too, *Uncle Tom's Cabin* has been criticized by militant abolitionists who find the character of Uncle Tom himself too meek and subservient. William Lloyd Garrison, the leader of those who demanded the immediate, unconditional, uncompensated abolition of slavery, did not like Tom's 'submission to tyranny' and thought him 'a disturbing model for a black hero'. More violent abolitionists would have preferred 'a hero who would have buried the hoe deep in the master's skull'. James Baldwin finds the figure of Tom as repellent as he is unlikely: 'he is phenomenally forbearing.' He has to be: 'he is black; only through this forbearance can he survive or triumph ... since he is black, born without the light, it is only through humility, the incessant mortification of the flesh, that he can enter into communion with God or man.' Mrs Stowe's 'only black man, has been robbed of his humanity and divested of his sex. It is the price for that darkness with which he has been branded.'[26]

The Death of Uncle Tom by Thomas W. Strong, 1853

But this is a melodramatic travesty of Stowe's character. Tom is resolute and energetic. When he is cast into fetters, he cheers up his fellow prisoners and restores their morale, as well as bringing them to Jesus. Nor is he submissive when it matters: he refuses to whip other slaves when the terrible Simon Legree commands him to; eventually Legree murders him when he refuses to give away the hiding place of his friends. Nor is he content to remain a slave. When his previous master, St Clare, promises him his freedom (St Clare's sudden death prevents him from filling in the necessary papers), he is disappointed by Tom's reaction:

... 'the sudden light of joy that shone in Tom's face as he raised his hands to heaven, his emphatic "Bless the Lord!" rather discomposed St Clare; he did not like it that Tom should be so ready to leave him.

"You haven't had such very bad times here, that you need be in such a rapture, Tom," he said, dryly.

"No, no, mas'r! 'tan't that, it's bein' a *free man!* That's what I'm joyin' for."

"Why, Tom, don't you think, for your own part, you've been better off than to be free?"

"No, *indeed*, Mas'r St Clare," said Tom, with a flash of energy. "No, indeed!'"

When he is sold off to Legree by St Clare's spoilt, hard-hearted widow, 'He drew his arms tightly over his bosom, and choked back the bitter tears, and tried to pray. The poor old soul had such a singular, unaccountable prejudice in favour of liberty, that it was a hard wrench for him.'[27] Tom can be seen as a model of passive resistance, a modest sort of Gandhi before Gandhi was born or thought of. Twentieth-century vitriol made 'Uncle Tom' a term of abuse. But in reality there is something of Uncle Tom in all the great non-violence movements which have brought about so many transformations in our own time. The tragedy for the United States was not that *Uncle Tom's Cabin* had too much influence but that it had too little. The slaughter in the American Civil War was of unparalleled ghastliness and left a legacy of loathing between North and South which took a century to dispel – and was ultimately dispelled only by the non-violent methods of Dr Martin Luther King – himself denounced as an Uncle Tom by Black Power militants. Our age has again and again fulfilled Blake's prophecy that 'the intellectual tear', rather than the sword and bow, would free the world from fear.

Secular-minded modern critics are put off, too, by the *tone* of the novel. They do not care for the frequent quotations from Scripture and the snatches of plantation hymns which pepper the text. But these spiritual interludes form the musical, poetic accompaniment to the often dark and brutal saga, and they are an integral part of the discourse of the day, lending authenticity rather than fakery to the narrative. This objection is bound up with the knee-jerk reaction that the whole thing is hopelessly sentimental. Baldwin, for example: 'Uncle Tom's Cabin is a very bad novel, having, in its self-righteous, virtuous sentimentality, much in common with Little Women. Sentimentality, the ostentatious parading of excessive and spurious emotion, is the mark of dishonesty, the inability to feel; the wet eyes of the sentimentalist betray his aversion to experience, his fear of life, his arid heart.'[28]

Nonsense. There never was a more sincere writer than Harriet Beecher Stowe, nor one more marked by experience. All her life she was as devoted to the Abolitionist cause as she was to her large family. Here's the letter she wrote a year after the death of her baby boy: 'I shall never love another as I did him – he was my "summer Child" – I cannot open his little drawer of clothes now without feeling it thro my very heart.'[29]

Her motives for writing Uncle Tom's Cabin are set out in her Concluding Remarks:

'For many years of her life, the author avoided all reading upon or allusion to the subject of slavery, considering it as too painful to be enquired into, and one which advancing light and civilization would certainly live down.' But the Fugitive Slave Act of 1850 changed her attitude: 'when she heard, with perfect surprise and consternation, Christian and humane people actually recommending the remanding of escaped fugitives into slavery, as a duty binding on good citizens – when she heard on all hands, from kind, compassionate and estimable people, in the free states of the North, deliberations and discussions as to what Christian duty could be on this head – she could only think these men and Christians cannot know what slavery is; if they did, such a question could never be open for discussion. And from this arose the desire to exhibit it in a *living dramatic reality*.'[30]

Readers of a more generous, open-hearted temper reacted to the book very differently, starting with Charles Dickens himself. She sent him a copy, and he replied: 'I have read your book with the deepest interest and sympathy, and admire, more than I can express to you, both the generous feeling which inspired it and the admirable power with which it is executed.'

George Orwell, so often a rescuer of battered literary reputations, wrote in Tribune:[31] 'Perhaps the supreme example of the "good bad" book is Uncle Tom's Cabin. It is an unintentionally ludicrous book, full of preposterous melodramatic incidents; it is also deeply moving and essentially true ... I would back Uncle Tom's Cabin to outlive the complete works of Virginia Woolf or George Moore, though I know of no strictly literary test which would show where the superiority lies.'

A few years later, the equally independent-minded Edmund Wilson declared that 'to expose oneself in maturity to Uncle Tom's Cabin may therefore prove a startling experience. It is a much more impressive work than one has ever been allowed to suspect.'[32] The first thing that struck Wilson was 'a certain eruptive force'. The story came so suddenly to Mrs Stowe and seemed so irresistibly to write itself that she felt as if some power beyond her had laid hold of her to deliver its message. The book had its faults, but 'out of a background of undistinguished narrative, inelegantly and carelessly written, the characters leap into being with a vitality that is all the more striking for the ineptitude of the prose that presents them'. What is most unexpected, Wilson goes on, unable to hide his surprise, is that 'the further one reads into Uncle Tom, the more one becomes aware that a critical mind is at work, which has the complex situation in a very firm grip and which, no matter how vehement the characters become, is controlling and co-ordinating their interrelations'. Contrary to earlier critics, Wilson maintains that the book is never a crude melodrama like the stage versions which were to wow audiences everywhere, and also that there is a good deal less sentimentality than you might have expected.

Throughout the book, the author makes it plain that the New Englanders are just as much complicit as the Southerners. Many of the vilest characters, including Simon Legree, were originally Yankees. Mrs Stowe brilliantly exposes the links between those passive Northern investors, whose debts and credits are paid in the proceeds from the sales of slaves. A similar process of exposure has taken place in Britain over the aristocratic investors in the Royal African Company, founded by Charles II, and other great slave-trading firms.

Despite its origins in 40 serialized episodes, the book also has a rather subtle structure. It begins at the outer reaches of the slave states, in Kentucky, which prides itself on the mild treatment of its slaves and where the blacks live in dread of being sold 'down river'. Only gradually does the action move South. We are carried along on the riverboat where Tom and his companions languish in irons below, while the gilded youth dine and dance on the upper deck. Simon Legree and his hellish plantation, amid the black moss and broken stumps of the Red River swamps, only appear three-quarters of the way through the book.

Mrs Stowe has, too, a strong sense of the *connectedness* of economic and social developments which one or two commentators have identified as anticipating Marx. According to St Clare, his ruthless brother Alfred believes that 'the American planter is only doing, in another form, what the English aristocracy and capitalists are doing to the lower classes, that is ... *appropriating* them, body and bone, soul and spirit, to their use and convenience'. St Clare himself says roundly, 'Talk of the *abuses* of slavery! Humbug! The thing itself is the essence of all abuse!'[33] The brilliantly rendered dialogue of the slave traders and slave catchers – as salty and vivid as Dickens at his best – is set within an ever-present awareness of the System which imprisons them all.

It remains only to mention the element in the book which Wilson does not really touch on, the element for which 'feminist' is almost too weak a word. This task is eloquently performed by Jane Tompkins in *Sensational Designs* (1985). Herself a professor at Temple and Illinois and married to the redoubtable modernist critic Stanley Fish, Tompkins lays into the way in which 'the male-dominated scholarly tradition' had excluded *Uncle Tom's Cabin* from the canon of American literature, preventing 'even committed feminists from recognizing the *value* of a powerful and specifically female novelistic tradition'. She laments that 'twentieth-century critics have taught generations of students to equate popularity with debasement, emotionality with ineffectiveness, religiosity with fakery, domesticity with triviality, and all of these, implicitly, with womanly inferiority'.[34] The sentimental novel was no mere vapid confection but represented 'a monumental effort to reorganize culture from a woman's point of view'.[35] Tompkins asserts that 'this body of work is remarkable for its intellectual complexity, ambition and resourcefulness', and 'in certain cases, it offers a critique of American society far more devastating than any delivered by better-known critics such as Hawthorne and Melville'. Hawthorne himself might inveigh against the 'trash' produced by 'this d****d mass of scribbling women',[36] and he and his allies might succeed in keeping Uncle Tom out of the literary canon, but they could not keep the book out of the minds of its millions of readers. Yes, Tompkins concedes, Stowe might be classified as a conservative, but her 'very conservatism ... is precisely what gives her novel its revolutionary potential', because 'applied universally not just to one segregated corner of civil life, but to the conduct of all human affairs, Stowe means to effect a radical transformation of her society'.[37] Stubborn critics, mostly of the male persuasion, refuse to accept this interpretation. Dr Keith Carabine, who quotes Tompkins at length in his invaluable introduction to the Wordsworth Classics edition of Uncle Tom's Cabin, scoffs: 'With sisters like Tompkins, who needs patriarchs?'[38]

What cannot be denied is that the book rates women far higher than men. Mrs Shelby, Mrs Bird and Ophelia St Clare are all persons of energy and moral courage, while their menfolk are flapping butterflies trapped in the net of the System. Then there is the underworld of slave traders and catchers and those planters who work them till they drop — all unspeakably vile and cynical creatures who rationalize what they do as 'just business'. Apart from the muscular Quaker backwoodsmen who offer unstinting assistance to runaway slaves, the only man of real moral worth in the book is Uncle Tom himself. Not since the novels of Samuel Richardson, I think, have we met a writer who insists so cogently on the superiority of women in all the departments of life that really matter. And not since the publication of Pamela a century earlier have we come across a book which evoked such a violent and immediate reaction from those who hated every word of it.

What swiftly became known as 'Anti-Tom Literature' (or sometimes 'Plantation Literature') was as plentiful as the anti-*Pamela* stuff. In both cases, between 20 and 30 novels were published. In both cases, too, the flood started the minute the original came out. Mrs Stowe's enemies had nearly a year to prepare their onslaughts during the serialization of the book. *The North and the South; or Slavery and its Contrasts, a Tale of Real Life*, by Caroline Rush, came out within a few months of *Uncle Tom*. So did *Life in the South; a Companion to Uncle Tom's Cabin*, by C. H. Wiley, as did the best-known and biggest seller, *Aunt Phillis's Cabin; or, Southern Life as it is*, by Mary Henderson Eastman. All of them claimed to be giving a true picture of Southern life and explicitly denounced the ignorant and biased slurs of Mrs Stowe. The Anti-Tom genre died off with the start of the Civil War, but while the vogue lasted, it kept Southern resentments on the boil, and helped to smother hopes of some fresh compromise between North and South.

Aunt Phillis's Cabin is typical of the genre. The Preface begins uncompromisingly: 'A writer on Slavery has no difficulty in tracing back its origin. There is also the advantage of finding it, with its continued history, and the laws given by God to govern his own institution, in the Holy Bible. Neither profane history, tradition, nor philosophical research are required to prove its origin or existence.'[39] This claim is based on Genesis 9.22, which is interpreted to mean that slavery was instituted by God as a curse on Ham and his son Canaan and their descendants. Thomas Newton, Bishop of Bristol in the eighteenth century and a notorious scholarly faker, popularized the belief that the whole continent of Africa was peopled by the descendants of Ham who lived there in wickedness and barbarity until they were scooped up by the slave traders and taken across the Atlantic. 'The Scriptures,' Mrs Eastman persists, 'evidently permit slavery, even to the present time.' Jesus Christ himself signally failed to emancipate slaves, or to condemn the divinely ordained institution. Mary Eastman is unrelenting towards Abolitionists, but she does concede that slavery was useless in the North; in the South, 'though an evil, it is one that cannot be dispensed with'.⁴⁰

The novel itself is concerned with events on the plantation of the benign Mr Weston, a widowed planter of English descent. Aunt Phillis is a pious, pipe-smoking elderly slave, married to tipsy old Uncle Bacchus. She has a glorious deathbed scene at the end, every bit as emotional as Uncle Tom's and a good deal longer. Unlike Tom, Aunt Phillis dies not only a good Christian, as she has lived, but a happy slave reconciled to her state. When Mr Weston offers to set her children free at his death, she refuses: 'As long as you, or Master Arthur and Miss Alice live, they would be better off as they are.' And Mr Weston agrees that they would.⁴¹

Mary Eastman ends with 'Concluding Remarks' to match those in Uncle Tom. Here she tackles Harriet Beecher Stowe head-on, asserting that 'most of our Southern slaves are happy, and kindly cared for'. She does not deny the evils of slavery, any more than she would deny the evils of the factory system in England or America. 'I only assert the necessity of the existence of slavery at present in our Southern States and that, as a general thing, the slaves are comfortable and contented, and their owners humane and kind.'⁴² There are constant sniping references to 'that interesting romance, Uncle Tom's Cabin'.⁴³ And she flatly denies the brutalities recounted by Mrs Stowe, of negroes being hunted with dogs and infants torn from the arms of their shrieking mothers and sold for five or ten dollars. 'It tells well, for the mass of readers are fond of horrors; but it is not true. It is on a par with the fact stated, that masters advertise their slaves, and offer rewards for them, dead or alive. How did the snows of New England ever give birth to such brilliant imaginations!'⁴⁴ She is referring here to the ad read out in Uncle Tom by George's old master, Mr Wilson. The ad itself is reproduced briefly in Aunt Phillis as a flagrant invention.⁴⁵ The full version in Uncle Tom reads:⁴⁶

'Run away from the subscriber, my mulatto boy, George. Said George, six feet in height, a very light mulatto, brown curly hair; is very intelligent, speaks handsomely, can read and write; will probably try to pass for a white man; is deeply scarred on his back and shoulders, has been branded in his right hand with the letter H. I will give four hundred dollars for him alive, and the same sum for satisfactory proof that he has been killed.'

This ad cannot help reminding us of the rather similar one inserted by Mr Thomas Jefferson of Monticello in the *Virginia Gazette* of 14 September 1769:

'Run away from the subscriber in *Albemarle*, a Mulatto slave called *Sandy*, about 35 years of age, his stature is rather low, inclining to corpulence, and his complexion light; he is a shoemaker by trade, in which he uses his left hand principally, can do coarse carpenters work, and is something of a horse jockey; he is greatly addicted to drink, and when drunk is insolent and disorderly, in his conversation he swears much, and in his behaviour is artful and knavish. He took with him a white horse, much scarred with traces, of which it is expected he will endeavour to dispose; he also carried his shoemakers tools and will probably endeavor to get employment that way. Whoever conveys the said slave to me, in Albemarle, shall have 40s. reward, if taken up within the county, 4l. if elsewhere within the colony, and 10 l. if in any other colony, from THOMAS JEFFERSON.'

The real-life advertisement gives a far harsher description of the runaway than the fictional one. Note also the other differences: British pounds and shillings instead of US dollars, and the differential rates that Jefferson offers to the slave-catchers. The huge sum, ten pounds sterling, offered for slaves brought back from another colony, would have given a rich incentive to the Markses and Lokers so marvellously evoked in *Uncle Tom* to press their searches deep into the free states, and so stem the leakage of slaves which threatened to undermine the whole system. There were more than 20 known escapes from Monticello between 1769 and 1819; between 1736 and 1783, there were no fewer than 3,000 such ads inserted in the *Virginia Gazette*. So, not as happy and contented as all that. Even in *Aunt Phillis* there are hints that slavery does have its terrors: the young lads are scared of being 'sold South', and recaptured slaves are, quite properly we are told, held in a place of confinement, which is delicately not described.

Later in life, Mary Eastman became a convinced Unionist. She even wrote a novel, *Jenny Wade of Gettysburg* (1864), in praise of a Union heroine who was killed while baking bread for the Union troops during the Battle of Gettysburg. Her husband Seth and her sons both fought for the Union. Seth even became commander of the compound for Confederate prisoners of war in New York, which was said to have the highest mortality rate of any such camp.

At the very end of *Aunt Phillis*, Mary Eastman claims that she knows no so-called good men in the North who are good enough to befriend negroes. 'They seem to me to have an unconquerable antipathy to them. Mrs Stowe says, *she* educates them in her own family with her own children. I am glad to hear that she feels and acts kindly toward them, and I wish others in her region of country would imitate her in this respect; but I would rather my children and negroes were educated at different schools, being utterly opposed to amalgamation, root and branch.'[47]

Yet when it came to Native Americans, Mary Eastman felt very differently — and for a striking reason. Seth Eastman was a West Point graduate, mapmaker and artist who rose to become a general. He served two terms at Fort Snelling, Minnesota, where he painted many scenes of native life. During his first posting, he married a 15-year-old girl, whose native name translated as 'Stands Sacred'; she was the daughter of Cloud Man, a chief of mixed French and Dakota ancestry. Seth and Stands Sacred had a daughter, Winona, also known as Mary Nancy Eastman. Seth abandoned Stands Sacred when he was reassigned. He did not mention her or their daughter in his memoir written after he became a general. Winona went on to marry a Sioux chief, who later also took the Eastman surname, as did their youngest child Charles Alexander, who became a celebrated physician, the first Native American to qualify in Western medicine. Charles Eastman was practising medicine at the local Indian reservation during the massacre at Wounded Knee in 1890, in which US army troops butchered hundreds of Native Americans, including their famous leader, Sitting Bull (despite the frustrated intervention of William F. (Buffalo Bill) Cody, who was also present). Dr Eastman is estimated to have saved the lives of more than 20 wounded Indians. This terrible event, the last and most ghastly episode in the Indian Wars, had some enthusiastic local support. The young editor of the local paper, the *Aberdeen Saturday Pioneer*, L. Frank Baum, wrote a few days after the massacre:

'The Pioneer has before declared that our only safety depends upon the total extirmination [sic] of the Indians. Having wronged them for centuries, we had better, in order to protect our civilization, follow it up by one more wrong and wipe these untamed and untameable creatures from the face of the earth.'[48]

When Frank Baum became famous as the author of *The Wonderful Wizard of Oz*, his fans claimed that he had meant this sarcastically, on the lines of Swift's *Modest Proposal* for eating Irish babies. But as he says himself, he had said it before, and it doesn't sound like sarcasm.

By then, Mary Eastman was already dead. But we can be sure that she would have been horrified. After she had married Seth – she was only 17 at the time – she took up the Native American cause, learned the Sioux language and published several books expressing her disgust at the maltreatment of the 'Red men' by American troops and missionaries. In *Aunt Phillis*, Mr Weston's son Arthur rebukes a Northern friend at Yale who is attacking slavery, by asking what right these smug New Englanders had to their farms: 'we all know how these transactions were conducted all over the country. We wanted the lands of the Red men, and we took them. Sometimes they were purchased, sometimes they were wrested, always, the Red men were treated with injustice. They were driven off, slaughtered and taken as slaves. Now, God as clearly gave these lands to the Red men as he gave life and freedom to the African.'[49]

The complicated family history of the Eastmans matches Mary's own complicated attitudes. Both are eloquent testimony to the whole tortured history of race relations in the United States. *Aunt Phillis's Cabin* is nowhere near as great a book as *Uncle Tom's*. It is slushy, chaotic and largely untrue. But it is all part of the same agonizing story.

VICTOR HUGO, HÉLAS!

For nearly 40 years now, the little windswept waif with the black cap on the back of her head has looked down from theatre billboards in London. In the full-length version, Cosette is half-naked, pushing a broom which is twice as big as she is. In the drawing by Émile Bayard in the first edition of Victor Hugo's novel, she is wading barefoot through the flooded cellar of the ghastly inn kept by the villainous Thénardiers. Cosette is France's Cinderella, bullied by the spoilt Thénardier daughters as she does the household chores. She is the heroine of the musical which the English-speaking world has taken to its heart. *Les Mis*, as we call it, is the longest running musical ever in London. As I write, productions are also playing in Belgium, Holland and Japan and across the United States. The show has been seen by 130 million people in 53 countries and through-sung in 22 languages.

'Cosette with her broom' from *Les Misérables*, Émile Bayard

Although its authors, Alain Boublil (lyrics) and Claude-Michel Schönberg (music) are French, its conception owes quite a lot to English musicals such as *Jesus Christ Superstar* and *Oliver!*. In fact, it was at a performance of *Oliver!* in the West End that Boublil really conceived the whole production: 'As soon as the Artful Dodger came on stage, Gavroche came to mind. It was like a blow to the solar plexus. I started seeing all the characters of Victor Hugo's *Les Misérables* – Valjean, Javert, Gavroche, Cosette, Marius and Eponine – in my mind's eye, laughing, crying and singing on stage.'[50]

Yet when the Royal Shakespeare Company launched its original production at the Barbican on 8 October 1985, the critics gave it a frosty and dismissive reception. Despite its distinguished RSC provenance – the show was directed by Trevor Nunn and John Caird – they really couldn't see much in it. Francis King in the *Sunday Telegraph* wrote it off as 'a lurid Victorian melodrama produced with Victorian lavishness'. In the *Observer*, Michael Ratcliffe described it as 'a witless and synthetic entertainment'. Many questioned the wisdom of trying to compress a 1,200-page novel into three and a half hours of stage time. In the *Daily Mail*, Jack Tinker compared it to 'attempting to pour the entire Channel through a china teapot'. Twenty-five years later, with *Les Mis* still flowing hot and strong through the West End, Michael Billington in the *Guardian* stuck to his original criticism: that '*Les Mis*, by ditching the spoken dialogue in favour of a through-composed score, led the musical down a false trail: away from the fun of wit, satire and romance toward the pomposities of pop-opera.'[51] Billington could not deny that audiences had never stopped loving the show, but he continued to shake his head over the fact that we might think we lived 'in a cool, smart, cynical age. Yet when the chips are down, what we really crave is a contest of good and evil and lashings of spectacle.' Just like our Victorian ancestors.

Ironically, much the same criticisms were made of Hugo's enormous novel when it came out in 1862. From the start, the public loved the book. But most of the literary critics were as sniffy as the theatre critics were to be a century later, with the added revulsion at what they saw as Hugo's approval of violent revolution and revolutionaries. Léon Gauthier wrote in *Le Monde* of 17 August 1862: 'One cannot read the book without an unconquerable disgust at all the details Monsieur Hugo gives regarding the successful planning of a riot.' In reality, the fascinating descriptions that the author gives of building a street barricade, cobblestone by cobblestone, are as much a contribution to social history as to literature, like his equally minute descriptions of the ramifications of the Paris sewers down which his hero, Jean Valjean, is pursued – a scene even more harrowing and intense than the Vienna sewer sequence in *The Third Man*. The Goncourt brothers in their celebrated diary found the book 'a great disappointment'. There was nothing alive in it. 'The characters are made of bronze or alabaster, everything but flesh and bones. The lack of observation is glaring and damages the whole book ... As for the style, it's inflated, overstretched, short-winded ... It's all fanfare and no music.'[52]

Like other hard-edged highbrows of the age, the Goncourts had no time for Hugo's morality: 'there is no morality in art. The book's humanitarian point of view leaves me cold.' This expulsion of morality from art was becoming an iron orthodoxy among writers who aspired to be taken seriously. In many spheres, that orthodoxy remains in force today.

But Hugo's reputation was already so gigantic that these damning judgements could be risked only in private, in diaries or letters, and among friends. Gustave Flaubert, for example, wrote from Croisset to his long-time correspondent, the actress Edma Roger des Genettes, in July 1862:

'Well! Our god is sinking. *Les Misérables* exasperates me and it is forbidden to speak ill of the book – you look like a sneak. The author's position is invulnerable, unassailable. For my own part, having spent my life adoring him, I am at present furious! I really must explode, none the less.'

And explode Flaubert certainly does: 'I find in this book neither truth nor greatness. As for the style, it seems to me intentionally incorrect and low. This is his way of flattering the public.' Hugo sucks up to everyone, has a kind word for every point of view. The book is stuffed with intolerable digressions. The characters are all sugary confections. Where in the world would you find a prostitute like Fantine, or a convict like Valjean? 'As for the dialogue, they make fine speeches, but *they all talk the same* ... Decidedly this book, although it has a few good patches, and they are rare, is infantile.'

As for the philosophy, 'he sums up the banal ideas of the epoch, and with such persistence that he forgets his work and his art … Anyway, that's my opinion. Of course, I'm keeping it to myself.'

The same fear of being seen to criticize a national treasure affected Charles Baudelaire. He was in low water financially at the time, and had to be grateful to be asked to write a review of the book for Le Boulevard. He sent a copy of the piece to his mother, explaining that 'This book is filthy and clumsy. I have shown, on the subject, that I possessed the art of lying. Hugo wrote me an absolutely ridiculous letter of thanks. Which proves that a great man can also be an idiot.' It is not surprising that Hugo should have written Baudelaire a thank-you letter, because, at first glance, the review seems pretty complimentary. The reader's eye falls on sentences such as: 'We simply want to do justice to the marvellous talent with which the author seizes the public attention and bends it, like the stubborn head of a lazy pupil, towards the prodigious abysses of social misery.' Yet on more careful reading, a subversive subtext reveals itself. Yes, it's a good thing that such books are written. But we have to ask at the same time 'whether the work of art must have no other goal but *art*, art ought to express adoration for anything except itself, or if some other goal, more or less noble, inferior or superior, can be imposed on it.'[53] And we know what Baudelaire's answer to that question is: art can only be for art's sake. The slogan 'l'art pour l'art' had been around for some time. It is first credited to Benjamin Constant at the beginning of the century. But by the time of Les Misérables, bolder spirits were openly advocating an art free of all social purpose, however noble.

None bolder than James Abbott MacNeill Whistler, who courted controversy more blithely than any other artist in history. When his painting The White Girl was among those rejected by the Salon of 1863 (it had already been rejected by the Royal Academy in London the year before), and the Emperor sportingly decreed that the rejected paintings should be exhibited in a separate room, Whistler wrote to Fantin-Latour: 'It's marvellous for us, this business of the Exhibition of Rejected Painters! Certainly my picture should be left there, and yours too.'[54] A few years later, in his little squib The Red

Rag, Whistler goes on to explain why his art aspires to the abstract harmony of music: 'Art should be independent of all claptrap – should stand alone, and appeal to the artistic sense of eye or ear, without confounding this with emotions entirely foreign to it, as devotion, pity, love, patriotism and the like. All these have no kind of concern with it; and that is why I insist on calling my works "arrangements" and "harmonies".'[55] The year before, Whistler's *Nocturne in Black and Gold – the Falling Rocket* had famously provoked the fury of the fiercest opponent of *l'art pour l'art*, John Ruskin: 'I have seen, and heard, much of Cockney impudence before now; but never expected to hear a coxcomb ask two hundred guineas for flinging a pot of paint in the public's face.'[56] This ferocious abuse panicked some owners of Whistler paintings. The artist, characteristically trigger-happy but also foreseeing his income disappearing, sued for libel. The case was chaotic. To start with, the painting was shown to the court upside-down, rather enhancing Ruskin's case. Whistler insisted that the work did represent a fireworks display in Cremorne Gardens, but failed to convince the judge, who awarded him a derisory farthing damages. Faced with huge legal bills, Whistler was forced to pawn or sell everything he possessed. But Ruskin's reputation too suffered for his intemperate words, not least from the young Henry James who said that Ruskin had overstepped the mark and become a tyrant. At the time, Ruskin was already on the verge of the first of the mental breakdowns which were to blight the rest of his life. And his words were ridiculously exaggerated. We can see perfectly well that the painting is a vivid evocation of a fireworks show at night, and that, like all Whistler's work, it is carefully composed and painted. Yet we might also be tempted to say that Ruskin's outburst was merely premature. If he had been around 80 years later to see one of Jackson Pollock's 'drip' paintings, he might have used much the same words.

Ruskin was a keen supporter of the Pre-Raphaelite Brotherhood. Like them, he aspired to return to the spirituality and devotion to Nature that he thought characterized Art before the chilly High Renaissance. He endorsed in particular the third of William Rossetti's Principles that were to animate the Brotherhood: 'to sympathise with what is direct and serious and heartfelt in previous art, to the exclusion of what is conventional and self-parading and learned by rote.' The Pre-Raphaelites did not care for what they saw as the materialism of Courbet and the Impressionists. They in turn were damned by the Modernists for their sentimentality. Their pictures often dared to tell a story, worse still, a story designed to bring a tear to the eye, of rejection or rescue or bereavement or disability: pictures such as John Everett Millais's *The Blind Girl* and *The Order of Release*, Holman Hunt's *The Awakening Conscience*, Ford Madox Brown's *The Last of England*, or Henry Wallis's *The Death of Chatterton*. The Blind Girl depicts two vagrant beggars, one of them a blind musician with her concertina on her lap. They are resting at the roadside after a storm which has left a rainbow in the background over the town of Winchelsea. The intense beauty of the landscape and the vivid rain-washed colours make an almost unbearable contrast with the poignant desolation of the two girls.

The Blind Girl by John Everett Millais, 1856

The Tate and the Birmingham and Manchester galleries which housed the cream of these pictures could not stop the public from adoring them, but the curators would not dream of laying on a single special exhibition throughout the years until 1948, the centenary of the Brotherhood's founding. Since then, there have been four blockbuster Pre-Raphaelite shows, every one a sell-out, despite the continuing disdain of the harder-edged critics.

Les Misérables was under attack from two opposite quarters: from the literary avant-garde (a term just coming into use) who felt an instinctive revulsion against art with any form of message or social purpose. But the book was also loathed by conservatives, who objected not to moralizing in art but to the particular moralizing that they thought Hugo was indulging in. From this angle Hugo's most indefatigable opponent was one of his oldest and closest friends, the poet-politician Alphonse de Lamartine.

At the age of 30, Lamartine's Méditations had made him the most famous of France's Romantic poets. Le Lac remains the most plangent ode of the age. He later moved into prose and into politics, becoming a liberal democrat in the Chamber of Deputies, then more of a republican in the last days of Louis-Philippe and briefly Foreign Minister in the turmoil of 1848. But he lost humiliatingly to Louis-Napoleon in the presidential election of December 1848 and returned to literature and a penurious old age. When Les Misérables was published, Lamartine was down on his luck, like Baudelaire only more so, and struggling to pay off his creditors by churning out endless monthly instalments of what he called his 'forced labour', the Cours Familier de Littérature. By contrast, although still only halfway through his 20-year exile on Guernsey, Hugo's star had never shone brighter.

The two men had been friends for over 30 years and had praised each other's work without rivalry or reserve. But all that changed with the publication of Les Misérables. Lamartine embarked on five enormous Entretiens, stretching over five months and 350 pages on the single subject of Hugo's novel and its failings.[57] There were a few morsels of praise scattered through this serial polemic, for example, on Hugo's huge digression on the Battle of

Waterloo: 'it's a triumph of the French language in flames ... you emerge from reading it intoxicated and annihilated, rather like a child who runs out of breath trying to keep up with a giant.' Yet even this praise comes barbed: 'splendid pages, but irrelevant to the structure of the whole, a wasted piece of bravura'. Only the passage describing the idyllic life of Cosette and her supposed father Jean Valjean in the rue Plumet come out unscathed: 'a marvel of freshness and innocence ... we know nothing more perfect or more real in any language ancient or modern.' Even here, though, we are told that it's a pity the passage comes too late in the book.

For the rest, the pejoratives pile up like the corpses in the sunken lane at Waterloo: exaggeration, witticisms that don't come off, faults of taste, cynical demagoguery. Unforgivable, in Lamartine's view, to devote so many pages to the vulgar language of the students and their tarts. Even worse to spell out 'le mot de Cambronne', that is, 'shit!', uttered by General Cambronne when refusing to surrender to the British at Waterloo – a filthy lapse in taste which 'soils the memory of the illustrious battle'. Indeed, several translators have shared Lamartine's *pudeur* and refused to spell out the *mot*.

Full of improbabilities. How could Valjean be sentenced to five years' hard labour for stealing a loaf of bread, and to death for stealing 40 sous? The character of the cheeky scamp Gavroche is another concession to the mob. And all the melodrama, which belongs in a popular pot boiler. Too many pages about nothing at all. And so on.

Lamartine simply refuses to believe that a lifelong crook like Valjean would ever repent and confess his crimes. Above all, he denounces the book as politically dangerous and destabilizing, encouraging sedition and revolt and destructive of personal responsibility. His characters are not *misérables* but *coupables*. The book should be called *The Criminals*. The indulgent, even hero-worshipping treatment of the young revolutionaries at the barricades is calculated to terrify the majority of law-abiding citizens and to encourage the utopian hopes of the poor which can never be realized. Lamartine still counts himself a liberal. He believes in trade unions and social security. But he also believes in Order, in a strong State with a powerful army. He is convinced that Hugo has written an 'unhealthy' book, likely to lead the People astray into anarchy, immorality and violence.

Hugo laconically described this relentless battering as 'like being bitten by a swan'. But Lamartine did not stop there. Not content with having torn his old friend's masterpiece to shreds, he sets out to construct an alternative *Les Misérables*, just as Fielding and a dozen others had constructed an alternative *Pamela*, and Southern writers like Mary Henderson Eastman attempted to rewrite *Uncle Tom's Cabin*. There appears to be some uniquely irritating quality in great sentimental literature which stings those who hate it into active retaliation.

In his novel *Fior d'Aliza*, Lamartine offered 'a true *misérable*, from his own knowledge', 'l'histoire de mon Misérable à moi'.[58] In a wretched cabin not far from Lucca, there lives an honest and peaceable family, composed of an old woman, a blind man, the pure young girl, Fior d'Aliza, and her cousin Hyéronimo who have loved each other since childhood. Believing Fior's life to be in danger, Hyéronimo accidentally shoots a low-life police agent, is sent to prison, condemned to death, then is helped to escape by Fior, who takes his place in disguise. Discovering her imposture, Hyéronimo gives himself up, their punishments are commuted by a forgiving judge, everyone returns to the cottage and gives thanks to God for his goodness. There is no injustice committed either by the characters or by Society, there are only mistakes and misunderstandings which are speedily rectified.

Fior did not make much of a splash when it was published in 1863, although it was turned into a four-act operetta that was staged in Paris in February 1866. The title survives today in the name of a boutique hotel on the rue Lamartine. Raymond Trousson describes the novel as 'an insipid, tearful idyll, a melodrama, in praise of big hearts and fine feelings, full of sloppy passages and improbabilities ... well below the mediocre'. In short, the product of an old man's blinkered bitterness towards his soaring rival.

But Lamartine's critique, as elephantine as the novel which it attempts to obliterate, should at least push us to examine *Les Misérables* itself more closely. By taking head-on the accusations most frequently levelled by Lamartine, Flaubert and the rest, we may be better able to assess the novel's claims to greatness.

First, the improbabilities. Like Harriet Beecher Stowe, Victor Hugo was not at all reluctant to divulge the real-life sources for some of his most dramatic episodes. He had himself witnessed a man being arrested for stealing a loaf of bread like Jean Valjean, while a grand lady in her coach looked on unmoved. The character of Valjean derived, pretty directly, from the legendary ex-con Eugène-François Vidocq, who later became founder of the Sûreté as the equivalent of the British CID, and also of France's first private detective agency. Like Valjean, too, under one of his many aliases Vidocq was a successful businessman, running a large paper factory employing other ex-convicts. Like Valjean again, he was possessed of amazing physical strength and saved one of the workers in his factory by lifting a heavy cart on his shoulders, as Valjean does in the novel. As Anthony Powell said of Charles Dickens's father, like all good characters Vidocq was good for several other fictional roles, appearing in Hugo's stories *Claude Gueux* and *Le dernier jour d'un homme condamné*, as well as being the model for Balzac's Vautrin.

Having enlisted in the Bourbon Regiment on his release, Vidocq challenged 15 men to duels and killed two of them. He fought at Valmy and Jemappes, deserted into the enemy camp, committed various frauds under various names, was jailed and escaped several more times, dressed as a nun and a sailor, was constantly being recognized and hauled in again. Valjean does not quite pale by comparison, but you can certainly acquit Hugo – and Balzac – of writing anything that couldn't happen.

By the mid-nineteenth century, ideas of rehabilitation and repentance for convicted criminals were common currency (we have seen their first stirrings in the penal reform movement in England). The amazing tales of how convicts transported to Australia became the leading (at first almost the only) lawyers and doctors in New South Wales quickly percolated back to Europe.

As early as 1805, Jacques Delille, 'Virgil Delille', wrote a poem, 'La Pitié', hymning these fabulous transformations: 'There, kindly laws turn dangerous men / Into skilled colonists and happy citizens / Stir them to penitence, stimulate industry, / And give them freedom, customs and a homeland. / On all sides, I see drained marshes, / Flowering deserts and cleared forests. / Follow this example! Take these bandits / From their sterile prison, make their punishment useful.'[59]

Then, the digressions. These are certainly enormous: 50 pages on the Battle of Waterloo, 36 pages on convents and the religious life, 20 pages on the virtues of slang, a dozen pages off and on about the techniques of constructing a street barricade, and 14 pages on the historical development of the sewers of Paris. If you are willing to surrender yourself, each of these is fascinating in its own right, and if you let them sink in, I think you begin to see how they do contribute to the structure and purpose of *Les Misérables*. Each digression takes you away from the simple human story – of Jean Valjean's unselfish love for Cosette, of Inspector Javert's insatiable thirst for justice, of Marius's shy courting of Cosette – and then returns you to them with a deeper understanding of the Paris they are enmeshed in and of the unpredictable, unstoppable flow of the history of which they are part.

Hugo's description of Waterloo is one of the most brutal and horrifying of any battle in literature. But beyond the endless spurting of blood and guts, Hugo brings home the immense chanciness of this battle, so decisive for world history, like so many other decisive battles which were also unpredictable: 'If it hadn't rained during the night of June 17–18, the future of Europe would have been different. A few drops of water, more or less, brought Napoleon to his knees. So that Waterloo could be the end of Austerlitz, Providence needed only a bit of rain, and a cloud crossing the sky out of season was enough for a whole world to disintegrate.'[60]

This chanciness seeped into the political after-effects of the battle, too. By bringing the Bourbons back 'in the baggage train of the Allies', Waterloo brought one revolutionary era to an end, but suppressed the beginning of another. During the unstable years of the Restoration and then the July Monarchy, the currents of revolutionary thought ran underground, breaking the surface in violent, chaotic, aborted events such as the riots of June 1832, which play such a large part in the later pages of the novel. Waterloo sets the conditions in which the lives of Valjean, Javert, Cosette and Marius are to be played out. It is not true either that Hugo's treatment of the motives of the young revolutionaries is excessively sentimental or pernicious, as Lamartine claims. He simply sets out to show how these garrulous, naive, impulsive young men find themselves driven to seek their progressive goals, which are entirely legitimate in themselves, by suicidally barricading themselves in sleazy cul-de-sacs. Hugo's own progressive instincts were not oblivious of practical and prudential limitations. After being elected to the National Assembly in 1848, he had, after all, supported the repression of the insurrectionists, siding with the forces of law and order against the young men behind the barricades. He had supported Louis-Napoleon's return from exile and his candidacy for President. It was only when 'Napoléon le Petit' seized power in his coup of 1852 that Hugo broke with him and went into exile himself. He had a generous heart, but never a soft head.

Nor are his digressions on the religious life of the convent which shelters Valjean and Cosette (he's posing as the convent gardener) open to the sort of criticisms that were thrown at him, whether from the irreligious – George Sand said 'there was too much Christianity' in the book, Flaubert slated Hugo for sucking up to the 'Catholic-socialist dregs' – or from the *croyants* who thought that Hugo was damaging the Church by his no-holds-barred critique. Yes, Hugo certainly admits that 'from the point of view of history, reason and truth, monasticism is absurd' and that 'all this shutting away in cloisters has had its day'.[61] At the same time, though, he readily declares that the religious life has a certain majesty: 'As for us, who do not believe what these women believe but live, like them, through faith, we have never been able to consider, without a kind of tender religious terror, without a sort of pity full of envy, those devout, quivering and trusting creatures, those humble and august souls who dare to live on the very brink of mystery, waiting there between the world that is closed and the sky that is not yet open, turned towards the light you can't see, having only the happiness of thinking they know where it is ...'[62] Hugo evokes the beauty of a monastic ideal which he does not share, and does so with a tenderness that I can't think of any other novelist surpassing.

Overarching all these apparent digressions, which in fact convey so powerfully what it is like to be alive in Paris at this particular historical moment, and which provide the background lighting to the simple, though dramatic stories of the half-dozen principal characters, lies Hugo's conviction that he has to *put everything in*. His little chapter entitled 'The Year 1817' piles up a heap of details (which no doubt he had jotted down in his voluminous notebooks), about the costumes, fashions, quarrels, catchwords, celebrities that were all the go that year, down to Chateaubriand's method of cleaning his teeth and the first appearance of a crummy piece of machinery that smoked and sloshed its way along the Seine from the Pont Royal to the Pont Louis XV 'with a noise like a dog swimming', to the general indifference of the locals, which was in fact the first steamboat. Hugo ends this divertissement, no more than four or five pages, with what is his dearly held credo: 'And that, willy-nilly, is what dimly survives of the year 1817, otherwise now largely forgotten. History neglects nearly every one of these little details and cannot do otherwise if it is not to be swamped by the infinite minutiae. And yet, the details, which are wrongly described as little – there are no little facts in the human realm, any more than there are little leaves in the realm of vegetation – are useful. The face of the century is made up of the lines of the years.'[63]

Other great writers specialize in selection. Hugo majors in inclusion, above all, in the inclusion of feelings, noble or vile, tepid or passionate, fleeting or ingrained. On page 1,001 of this vast epic, he opens up a grand tirade against the maestros of the unruffled serene, the artists who pride themselves on the classical virtue of *ataraxia*, the geniuses who smile but never weep. We shall quote from it at some length here, by way of a leave-taking of this *chef d'oeuvre* of sentimental literature:

'There are those who ask for nothing more, living beings who, having bright blue skies above, say: This is enough, dreamers absorbed in wonder, drawing from nature-worship an indifference to good and bad, contemplators of the cosmos radiantly distracted from mankind who just don't understand how anybody can worry about the hunger of some, the thirst of others, the nakedness of the poor in winter, about the lymphatic curvature of a tiny spine, about the straw pallet, about the garret, the dungeon, and the rags of shivering young girls, when a person can just dream away idly under the trees, peaceful and terrible souls, mercilessly content ...

'These thinkers forget to love. The Zodiac is such a big thing for them that it prevents them from seeing the child crying. God eclipses their souls. This is a family of minds, at once both small and great. Horace was one of them, Goethe was another, La Fontaine perhaps, magnificent egoists of the infinite, unruffled onlookers of pain, who don't see Nero if the weather's nice, people for whom the sun hides the stake ... These are the darkly radiant. They have no idea they are to be pitied, Of course they are. Whoever does not weep, does not see.'

In its popular musical version, *Les Misérables* lives on, like no other nineteenth-century novel. In the estimation of the literati, it has fallen under the dread exclusion from the canon, largely prompted by André Gide's famous response when he was asked who was France's greatest poet: *Victor Hugo, hélas!*. Gide never resiled from this snap judgement, first given in 1902. Indeed, he enlarged on it in a series of further responses given over succeeding decades and collected in a little book, entitled – what else? – *Hugo, hélas!*, and published a century later, in 2002. Here are a few samples: 'I no longer understand Hugo at all and, in his entire work, see nothing but rhetoric and vain agitation of big words; I have come to be astonished that I was once captivated by his meaningless eloquence.'[64] 'From my earliest years, his faults always bothered me: his systematic turgid inflation, forced antitheses, the almost constant and transparent insincerity underneath, the deployment of the prettiest and boldest metaphors! ... even his finest verses reeked of the manufacturing process: given birth to without pain and as though in play, while playing with us.'[65] As late as 1941, when quizzed about his notorious phrase, he said he would say it again: 'I am ill at ease with his pathos, feeling it to be artificial, everywhere and ceaselessly, rhyming with nothing, or rather doing nothing but rhyme. Yes, this kind of thinking, always swimming to suit the verse, leaves me longing for more rigour and more authenticity.'[66]

There, I think, we have it. Hugo is simply *too much*, too abundant. The dry classical mind of a Gide or a Flaubert recoils from this unstoppable flow of feeling. The thin lips purse, the hard eyes look coldly down at this leaky colossus. Art must be hard-won, forged, filtered. To find an alternative role model, we need look no further than Théophile Gautier, that great mid-century proponent of *l'art pour l'art*, the brightest of the Parnassiens, the anti-Romantic school who believed in objective, impersonal, 'scientific' poetry. His most famous poem, entitled simply 'L'Art', begins: 'Yes, Art comes out best / from a medium which is hard to work: / Verse, marble, onyx, or enamel. / No false constraints! / But to walk straight, / Muse, you must put on/ A tight-fitting shoe.'

No, you mustn't, you can hear Hugo roar, art flows from the heart, and it flows in torrents, and you must gallop through the mud in seven-league boots to catch up with it. Hugo wrote to his Italian publisher about the book in terms which would have confirmed the worst fears of all his critics:

'I don't know whether it will be read by everyone, but it is meant for everyone. It addresses England as well as Spain, Italy as well as France, Germany as well as Ireland, the republics that harbour slaves as well as empires that have serfs. Social problems go beyond frontiers. Humankind's wounds, those huge sores that litter the world, do not stop at the blue and red lines drawn on maps. Wherever men go in ignorance or despair, wherever women sell themselves for bread, wherever children lack a book to learn from or a warm hearth, *Les Misérables* knocks at the door and says: "open up, I am here for you".'

SIX

The Great Estranging

THE DILEMMA OF THE DOCTOR

It was one of the first paintings to hang in Sir Henry Tate's National Gallery of British Art. In fact, Tate himself had commissioned the picture from Luke Fildes, and *The Doctor* still hangs in the permanent collection at Tate Britain, one of the gallery's most popular works, along with Fildes's equally poignant picture, *Applicants for Admission to a Casual Ward*, painted 16 years before, in 1874, after his earlier wood engraving, *Houseless and Hungry*. Tate was a sugar baron, but he was also an energetic and open-handed philanthropist, not least to the workmen in his own refineries. He admired Fildes's passionate concern for the poor and sympathized with his hope that his celebrated illustrations for *The Graphic* would inspire individual acts of charity and collective social action. John Everett Millais showed *Houseless and Hungry* to Charles Dickens, who was so impressed that he immediately commissioned Fildes to illustrate his new novel *The Mystery of Edwin Drood*. Fildes's line drawings for the book are of an unrivalled intensity and menace, especially 'In the Court', depicting the opium den in which the book begins.

One young student who was deeply impressed by the work of Fildes and the other Dickens illustrators was Vincent van Gogh, who was spending three years in London training to be an art dealer and who had become an obsessive Dickens fan. Unfortunately, Dickens died in 1870, before the serial numbers of *Edwin Drood* had been completed. Luke Fildes was invited by the

Dickens family to the funeral at Gad's Hill, and he was deeply touched to be shown the author's empty chair in his study. He was immediately inspired to draw the poignant scene for *The Graphic*, and the drawing quickly went viral all over the world. Van Gogh acquired a woodcut of *The Empty Chair* and couldn't wait to show it to his brother Theo. Ten years later, the illustration still haunted him; he reminded his brother of the story of how Fildes came to draw the melancholy scene, and added: 'Empty chairs – there are many more to come, and sooner or later instead of Herkomer, Luke Fildes, Frank Holl, William Small &c., there will only be Empty chairs.'

And there were, in another sense, too. Van Gogh's empty *Yellow Chair*, painted in 1888 and now in the National Gallery, was to become one of the iconic masterpieces of modern art. Van Gogh painted a companion piece, too, *Gauguin's Armchair*, this chair not unlike Dickens's, also painted in 1888, in recollection of his absent friend and now in the Van Gogh Museum, Amsterdam.

The Empty Chair by Luke Fildes, 1870

Gauguin's Chair by Vincent van Gogh, 1888

The scene set in *The Doctor* is equally poignant. A child lies desperately ill in a tumbledown cottage, with his distraught parents standing by. The Doctor is sitting by the side of the bed (which is no more than a couple of chairs covered by a blanket). The light from a single oil lamp falls on the child's pillow and on the pale brow of the Doctor, who leans forward lost in thought. Is he thinking what he can tell the parents, or pondering the child's chances of coming through the crisis? The scene is deathly quiet and sad, dominated by dark umber tones, and painted in a masterfully understated way. The picture is influenced by Fildes's memory of the doctors who attended his young son Philip who had died of typhoid ten years earlier.

Ever since, this picture has been commandeered for medical adverts and medical journals, even for the US stamp to commemorate the centenary of the American Medical Association in 1947. It has come to represent the ideal of the dedicated practitioner, who, despite his stiff collar and smart suit, is ready to sit up all night with his patient.

The Doctor by Luke Fildes, 1891

Yet it is *The Doctor* which, of all the pictures in the world, the critic Clive Bell chooses to illustrate what Art is *not*. Bell was married to the painter Vanessa Stephen, Virginia Woolf's sister, and he became the house art critic of the Bloomsbury Group. He has gone down to posterity as one of the least appealing of the Bloomsberries: cold, snobbish, racist, anti-Semitic, a ruthless adulterer, living off the profits of the family coal mines in Merthyr Tydfil. But he was a forceful advocate of modernism in art, and his definition of art as 'significant form' was enormously influential. Almost as influential was his definition of what was to be excluded from genuine art. And in his essay 'The Aesthetic Hypothesis' (1914), he takes *The Doctor* as 'the most flagrant example':

'Of course "The Doctor" is not a work of art. In it form is not used as an object of emotion, but as a means of suggesting emotions. This alone suffices to make it nugatory; it is worse than nugatory because the emotion it suggests is false. What it suggests is not pity and admiration but a sense of complacency in our own pitifulness and generosity. It is sentimental.'[1]

Of all the artists in the world to accuse of false emotion and sentimental fakery, Luke Fildes must be about the least plausible. His passion through life for improving the lot of the poor, his memory of his son's death, his dedication to his art – no, it just won't wash. But Bell goes further. He finds the picture actively 'unpleasant': 'Not being a work of art, "The Doctor" has none of the immense ethical value possessed by all objects that provoke aesthetic ecstasy; and the state of mind to which it is a means, as illustration, appears to me undesirable.'[2]

Even if it's a compelling representation of the scene, it's still beyond the pale of Art: 'The representative element in a work of art may or may not be harmful; always it is irrelevant. For to appreciate a work of art we need bring with us nothing from life, no knowledge of its ideas and affairs, no familiarity with its emotions.'[3] This is a breathtaking claim. But Bell hammers home his assertion: 'What I have to say is this: the rapt philosopher, and he who contemplates a work of art, inhabit a world with an intense and peculiar significance of its own; that significance is unrelated to the significance of life. In this world the emotions of life find no place. It is a world with emotions of its own.' Bell's aesthetic contemplative travels light: 'To appreciate a work of art we need bring with us nothing but a sense of form and colour and a knowledge of three-dimensional space.'[4]

This is Whistler's credo carried to the extreme. 'Devotion, pity, love, patriotism and the like' are all to be firmly excluded from the realm of Art. Our aesthetic ecstasies are to come from pleasing arrangements of line and colour, and from nothing outside.

For Bell, the actual subject of the picture is supremely irrelevant. 'You will notice that people who cannot feel pure aesthetic emotion remember pictures by their subjects; whereas people who can, as often as not, have no idea what the subject of a picture is. They have never noticed the representative element, and so when they discuss pictures they talk about the shapes of forms and the relations and quantities of colour.'[5]

Really? Do these superior aesthetes not notice the Magdalen's tears or the Cavalier's laugh? Do they really not remember whether the painting they admired depicted the Crucifixion or the Rape of the Sabine Women?

Well, no, they don't. That's why primitive art is so great. 'Most people who care much about art find that of the work that moves them most the greater part is what scholars call "Primitive".'[6] 'As a rule primitive art is good – and here again my hypothesis is helpful – for, as a rule it is also free from descriptive qualities. In primitive art you will find no accurate representation, you will find only significant form. Yet no other art moves us so profoundly.'[7] But, of course, it is also true that the Western aesthete has little knowledge of, and even less interest in, the gods and myths that are represented, clumsily by our lights, in 'Primitive art'. Such works move us partly, it seems, because we don't understand what they are about.

This much is certainly true: that the dawn of modernism occurs simultaneously with a new enthusiasm for primitive art and for attempting to imitate or somehow to incorporate something of its supposed grandeur and innocence – and strangeness – as Picasso, Brancusi and a host of lesser lights have tried to do. For modernism is preoccupied with breaking away from the familiar world and the long-standing efforts to represent it, and into an entirely fresh enterprise, that of 'making strange', *ostranenie*, to use the term coined by the Russian Formalist critic Viktor Shklovsky, in his essay 'Art as Technique', three years after Bell's *Art*. Later writers and artists have refined or repeated this ambition. In the 1930s, Bertolt Brecht's *Verfremdungseffekt*, or 'alienation effect', carries the idea into the theatre. The old-fashioned bourgeois play sets out to tug at the audience's heartstrings; the Brechtian playwright or director aims to leave them cold, but to persuade them of the truth of the moral fable of socialism which is being acted out in front of them. Brecht's modern successors deter their audiences from too much sentimental identification with the plight of the hero/heroine by having women play men, white men play black men and vice versa and so on, with wilfully inappropriate costumes and sets, all combining to intensify the sense of strangeness, and to distance the viewer from the action. These refrigerating techniques were described back in 1925 by Ortega y Gasset in *The Dehumanization of Art*: 'Far from going more or less clumsily towards reality, the artist is seen going against it. He is brazenly set on deforming reality, shattering its human aspect.'[8] We are wrenched out of the old familiar environment into a world which exults in its strangeness: 'This new way of life which presupposes the annulment of spontaneous life is precisely what we call understanding and enjoyment of art.'[9] This new way of life has its own strict rules, its particular exclusion zone, to stop the old sentimentality seeping in: 'Art must not proceed by psychic contagion, for psychic contagion is an unconscious phenomenon, and art ought to be full clarity, high noon of the intellect. Tears and laughter are, aesthetically, frauds. The gesture of beauty never passes beyond smiles, melancholy or delighted. If it can do without them, better still. "*Toute maîtrise jette le froid*"' (Mallarmé) – 'every form of mastery casts a chill'.[10]

As Victor Hugo has already told us, the maestros of the unruffled serene do not weep. They experience only a chilly sort of sublime, the frosty exhilaration of tramping the high peaks. As John Carey points out in his marvellous study *The Intellectuals and the Masses* (1992), the modernist aesthete follows Nietzsche's metaphor of the icy peaks as the realm of liberty for those who have the courage to scale them: 'So we find, for example, Clive Bell hymning "the austere and thrilling raptures of those who have climbed the cold, white peaks of art," and contrasting them with the herd who frequent the "snug foothills of warm humanity".'[11]

Alas, even the dedicated aesthete can be in danger of falling off the cliff edge. In the same passage, Bell describes how his concentration sometimes slides at a concert: 'Tired or perplexed, I let slip my sense of form, my aesthetic emotion collapses, and I begin weaving into the harmonies, that I cannot grasp, the ideas of life. Incapable of feeling the austere emotions of art, I begin to read into the musical forms human emotions of terror and mystery, love and hate, and spend the minutes, pleasantly enough, in a world of turbid and inferior feeling. At such times, were the grossest pieces of onomatopoeic representation – the song of a bird, the galloping of horses, the cries of children, or the laughing of demons – to be introduced into the symphony, I should not be offended.'[12]

Alas, so often the composer is the accomplice in this slippage. He may drop an explicit hint of what is called 'programme music', suggest that he intends in this passage to evoke the sights and sounds of real life. Programme music is much derided, but even the greatest composers have dallied with it. Beethoven marks the movements of his Symphony No. 6 – the 'Pastoral' – as being designed to evoke bird calls, a babbling brook, a storm. The score is marked with the bars intended to imitate the cuckoo, the quail and the nightingale. Modern composers – Honegger, Grainger, Villa-Lobos – have written music to imitate the sounds of trains. In the Soviet era, Russian composers such as Prokofiev evoked the sounds of steel mills. These effects may be intended as direct imitations of nature, or to evoke a mood or an event – a country wedding, a lovers' parting, a hunt – again sometimes accompanied by a programme note. Such pieces often win lasting popularity – and the scorn of the cognoscenti, none more so than Vaughan Williams's *The Lark Ascending*, which regularly tops the radio polls of classical music.

But after deploring the vulgarity of the public's taste, the rigorous aesthete is still left with the unanswered question: why shouldn't Art mix the familiar and the strange, achieve a fresh fusion between the sentimental and the technical, even in music, generally regarded as the most 'abstract' of the arts? It is a tortuous and never properly defended theory that excludes, in advance, any human dimension.

If van Gogh loved *The Empty Chair* and responded to the ghost of Charles Dickens by painting his own version, why shouldn't we? Might we even be allowed to linger a moment or two in front of *The Doctor*, too, and perhaps experience just a hint of rapture?

If *The Doctor* is still off limits for art lovers, then we might instead take a look at another work in oils, finished six years later by a young Spanish artist. Pablo Picasso was still only 16 when he painted *Science and Charity*, which now hangs in the Museu Picasso in Barcelona. The composition bears a weird resemblance to that of *The Doctor*, although it's unlikely that Picasso had any knowledge of Fildes's work. His biographer, John Richardson, points out that 'there are at least three well-known Spanish paintings of the period that could have inspired this maudlin sickroom set piece'.[13] Thus Richardson is just as hard on Picasso as Bell was on Fildes. Indeed, the emotion in the picture recalls Fildes just as much as the composition: the doctor in frock coat and stiff collar (the model was Picasso's father, Don José) is taking the patient's pulse, while a nun holding a toddler clasps her other hand. The huge canvas, 200 x 250 cm, filled Picasso's tiny studio, barely leaving room for the truckle bed and the patient, modelled by a local beggar woman who was paid ten pesetas and afterwards stole the sheets off the bed. The message in the two paintings is exactly the same: the doctor's devotion to even his poorest patient.

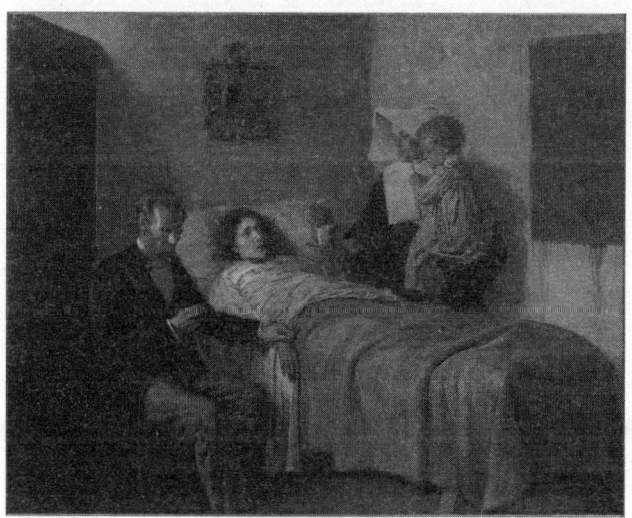

Science and Charity by Pablo Picasso, 1897

The drubbing Richardson handed out to the teenage Picasso is not untypical of the verdicts passed by later critics on the early work of Modernists before they discovered modernism. For the explosion of -isms that swept across Europe before the outbreak of the First World War transformed critical orthodoxies, too. We need only list a few of the new movements and their prime movers to see how overwhelming it all was: Fauvism (Matisse and Derain), 1905–10; Cubism (Picasso and Braque), 1907–8; Futurism (Marinetti), 1909; Orphism (dubbed by a poet, Guillaume Apollinaire, who also coined Surrealism five years later), 1912; Abstractionism (Kandinsky), 1910–13; Constructivism (Tatlin), 1913; Suprematism (Malevich), 1913; Vorticism (Wyndham Lewis), 1914. What were they all up to? However original each might think itself, Malevich can speak for them all: 'In the year 1913, trying desperately to free art from the dead weight of the real world, I took refuge in the form of the square.' Whether the focus was to be on line, or colour, or shape, the aim was always to break free of realism. But before their several flashes of light, each of these artists had painted hundreds of more or less realist landscapes and portraits, drenched in feeling and atmosphere: Kandinsky's *Odessa Port* of 1898, Malevich's *Flower Girl* of 1903, for example.

Even more emotional than *Science and Charity* is Picasso's *First Communion*, painted the year before and now also in the Museu Picasso. It shows Pablo's sister Lola kneeling at the altar, clutching a missal, in a white dress with a chaplet of white flowers. The picture was conceived under the supervision of Don José during Pablo's apprenticeship to a local painter who specialized in sacred subjects, and aimed at an art exhibition in Barcelona's Palace of Fine Arts. Richardson calls it 'a sanctimonious scene'. But he has to admit that, though Picasso later became a confirmed atheist, he remained proud of the picture and thought that he had hit on something 'real', more so perhaps than in his later Blue Period and Rose Period pictures of hunched waifs and starving acrobats. In fact, 20 years later, in an affectionate backward glance, he painted a couple of neoclassical variations on the subject.[14] Thus, all through his precocious teens and most of his twenties, Picasso was putting not only his amazing technique but also his heart into scenes calculated to stir pity and sympathy. If ever there was an artist whose oeuvre could properly be called 'sentimental', it was Picasso-before-Cubism. He remained indulgent towards his earlier works and would, I fancy, have been taken aback to be told that they did not count as works of art. He had simply moved on from them.

Pablo Picasso, First Communion, 1896

ON OR ABOUT DECEMBER 1910

It is a startling claim, breathtaking in its sweep and unnervingly precise in its dating. 'On or about December 1910 human character changed.' Virginia Woolf was giving a talk in 1924 to the Heretics, an avant-garde, anti-religious society of Cambridge undergraduates. She herself was now in her early forties, and she was setting out to shake up her young audience: 'All human relations have shifted – those between masters and servants, husbands and wives, parents and children. And when human relations change, there is at the same time a change in religion, conduct, politics and literature.'[15]

Woolf rather liked identifying watershed moments. In her memoir 'Old Bloomsbury',[16] she recalls a scene in the drawing room of 46 Gordon Square on a spring evening in 1907: 'Suddenly the door opened and the long and sinister figure of

Lytton Strachey stood on the threshold. He pointed his finger at a stain on Vanessa's dress.

'"Semen?" he said.

'Can one really say it? I thought and we burst out laughing. With that one word all barriers of reticence and reserve went down. A flood of the sacred fluid seemed to overwhelm us. Sex permeated our conversation. We discussed copulation with the same excitement and openness that we had discussed the nature of good.'

Not for the first or last time, sexual relations, sexual freedom and the nature of marriage were up for discussion. But the shift in human character that Woolf claimed to have spotted was of a different sort, to do with art and literature, not so much with life. Gottfried Benn, the German Expressionist poet and for a time Hitler's pet, also identified 1910 as 'indeed the year when all the timbers started creaking'.[17]

Woolf admits that she finds it hard to pin down the exact nature of the great shift. The way she goes about her task is to make a sharp distinction between 'the Edwardians', the old guard of Arnold Bennett, John Galsworthy and H. G. Wells, and 'the Georgians', 15 or 20 years younger, consisting of E. M. Forster, D. H. Lawrence, Lytton Strachey, James Joyce and T. S. Eliot, and by implication, though she is too modest to add her name, Virginia Woolf herself.

She pays a back-handed tribute to the progressive intentions of the old guard. 'After the creative activity of the Victorian age it was quite necessary, not only for literature but for life, that someone should write the books that Mr Wells, Mr Bennett and Mr Galsworthy have written.' Which reminds one of the patronizing things that Baudelaire said about Victor Hugo. But Woolf hastens on to express an unmitigated disdain: 'Yet what odd books they are! Sometimes I wonder if we are right to call them books at all. For they leave one with so strange a feeling of incompleteness and dissatisfaction.' They are not self-contained works of art. They tell you all about the houses the characters live in, the furniture in their living rooms, the fabrics they wear, how much they have in their bank accounts. But they tell you nothing about their inner lives. The old guard are fatally materialist, insensitive, ultimately nothing but philistines.

She acknowledges that 'Mr Bennett has some reason when he complains that our Georgian writers are unable to make us believe that our characters are real.' You may be put off by the indecency of Mr Joyce or the obscurity of Mr Eliot. But we are in a time of violent experimentation. 'Thus it is that we hear all round us, in poems and novels and biographies, even in newspaper articles and essays, the sound of breaking of falling, crashing and destruction. It is the prevailing sound of the Georgian age.' But we have to put up with it if we are to break through. 'We must reconcile ourselves to a season of failures and fragments ... Tolerate the spasmodic, the obscure, the fragmentary, the failure.' It will be worth it. For 'we are trembling on the verge of one of the great ages of English literature'. And we shall be able to relegate Mr Bennett and his kind to the dustbin of literary history.

Now, as John Carey points out in his superb defence of Arnold Bennett, this contrast is grotesquely unfair. In all Bennett's novels, he is intensely alert to the singularity of 'ordinary' people; 'the sense of delicacy' in the superficially, clumsy, ignorant Edwin Clayhanger; Constance and Sophia, the unremarkable daughters of a draper in *The Old Wives' Tale*, who are 'like racehorses, quivering with delicate, sensitive, luxuriant life'; the housemaid, Elsie Sprickett, 'a dull, slow, heavy ex-charwoman' but a woman who is also alert, wise and frightened – more alert and alive than the other characters in the two stories she appears in.[18] For my own part, I have seldom been more moved by any English novel than *The Old Wives' Tale*; I remain deeply admiring, too, of *Riceyman Steps* and the Clayhanger series.

Nor was Arnold Bennett himself any sort of philistine. He was an early enthusiast for Dostoevsky, Turgenev and Chekhov. When the audience walked out at the first performance of *The Cherry Orchard*, Bennett defended the play's 'daring naturalism'. He championed Mallarmé, Gide and Valéry. He even admired and spoke up for Mrs Woolf's Georgians, for D. H. Lawrence – 'far and away the best of the younger school' – and for Joyce, Forster and Eliot. He also warmed to modernism in art. He enthusiastically welcomed the 1910 Post-Impressionist Exhibition which gave Londoners their first sight of Cézanne and van Gogh, and wrote an introduction to the catalogue for a 1919 show which included Picasso and Matisse, and which he said provided 'an education for the islanders; and of course it is equally a joy'.[19]

How then does Woolf come to caricature him in this utterly wrong-headed fashion? The answer, I'm afraid, lies in a squalid and all-consuming snobbery. Bennett had left school at 16, worked as a clerk and then got a job on *Woman* where he wrote 'Gwendolen's Column'. John Carey rightly homes in on the intellectuals' obsession with Bennett's lower-middle-classness. Woolf's brother-in-law Clive Bell described him as 'an insignificant little man and ridiculous to boot ... he was the boy from Staffordshire who was making good, and in his bowler hat and reach-me-downs he looked the part'. Woolf herself mocked his 'shopkeeper's view of literature', Wyndham Lewis sneered at his 'grocer origins'. Bertrand Russell found him so 'vulgar' that he could not bear to be in the same room with him. T. S. Eliot was furious to have his conversation with W. B. Yeats interrupted by a red-faced man 'with an air of impertinent prosperity and the aspect of a successful grocer', not to mention 'a most disagreeable cockney accent' (hardly likely in a Staffordshire man).[20]

This looking down on Bennett, and on Wells, too (Galsworthy went to Harrow and New College, Oxford, so he was all right), was not just an unlovely quirk; it was at the heart of the upper-middle-class intelligentsia's view of itself as a superior caste. These terms of demarcation – intelligentsia, highbrow/middlebrow/lowbrow, avant-garde/bourgeois – are intensively deployed from the 1920s onwards. By contrast, the commercial success of the lower-middle-class authors was seen as another marker of their inferiority, their unfitness for the high peaks of art. D. H. Lawrence described Bennett as 'a pig in clover'. The Edwardians were unforgivably popular.

Ortega y Gasset frankly declares in *The Dehumanization of Art* (1925) that modern art 'will always have the masses against it. It is essentially unpopular; moreover, it is antipopular ... the work of art acts like a social agent which segregates from the shapeless mass of the many two different castes of men'.[21] This unpopularity is not confined to any particular art form: 'the unpopularity of the new music has its counterpart in a similar unpopularity of the other Muses. All modern art is unpopular, and it is so not accidentally and by chance, but essentially and by fate.'[22]

As art retreats from the real, it also retreats from the deplorable messy feelings of the masses. 'The first consequence of the retreat of art upon itself is a ban on all pathos.' No question of shedding a tear in front of a landscape by Gainsborough, or by anyone else, or in front of any sort of work of art at all. 'Whatever the content,' Ortega insists, 'the art itself is jesting. To look for fiction as fiction ... is a proposition that cannot be executed except with one's tongue in one's cheek ... I much doubt that any young person of our time can be impressed by a poem, a painting or a piece of music that is not flavoured with a dash of irony.'[23] The new movements such as Dada and Surrealism revelled in jokey transformations of reality: watches and buildings which melt; a picture of a pipe captioned 'This is not a Pipe'; a porcelain urinal signed and exhibited as a work of art. The surrealists claimed to be bringing the subconscious back to the surface, translating the language of dreams onto the canvas. But these excursions into dreamland were always laced with irony. And that's still true today. Exactly a century after Ortega, *The Times* straplines its Survey of the first 25 years of Tate Modern: 'it's the gallery that showed us that art was fun.' (*Times*, May 3, 2025) In Ortega's words, Art's 'mission is to conjure up imaginary worlds. That can only be done if the artist repudiates reality and by this act places himself above it. Being an artist means ceasing to take seriously that very serious person we are when we are not an artist.'[24]

But is this quite true? Could not the methods of Cubism and Futurism, say, be applied to serious, even tragic subjects, including the most tragic of all subjects, the Great War, in which the world was about to be engulfed while the artists were busily devising their -isms?

At first sight, most Modernists of all schools would seem to have shied away from the subject, even if they did not shy away from the war, in which Braque and Kokoschka were badly injured among millions of others. They did not directly address the subject in their art, any more than, say, Matisse and Picasso did. Their war work was to do no war work, the sole mission to keep the flag of Art flying above the human swamp.

Yet there were one or two exceptions, in England at least. Among the war artists sent out to record the terrible events in Flanders and the Middle East were two young Modernists of remarkable talent. Paul Nash (1889–1946) had links with the Vorticists before the war and with the surrealists after it. He is rare in covering both world wars as an official war artist. His work in the trenches uses Modernist techniques to convey the unbearable desecration of the peaceful countryside of Flanders. Nash came under fire during the Third Battle of Ypres and wrote an unforgettable letter home to his wife, equalling in his passionate detestation of the war any poem by Sassoon or Owen:

'I have just returned, last night from a visit to Brigade Headquarters up the line and I shall not forget it as long as I live. I have seen the most frightful nightmare of a country more conceived by Dante or Poe than by nature, unspeakable, utterly indescribable. In the fifteen drawings I have made I may give you some idea of its horror, but only being in it and of it can ever make you sensible of its dreadful nature and of what our men in France have to face. We all have a vague notion of the terrors of a battle, and can conjure up with the aid of some of the more inspired war correspondents and the pictures in the *Daily Mirror* some vision of battlefield; but no pen or drawing can convey this country – the normal setting of the battles taking place day and night, month after month. Evil and the incarnate fiend alone can be master of this war, and no glimmer of God's hand is seen anywhere. Sunset and sunrise are blasphemous, they are mockeries to man, only the black rain out of the bruised and swollen clouds all through the bitter black night is fit atmosphere in such a land. The rain drives on, the stinking mud becomes more evilly yellow, the shell holes fill up with green-white water, the roads and tracks are covered in inches of slime, the black dying trees ooze and sweat and the shells never cease. They alone plunge overhead, tearing away the rotting tree stumps, breaking the plank roads, striking down horses and mules, annihilating, maiming, maddening, they plunge into the grave, and cast up on it the poor dead. It is unspeakable, godless, hopeless. I am no longer an artist interested and curious, I am a messenger who will bring back word from the men who are fighting to those who want the war to go on for ever. Feeble, inarticulate, will be my message, but it will have a bitter truth, and may it burn their lousy souls.'[25]

The Menin Road by Paul Nash, 1919

I quote this message at such length to demonstrate that, whatever Bell or Ortega might say, it was possible to be a devoted Modernist and still to show both in your art and in your life an undiminished capacity for pity and love. For Nash gave vivid life to that message in a series of paintings and drawings, such as Wire, The Ypres Salient at Night, The Menin Road, and the vista of blasted tree stumps and foul bogs left by the shells, bitterly entitled We Are Making a New World.

No less bitter and no less powerful was the wartime work of his fellow Slade student and exact contemporary C. R. W. Nevinson (1889–1946). After leaving the Slade, he became a friend of Marinetti, the leader of the Italian Futurists who was much in London at the time. In fact, he seems to have been the only English artist who signed up to the Futurist movement. He was also a friend of Wyndham Lewis, the founder of the rival Vorticism, though he fell out with Lewis (who didn't?) and was excluded from the Vorticist group because of his support for the Futurists. But his work remained strongly influenced by Futurism and by Cubism, and he produced some amazing work, both during his brief spell as an ambulance driver on the Western Front and then, after being invalided out, on home service with the Royal Army Medical Corps. Among the most telling are: *La Mitrailleuse*, the machine gun, which Walter Sickert, as good a critic as an artist, said 'will probably remain the most authoritative and concentrated utterance on the war in the history of painting'; *Paths of Glory*, another bitter title for a picture of dead soldiers tangled in barbed wire; *La Patrie*, a large study of wounded soldiers lying in a darkened shed; and *A Taube*, which shows a dead child lying on shattered cobbles outside a bombed-out house – 'Taube' is the German for 'dove', and the name given to a German reconnaissance plane, in which the pilot could chuck bombs out of the cockpit. It was a Taube that dropped the first aerial bomb in history. With its pleated wings and tail, it did look rather like a dove. Thus another hideous irony, mocking Picasso's far more famous dove of peace several decades later.

La Patrie by C. R. W. Nevinson, 1916

Guernica by Pablo Picasso, 1937

These are wonderful pictures, as harsh in their impact as anything since Grünewald's *Crucifixion*. Yet they remain little known except to enthusiasts. A few of them hang in the Tate, but most of them are today in the Imperial War Museum. Thus they are classified primarily as part of the history of warfare rather than the history of art.

Far more famous is the huge canvas (25 x 11 ft) which Picasso painted to commemorate the German bombing of Guernica in 1937 during the Spanish Civil War. Partly perhaps because the name suggests war, but mostly because of Picasso's unrivalled celebrity, it immediately became the greatest anti-war icon ever. The canvas is a jumble of screaming women's heads thrown back in agony, dead soldiers and horses' heads neighing in terror. Not everyone liked the painting at the time. Marxists complained that it failed to offer a positive vision for the future. Clement Greenberg, the supreme Modernist guru, called it 'jerky' and 'too compressed for its size'; he preferred Picasso's later anti-war picture *The Charnel House*. Nevertheless, the painting remains as firmly etched on the public imagination as Picasso's dove.

For my own part, I cannot help feeling that the fragmented figures are somehow gestural, fabricated things, distanced from the realities they point at. Paradoxically to me at least, this supreme expression of pacifist agony seems rather to reinforce Ortega's scandalous assertion, that Modernist artists cannot weep and that it is not in their repertoire to make others weep either. If you did not know the painting's title and occasion, its, well, its gaiety might even make you smile a little. This opinion goes dead against the orthodoxy that Guernica is an intensely moving work. I can only ask the reader to look again.

For me, Nevinson's *La Patrie* is an infinitely more moving work. I cannot resist noting that when it was shown at the Leicester Galleries, it was bought by that vulgar little man, Arnold Bennett (he supported Paul Nash, too).

But there is one great exception to the inescapable irony of modernism. Photography has never ceased to enjoy the right to be serious, and to confront the sufferings of humanity directly. It was recognized from the first that the new medium would offer formidable competition to the traditional arts of painting and sculpture. As early as 1840 or thereabouts, the French painter Paul Delaroche is said to have exclaimed on seeing a daguerreotype, 'From today painting is dead'.[26] It is significant that it was Delaroche who said it, because he was a leader of the Realist school. His grand historical canvases – 'The Princes in the Tower', 'The Death of Queen Elizabeth' – attempted to portray the scene as it might actually have looked. His 'Napoleon Crossing the Alps', for example, consciously undercut David's famous image of the handsome Emperor on his prancing white steed; Delaroche's Napoleon is a seedy-looking fellow bumping over the rocky snowpath on a humble mule (which was how in fact Napoleon did cross the Alps). But Delaroche feared that all his efforts to be authentic would be outclassed by the immediacy of the new medium – by the clear window on reality that it appeared to offer.

On the other hand, though, for years, the new art or science was hobbled by the technical difficulties of taking a 'snapshot'. A photogravure like Oscar Rejlander's *Homeless* would have taken hours to set up, shoot and process. Roger Fenton in the Crimean War and Mathew Brady and his rivals in the American Civil War were the first to try to render the horrors of war in photographs. But their apparatus was too cumbersome to capture much more than the battlefield after the battle – generals posed with their staffs, troops sitting in front of their tents with their arms stacked beside them. Fenton did achieve a memorable effect with his photo of *The Valley of the Shadow of Death* (April 1855), which simply shows a rocky hillside littered with spent cannon balls. Only in the First World War was it possible to show the horrors of trench warfare 'in real time' with a directness that has seared the Western mind forever. Similarly in the 1930s, Dorothea Lange's poignant pictures conveyed the misery of the Depression for migrants in the Midwest. In Britain, Bill Brandt immortalized the Jarrow March, the Blitz and the miners in Northumberland. After the war, Don McCullin has brought home the brutality of conflicts all over the world from Vietnam to Biafra. Cynics who are uncomfortable with the powerful emotional effect of these iconic photographs have often claimed that they were staged – the raising of the US Flag on Iwo Jima, for example, and Robert Capa's *Falling Soldier* in the Spanish Civil War. Fenton was suspected of shifting the cannon balls to make a more picturesque effect. But in most cases, the photographic evidence is unfakeable; it stares you in the face and it sticks in your mind. Photography and pathos remain inseparable.

THE REVOLT AGAINST THE MASSES

It may seem like a coincidence that so many of the literati who looked down on Bennett should have also been among the 'Georgians', singled out by Woolf as the first wave of 'one of the great ages of English literature', such as T. S. Eliot and D. H. Lawrence. But these are only a subset of the intelligentsia as a whole, which shared a contempt and loathing for the lower orders, especially the lower middle class, or petty bourgeoisie, which had been getting it in the neck well before Arnold Bennett was born or thought of.

This distaste can be found in *The Communist Manifesto*. Marx and Engels single out for special scorn the petty-bourgeois philistines, with their 'sickly sentiment' and 'villainous meanness'. You find it, too, in Nietzsche's *Will to Power*, which tells us that 'everywhere the mediocre are combining in order to make themselves master'. The tyranny of the least and dumbest will lead to socialism, a hopeless and sour affair that negates Life. Nietzsche was everywhere among early twentieth-century intellectuals, recommended by all sorts of people like W. B. Yeats and George Bernard Shaw (quite a few of them, like

Shaw, were themselves socialists, which did not stop them looking down on their intellectual inferiors). Nietzsche also implanted the idea that in order to breed a master race it was necessary to weed out the duds. This was the heyday of the fashion for dabbling in eugenics, Yeats and Wells being among the notable enthusiasts. Sooner or later, Yeats warned, we must limit the families of the unintelligent classes because they have been breeding so rapidly: 'Since about 1900 the better stocks have not been replacing their number, while the stupider and less healthy have been more than replacing theirs.'[27]

This was necessary, not only to purify the race but also to roll back the overpopulation which was causing the phenomenon that the intelligentsia loathed above all: the relentless spread of suburbia. You can find the revulsion almost everywhere in the 1920s and 1930s, in the novels of Graham Greene and Evelyn Waugh, in the essays of Cyril Connolly and the leader columns of *The Times*. T. S. Eliot, when announcing the aims of his new periodical *The Criterion*, declared that it would be directed against 'suburban democracy'. The suburbs not only ruined the view; they also ruined the mind. Connolly famously declared that 'Slums may well be breeding grounds of crime, but middle-class suburbs are incubators of apathy and delirium.' These settlements were an offence to the eye and to the spirit, too. They could never be part of the true England. As late as 1998, Roger Scruton was deploring 'these suburbs dropped from nowhere'. He complained that 'the commuter suburbs violate the landscape partly because they violate the sense of rural time. Even if they remain there for ever, people feel, it will be with a stagnant impermanence.'[28]

The suburbs bred suburban types, low-bred characters like Leonard Bast, the bank clerk in E. M. Forster's *Howards End*, whose mind is as stunted as his spine, or Eliot's cocky, carbuncular young house agent's clerk in *The Waste Land*. What the suburbs bred in particular was conformity of mind, so memorably derided in the song 'Little Boxes', made famous by the left-wing folk singer Pete Seeger in 1963:

> Little boxes on the hillside,
> Little boxes made of ticky tacky,
> Little boxes on the hillside,

Little boxes all the same....
And the people in the houses
All went to the university,
Where they were put in boxes
And they came out all the same.

The most memorable of such jeremiads is perhaps Ortega y Gasset's *The Revolt of the Masses* (1930), a prolonged tirade which might be better titled *The Revolt Against the Masses*, or *The Revolt of the Intellectuals*. For it is among the intelligentsia that you find the passions stirring that typically inspire revolts: the resentment against The Other, the fear of being swamped or overshadowed, the fear of losing your place in the world. The masses have taken over, the world is too crowded for the exceptional person to think, even to breathe: 'The characteristic of the hour is that the commonplace mind, knowing itself to be commonplace, has the assurance to proclaim the rights of the commonplace and to impose itself everywhere. As they say in the United States: "To be different is to be indecent." The mass crushes beneath itself everything that is different, everything that is excellent, qualified and select. Anybody who is not like everybody, who does not think like everybody, runs the risk of being eliminated.'[29] The masses have lost the art of being ruled by their betters, which is the indispensable precondition of a society that works.

There is in all this a noticeable *hardening* of politics. The old compromises and adjustments will no longer suffice, the traditional concordats between parties and classes no longer hold. And so it is that the more anguished members of the intelligentsia begin to turn to more desperate remedies. A taste for Nietzsche is often the first symptom. In the United States, perhaps the most besotted follower of the German sage was the essayist H. L. Mencken (1880–1956). Mencken was famous for his contrarian views and his contempt for what he called 'the booboisie', that is, a fair proportion of his readers. His reverence for Nietzsche came close to hero worship. He wrote *The Philosophy of Friedrich Nietzsche* when he was still in his twenties, and ten years later translated Nietzsche's scorching polemic against Christianity, *The Anti-Christ*.

In his remarkable introduction, Mencken applauds every word of the book. 'The fact is that Nietzsche had no interest whatever in the delusions of the plain people – that is, intrinsically. It seemed to him of small moment what they believed, so long as it was safely imbecile. What he stood against was not their beliefs, but the elevation of those beliefs, by any sort of democratic process, to the dignity of a state philosophy – what he feared most the pollution and crippling of the superior minority by intellectual disease from below.'[30] Mencken praises Nietzsche's hardness and courage: 'he seldom allowed sentimentality to turn him from the glaring fact ... The mob and its maudlin causes attract only sentimentalists and scoundrels.'[31] Nietzsche is merciless on the poisonous nonsense of Christianity, 'the greatest of all imaginable corruptions'.

But Mencken goes rather further than his master, by also denouncing the race that spawned this nonsense. 'The case against the Jews is long and damning; it would justify ten thousand times as many pogroms as now go on in the world.'[32] Attempts have been made to water down the charge of anti-Semitism, mostly on the grounds that some of his best friends really were Jewish. I don't think that these excuses begin to work, any more than the efforts to deny that Mencken was soft on Hitler. His review of *Mein Kampf* in the *American Mercury*, just after Hitler had taken power in 1933, tells us that 'what Hitler says in it is often sensible enough – for example, when he argues that Germany's first big task is to collar Austria and so consolidate the German people, and again when he argues that its natural route of expansion is along the Baltic, and yet again when he argues that it can never hope to make an honest friend of France' – so a green light for the *Anschluss*, the invasion of Poland, and indeed for the invasion of France. As for the Jews, 'Hitler's anti-Semitism, which has shocked so many Americans, is certainly nothing to marvel over.' Mencken goes on to tell us that the anti-Semitism will probably calm down, and anyway Hitler won't last unless he moderates his programme.

Mencken's indulgence of Hitler, though, pales beside that of Wyndham Lewis, who wrote no less than three books in the 1930s endorsing the Führer: he was essentially a 'man of peace', who, if he obtained power, would show 'increasing moderation and tolerance'. His anti-Semitism was 'a mere bagatelle', and the Nazi stormtroopers were much misunderstood:

> 'These hefty young street-fighting warriors have not the bloodshot eyes and furtive manners of the political gutter-gunmen, but the personal neatness, the clear blue eyes, of the police. The Anglo-Saxon would feel reassured at once in the presence of these straightforward young pillars of the law.'[33]

Manliness was crucial to Lewis. He hated 'the increasingly feminine world', in which 'the natural feminine hostility to the intellect' was rampant. Hitler and Mussolini alone stood out against the degenerate female flux. Lewis himself treated women rough, and abandoned four or five of his illegitimate children.

At least Lewis did not emigrate to Germany and become a paid propagandist for the Nazis, as Ezra Pound did for Mussolini after he decamped to Rapallo and chummed up with the Duce, or 'the Boss', as he called him. Pound's anti-Semitism was already well entrenched and more profoundly felt than Mussolini's. Back in 1910, he had written in *Patria Mia*: 'The Jew alone can retain his detestable qualities, despite climatic conditions.' His broadcasts for Italian radio during the war included praise for Hitler as well as Mussolini, and referred to the Jews as filth. Even after the German surrender, Pound was telling his American captors that 'Hitler and Mussolini were simple men from the country. I think that Hitler was a saint and wanted nothing for himself.' Later the same day, he told an American reporter that 'Hitler was a Jeanne d'Arc. Like many martyrs, he held extreme views.' All through the 1950s, he went on writing anti-Semitic, pro-Hitler, pro-racial segregation stuff. The nearest he came to repentance was when he told Allen Ginsberg that 'the worst mistake I made was that stupid, suburban prejudice of anti-Semitism'. Even at the last, he blamed it all on suburbia.

In fact, you are just as likely to find the most vicious instances of anti-Semitic talk in Bloomsbury as in the suburbs, nowhere more shockingly than in the early work of T. S. Eliot. It is hard to forget the shock of coming across the lines in 'Gerontion' (1920) about the Jew squatting on the windowsill, or the lines in 'Burbank with a Baedeker,

Bleistein with a Cigar', of the same year, about the rats underneath the piles and the Jew underneath the lot. Even today, the Eliot estate is reluctant to grant permission for these lines to be quoted.

To dismiss these ugly squirts of prejudice as merely voices in the poem won't survive the more considered argument that Eliot puts forward in a lecture he gave at the University of Virginia a decade later, in 1933, just as Hitler is coming to power: 'The population should be homogeneous; when two or more cultures exist in the same place, they are likely either to be fiercely self-conscious or both to become adulterate. What is still more important is unity of religious background; and reasons of race and religion combine to make any large number of free-thinking Jews undesirable.' The lecture was published in *After Strange Gods*, but Eliot forbade any second edition of the book, on the grounds that these sentiments expressed his own disturbed state of mind at the time.

We could trawl further and deeper into the unsavoury utterances of the intelligentsia between the wars. But what is clear is the monotonous uniformity of those views: the belief in the rule of a heroic master race, in selective breeding and extermination of the unfit, the contempt for suburbia and the dead souls of the masses, and always the identification of the Jew as the corrupter of modern society.

It may seem odd that one or two intellectuals, such as the Scottish poet Hugh MacDiarmid, should have wandered from fascism to communism (MacDiarmid's lasting passion was for Scottish Nationalism), or vice versa. But what these extremes have in common is the worship of hardness, the disdainful refusal of softer options such as social democracy.

It is this hardness which attracts the self-appointed guardians of art, and which drives their corresponding hatred of sentimentality. Hardness is seen as noble and authentic. The Artist must at all costs eschew the half-measure, the comfortable, the suburban. If he is to follow Nietzsche to the icy peaks, he must be pitiless. He must distance himself from the common herd. His estrangement is the sign that he is the Real Thing.

No more flamboyant exemplar could be imagined than the founder of Futurism, Filippo Tommaso Marinetti (1876–1944).

He loved speed and machines and hated museums, the Church and anything stuffy or fuddy-duddy. He wanted the canals of Venice to be filled with the rubble of the crumbling palaces and a glorious new industrial city to be built on the site. In his stay in England, his exuberance captivated the intelligentsia, including James Joyce, Ezra Pound and, as we have seen, Christopher Nevinson. In the Great War, he fought first in the mountains with the Lombard Volunteer Cyclists, then took part in the decisive Italian victory of Vittorio Veneto.

The party he founded in 1918, the Partito Politico Futurista, quickly merged with Mussolini's Fasci Italiani di Combattimento, and he actually co-wrote the manifesto of Italian Fascism a year later. He remained a devoted follower of Mussolini to the end, but he never managed to persuade Mussolini to make Futurism the official state art of Italy. The Duce was a wily enough politician to realize that he had to conciliate the forces of reaction, not least the Catholic Church.

So Marinetti's enduring legacy remains the *Manifesto of Futurism* which he had written back in 1909. To get some idea of its frenetic, crazy exhilaration, it is worth quoting the brief document in full:

'1. We want to sing the love of danger, the habit of energy and rashness. 2. The essential elements of our poetry will be courage, audacity and revolt. 3. Literature has up to now magnified pensive immobility, ecstasy and slumber. We want to exalt movements of aggression, feverish sleeplessness, the double march, the perilous leap, the slap and the blow with the fist. 4. We declare that the splendor of the world has been enriched by a new beauty: the beauty of speed. A racing automobile with its bonnet adorned with great tubes like serpents with explosive breath ... a roaring motor car which seems to run on machine-gun fire, is more beautiful than the Victory of Samothrace. 5. We want to sing the man at the wheel, the ideal axis of which crosses the earth, itself hurled along its orbit. 6. The poet must spend himself with warmth, glamour and prodigality to increase the enthusiastic fervor of the primordial elements. 7. Beauty exists only in struggle. There is no masterpiece that has not an aggressive character. Poetry must be a violent assault on the forces of the unknown, to force them to bow before man. 8. We are on the extreme promontory of the centuries! What is the use of looking behind at the moment when we must open the mysterious shutters of the impossible? Time and Space died yesterday. We are already living in the absolute, since we have already created eternal, omnipresent speed. 9. We want to glorify war — the only cure for the world — militarism, patriotism, the destructive gesture of the anarchists, the beautiful ideas which kill, and contempt for woman. 10. We want to demolish museums and libraries, fight morality, feminism and all opportunist and utilitarian cowardice. 11. We will sing of the great crowds agitated by work, pleasure and revolt; the multi-colored and polyphonic surf of revolutions in modern capitals: the nocturnal vibration of the arsenals and the workshops beneath their violent electric moons: the gluttonous railway stations devouring smoking serpents; factories suspended from the clouds by the thread of their smoke; bridges with the leap of gymnasts flung across the diabolic cutlery of sunny rivers: adventurous steamers sniffing the horizon; great-breasted locomotives, puffing on the rails like enormous steel horses with long tubes for bridle, and the gliding flight of aeroplanes whose propeller sounds like the flapping of a flag and the applause of enthusiastic crowds. It is in Italy that we are issuing this manifesto of ruinous and incendiary violence, by which we today are founding Futurism, because we want to deliver Italy from its gangrene of professors, archaeologists, tourist guides and antiquaries.'

The *Manifesto of Futurism* is perhaps the ultimate document of modernism. In its worship of violence and hardness, its loathing of soppy old stuff and its contempt for women, it ticks all the boxes. It is also the ultimate document of anti-sentimentalism. Item 9 praising war as the world's only hygiene, 'sola igiene del mondo', is a repeat of Hegel's claim that 'war protects the people from the corruption which an everlasting peace would bring upon it'. In peace, people stagnate: 'let insecurity finally come in the form of Hussars with glistening sabres, and show its serious activity!' Mercy is for milksops. Hard steel is the substance of the new world. The future is hard-edged. The school of abstract painters who called themselves 'hard-edged' did not emerge until the early 1960s, but Marinetti was in their genes.

SEVEN

The Third Sentimental Revolution

1963 AND ALL THAT

The First Sentimental Revolution started with a date and an explosion of troubadour songs. The Second Sentimental Revolution kicked off with a date and a novel. The Third Sentimental Revolution, the one we are still living through the tail-end of, announced itself with a date and a poem.

Philip Larkin called his poem 'Annus Mirabilis'. Its opening lines are as memorable as any:

Sexual intercourse began
In nineteen sixty-three
(Which was rather late for me) –
Between the end of the Chatterley ban
And the Beatles' first LP.

The poem was written in 1967, exactly 300 years after John Dryden wrote his own 'Annus Mirabilis' to celebrate London's survival after the Great Plague and the Great Fire. Larkin's poem is, as usual, full of ironies, not least his disingenuous references to his own experience. Andrew Motion points out in *Philip Larkin: A Writer's Life* that the disingenuous poet had in fact been enjoying sexual intercourse since about 1945, with several women, often concurrently. But what the poem sets out to recapture is that feeling of liberation which was approaching its zenith as he wrote – 1967 was the famous Summer of Love. And by linking two distinct events — the virtual end of literary censorship and the rise of popular music — he brilliantly incapsulates the cultural shifts which were gathering pace, more or less simultaneously, and after periods of long and often fitful gestation.

The Beatles receive their MBEs, 1965

Since the early 1950s, the Society of Authors had been campaigning for a wholesale reform of the laws of censorship. The campaign was led by the flamboyant Norman St John-Stevas, later to be a Tory MP and Secretary of State for the Arts, and it eventually sparked a Private Members' Bill, sponsored by the rising Labour MP Roy Jenkins, later in his two spells as Home Secretary (1965–7, 1974–6) to be lauded or lambasted as the godfather of the Permissive Society — he preferred to call it 'the civilized society'. The Jenkins Bill re-emerged as the Obscene Publications Bill, which became law in 1959. Previously the law on obscenity had been governed by a common-law case, *R. v Hicklin*, which allowed no defence to the charge on grounds of artistic merit or the public good. The Act introduced two new defences: 'innocent dissemination', which let booksellers off the hook, and 'the public good', defined as 'the interests of science, literature, art or learning'. Even before the Act had come into force, Vladimir Nabokov's *Lolita* had been published in the UK by Weidenfeld & Nicolson and had escaped prosecution. But when Penguin published D. H. Lawrence's *Lady Chatterley's Lover*, unexpurgated, the DPP felt compelled to act. Various literati gave evidence for the defence, including E. M. Forster, the Bishop of Woolwich, John Robinson, who declared that Lawrence, though not a Christian, intended 'to portray the sex relationship as something essentially sacred', and Richard Hoggart, author of *The Uses of Literacy*, who claimed that the book was 'highly virtuous if not puritanical'.

The defence won hands down, hugely helped by the laughter in court when the prosecuting counsel, Mervyn Griffith-Jones, asked the jury, 'Is it a book that you would have lying around in your own home? Is it a book you would even wish your wife or your servants to read?' The initial print run of 200,000 sold out on the first day of publication. Penguin Books quickly sold three million copies. Within 20 years, the book was on many an Eng. Lit. syllabus.

While the censorship of books was left to the common law, the theatre had been subject since the days of Sir Robert Walpole to the often capricious mercies of the Lord Chamberlain, the most senior functionary at Court, and someone who need have no interest in or knowledge of the theatre. From 1963 to 1971, this office was held by the portentous, genial former Governor of the Bank of England, Lord Cobbold. Under his watch, a prosecution was launched against the Royal Court Theatre's production of *Saved*, Edward Bond's merciless play which featured the stoning to death of a baby and which has proved rather too daunting to be produced much in subsequent years. John Osborne's play *A Patriot for Me* was also staged at the Royal Court but evaded Cobbold's veto by the theatre turning itself into a private club for the duration of the run, a loophole which in fact had no legal standing.

There had been previous campaigns against the quaint and arbitrary survival of the Lord Chamberlain's veto — most notably the reform group in 1909 led by W. S. Gilbert, J. M. Barrie and George

Bernard Shaw. In fact, the Lord Chamberlain himself read few of the plays, being occupied with other duties, such as organizing royal garden parties and the annual upping of the royal swans. The assistants who did the reading would not have had much expertise either. The whole system had been devised in the first place, back in the eighteenth century, not to protect public morals but to protect Walpole's ministry against *political* attacks.

The system looked even more ridiculous when the Lord Chamberlain banned plays by Arthur Miller and Tennessee Williams that had already been produced on Broadway. Eventually, Bond, Osborne, the critic Kenneth Tynan and the directors of the Royal Court and the Royal Shakespeare Company launched a combined assault, and the rickety edifice crumbled. In 1968, the Theatres Act simply swept it away.

The Arts Council claimed that the censorship had had 'a contraceptive effect' on the development of British drama. But it had had a political effect, too. In the 1930s, the then Lord Chamberlain had banned plays which showed the Nazis in a bad light, although he acknowledged in 1934 that 'the brutality of the Nazi regime is, I imagine, beyond question', and pointed out that disapproval of the Nazis 'can perfectly well be done in books and novels, and even published plays, but not by plays acted on the English stage', if Britain was to remain officially neutral and disengaged. This weird inconsistency could not endure. It's amazing it lasted so long.

The opening night of *Hair!*, the American hippie rock musical, had been delayed until 27 September 1968, after the Theatres Act became law, so that the show could feature nudity and profanity without fear. Among the young actors taking part was Floella Benjamin, later presenter of *Play School*, Chancellor of the University of Exeter and eventually a member of the House of Lords and of the Order of Merit. The following year, Tynan staged the avant-garde, sex-drenched revue *Oh Calcutta!* – the title is adapted from a saucy collage by a French surrealist 'O! Quel cul t'as' – 'oh, what an arse you have!' Sketches for the show were written by, among others, Samuel Beckett, John Lennon, Edna O'Brien and Tynan himself. The brilliant young painter Pauline Boty was dying of cancer when

Tynan commissioned her to make a series of paintings of erogenous zones for the show. She only lived long enough to complete one, her last painting: BUM. The painting was sold by Tynan's estate at Christie's in 2017 for £632,750.

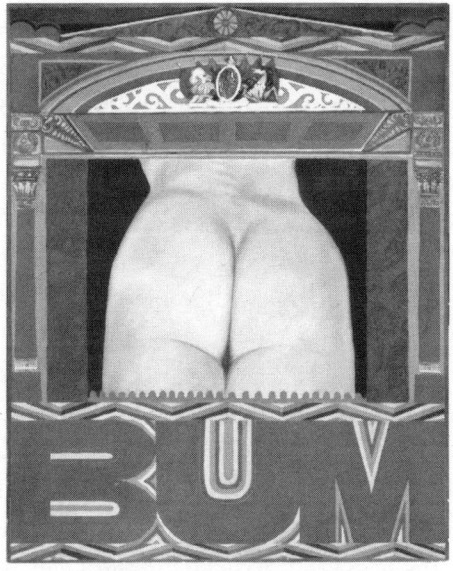

BUM by Pauline Boty, 1966

Oh Calcutta! ran for nearly 4,000 performances in the West End. Its revival on Broadway was the longest running revue there ever. The Director of Public Prosecutions sent a panel of experts, including two retired headmistresses, to see the first London production at the Round House. The panel concluded that the show was not obscene, allowing it to transfer to the West End.

These joustings with the often reluctant censors had their absurd side. The Lord Chamberlain and the DPP might have been comic butts in a Gilbert & Sullivan opera. But they were only the most visible puppets in what looked to young people like a sclerotic society — indeed, it's in these years that the adjective 'sclerotic' is first used to describe the hidebound, clogged-up character of so many British institutions. The laws governing sexual conduct were as old as the Victorian sewers and, like them, were beginning to crack up and smell rather nasty. The laws on homosexual conduct, for example, dated back to the Labouchere Amendment to the Criminal Law Amendment Act of 1885. The laws forbidding abortion remained essentially unchanged since the Offences Against the Person Act of 1861. There had been repeated efforts to modernize the divorce laws, notably by A. P. Herbert's 'Holy Deadlock' campaign in the 1930s, but nothing much had really changed since the Matrimonial Causes Act of 1857, which had moved divorce litigation from the ecclesiastical to the civil courts.

There was a widespread feeling that the State exercised too much control over the private lives of ordinary people, especially the poor who could not afford expensive lawyers or fancy doctors. This was particularly glaring in the curbs on working-class pleasures. Far from loosening in the twentieth century, these had actually been tightened. Nonconformist Liberals engineered the Street Betting Act of 1906, which outlawed the only sort of flutter open to the working man, while the upper classes continued to gamble in their clubs and over the phone to their bookies. More painful still, the Defence of the Realm Act of 1914 included a clause severely restricting the opening hours of pubs, on the grounds that too much boozing would harm the proles' contribution to the war effort. These puritanical restrictions were continued even after the sufferings of the Great War and went on unchanged after the Second World War.

As the 1960s dawned, these restrictions began to crumble. Governments felt under pressure to deliver more liberty and more choice. Most conspicuous was the arrival of commercial television in the mid-fifties. Despite Establishment efforts to reassure elite opinion by making Sir Kenneth Clark, 'Lord Clark of Civilisation' as *Private Eye* dubbed him, the first chairman of the Independent Television Authority, as the channels multiplied, their content inevitably became more popular, more irreverent, more vulgar. The public got what it wanted and switched off what it didn't, and the BBC had to chase ratings or risk losing its licence fee.

The elite had lost its self-confidence, and no longer felt that it had the right to tell people how to lead their lives or what to watch.

Besides, there might be votes in liberalization. The Conservative Party slipped into its 1959 manifesto pledges to extend licensing hours in pubs and to legalize off-course betting, thus extending to the working classes those privileges which had been freely available to the rich in their all-day drinking clubs and personal accounts with their bookmakers. These pledges were amply fulfilled in the Betting and Gaming Act of 1960 and the Licensing Act 1961, and no government since has dared to think of reversing them. Harold Macmillan was now caricatured as a bookie in loud tweeds, but he didn't care if he could secure another thumping victory like the one he got in 1959.

There were other reforms, of a more thoughtful nature, indicating a widening of sympathy in British politics, notably the Mental Health Act of 1959. The idea was, as far as possible, to take psychiatric patients out of what Enoch Powell, Minister of Health at the time, called 'those isolated, majestic, imperious asylums, brooded over by its gigantic water-tower and chimney combined, rising unmistakable and daunting out of the countryside'[1] and treat them as voluntary patients in the community. It swept away a swathe of the old Lunacy Acts, and abolished the category of 'moral imbecile', a catch-all term which had allowed vulnerable single mothers (unmarried mothers, as they were then called) to be locked up in bins without their children. The trouble was that the community facilities were not yet in place to receive the patients, who were soon seen wandering the streets, lost and disconsolate. But the trend to more humane treatment of mental illness continued, picking up from the first emergence we saw in the 1790s. Psychiatric patients were now to be treated as human beings, deserving of sympathy and dialogue.

A similar softer mindset was behind the Suicide Act of 1961, which decriminalized the act of killing yourself – always an absurdity, being the only known crime in which success renders the offender invulnerable to prosecution. Macmillan affected not to be able to see the point of it. He asked his reforming Home Secretary, Rab Butler: 'Must we really proceed with the Suicides Bill? I think we are opening ourselves to chaff if, after ten years of Tory Government, all we can do is to produce a Bill allowing people to commit suicide.'[2] But no serious objections were raised. By contrast, the objections to assistance being given deliberately to someone who wished to end his or her life remained fierce, both among religious groups and the doctors who would have to administer the lethal pill or injection, and also at first among the general public. It took another half-century of heart-wringing end-of-life stories before public opinion shifted decisively and the incoming Labour government of 2024 felt confident enough to make time for a Bill to permit assisted dying in certain carefully defined circumstances.

IT'S A PRIVATE MATTER
But the regulation of sexual behaviour was a more daunting proposition for Parliament to tackle. Even if MPs knew their own minds, which they often didn't, they were faced with the flinty opposition of all the Churches to any loosening at all. It required some hard cases and some scandalous miscarriages of justice to generate any momentum for change.

In the case of homosexual law reform, it was undoubtedly the 1954 case of Lord Montagu of Beaulieu, his cousin Michael Pitt-Rivers and the playwright Peter Wildeblood. The three of them were convicted at Winchester Assizes and sentenced to jail terms of up to 18 months for having consensual sex with a couple of young RAF men in a beach hut near Montagu's estate. They were not the only ones. It's estimated that there were over 1,000 men in jail at the time for various homosexual offences. Far from turning a blind eye, the police were increasingly haunting public lavatories and bars with an eye to detecting or even provoking misconduct. This was no accident. Orders had come from the Home Secretary himself, Sir David Maxwell Fyfe, to 'rid England of this male vice ... this plague'. As a result, prosecutions of all homosexuality offences rocketed from 1,276 in 1939 to 5,443 in 1952.[3]

But the Montagu case was the last straw. The social prominence of these offenders, the mildness of the offence and the severity of the sentence at last convinced the government that the law needed to be looked at. Sir John Wolfenden, former headmaster of Uppingham and Shrewsbury, was appointed by none other than Maxwell Fyfe to conduct a review of the laws on homosexuality and prostitution. The Home Secretary obviously thought that Wolfenden would endorse the status quo. He told Bob Boothby (himself a well-known closet bisexual) that 'I am not going down in history as the man who made sodomy legal.'[4] But Maxwell Fyfe had picked the wrong man. Wolfenden's son Jeremy, the *Daily Telegraph* correspondent in Moscow and Washington, was a brilliant, extravagant gay who probably drank himself to death. His father was therefore not unacquainted with the subject, as well as being a man of strong liberal instincts. He and his team approached their task with extreme delicacy. Wolfenden suggested that, for the sake of the ladies in the room, they should use the word Huntleys when referring to homosexuals and Palmers when referring to prostitutes, after the biscuit manufacturers. But their conclusions were robust: 'It is not, in our view, the function of law to intervene in the private lives of citizens, or to seek to enforce any particular pattern of behaviour.' This was not to be taken as a licence for homosexuals to behave exactly as they pleased, certainly not in public, but same-sex activity in private between consenting adults ought not to be illegal.

There was fierce opposition to these proposals among Conservative MPs and in the House of Lords, less so, oddly, in the national press, although columnists at the rougher end denounced 'the Pansies Charter'. Lord Denning, the most celebrated judge in the country, was in no doubt: 'The Bible calls it "an abomination"; the Statute Book describes it as an "abominable crime"; and the old lawyers, when they framed their indictments, thought it was a disgrace even to name it. So it is wrongful ... Is this conduct so wrongful and so harmful that, in the opinion of Parliament, it should be publicly condemned and, in proper cases, punished? I would say that the answer is, Yes; the law should condemn this evil, for evil it is, but the judges should be discreet in their punishment of it.'[5]

So the government funked it. Rab Butler told the Commons on 24 November 1958: 'I do not think we have yet a general sense of opinion which would regard it as right to alter the criminal law in the sense suggested by the Committee.' For the liberal-minded Butler, the emphasis was on the 'not yet'. For many of his backbench colleagues, 'never' would have been a better word. And when the Commons voted heavily against Wolfenden on a free vote by 213 to 99 on 29 June 1960, Macmillan, who found these questions of conscience an embarrassing bore, wrote in his diary with evident relief: 'this should end the Parliamentary controversy for a time.'[6]

But the debate outside Parliament had only just begun. The Report itself was the starter's pistol for an argument which was to continue for years. The opening salvo came from Sir Patrick Devlin, an eminent judge often called on by government to sort out tricky questions. In his British Academy lecture of 18 March 1959, he roundly asserted that Wolfenden had been mistaken. The law could and should intervene to suppress vice:

'an established morality is as necessary as good government to the welfare of society. Societies disintegrate from within more frequently than they are broken up by external pressures. There is disintegration when no common morality is observed and history shows that the loosening of moral bonds is often the first stage of disintegration, so that society is justified in taking the same steps to preserve its moral code as it does to preserve its government and other essential institutions. The suppression of vice is as much the law's business as the suppression of subversive activities.'[7]

This trumpet blast was replied to by Herbert Hart, Professor of Jurisprudence at Oxford. In a radio talk,[8] he argued that State power could be invoked to punish a private activity only where the test of harm to others was passed. It was not the mark of a civilized society to invoke the criminal law just because conventional morality was affronted. It was plain wrong to liken 'immoral' conduct in private to treason. In his Stanford lectures, *Law, Liberty, and Morality* (1963), Hart amplifies his attack on Devlin. 'Laws enforcing a sexual morality ... may create misery of a quite special degree. For both the difficulties involved in the repression of sexual impulses and the consequences of repression are quite different from those involved in the abstention from "ordinary" crimes.'[9] It was dangerous to invoke 'the people' and their views on crime and punishment: 'It seems fatally easy to believe that loyalty to democratic principles entails acceptance of what may be called moral populism: the view that the majority have a moral right to dictate how all shall live.'[10]

The Hart–Devlin debate was, as both men acknowledged, only a reprise of the debate a century earlier between John Stuart Mill and Virginia Woolf's uncle, James Fitzjames Stephen, whom we have already encountered as the fierce critic of Mr Popular Sentiment, alias Charles Dickens. In *On Liberty*, Mill famously laid down the doctrine: 'The only purpose for which power can rightfully be exercised over any member of a civilized community against his will is to prevent harm to others ... His own good, either physical or moral, is not a sufficient warrant.'[11]

To which Stephen, another eminent unbending judge, who like Devlin was deployed in colonial affairs, riposted in *Liberty, Equality, Fraternity* (1873): the purpose of the common law was to give 'distinct shape to the feeling of anger', felt in the community in relation to immoral conduct, and also 'distinct satisfaction to the desire for vengeance'.[12] So, not reform and rehab, or even deterrence to future immoral acts, though these might be welcome consequences, too, but unvarnished disgust and retribution.[13] Hart quotes this ferocious passage from Stephen's *A History of the Criminal Law of England*:[14] '... the infliction of punishment by law gives definite expression and solemn ratification and justification to the hatred which is excited by the commission of the offence and which constitutes the moral, or popular, as distinct from the conscientious, sanction of that part of morality which is also sanctioned by the criminal law.' The judge's sentence was like hot wax sealing the public's disapproval.

I compare these two titanic tussles to make a simple point: that in the first, the Mill–Stephen argument, in practical terms Stephen came out victorious. No Victorian Parliament would have dared to soften the laws against immorality in general, or homosexuality in particular. Only ten years after Stephen's polemic, the notorious Labouchere Amendment to the Criminal Law Amendment Act of 1885 made it illegal for any man to commit an act of 'gross indecency' with another man (women were excluded, allegedly after interference from Queen Victoria). Sodomy had always been a serious crime, subject to life imprisonment (death until 1861), but the punishment was so harsh and the offence so difficult to prove that successful prosecutions were rare. The new Act was much more enforceable. Oscar Wilde was convicted under it and sentenced to two years' hard labour; so was Alan Turing, who was sentenced to oestrogen injections as an alternative to jail; so was Sir John Gielgud as late as 1953, as were thousands of others who were picked up by police provocateurs in parks, pubs and public lavatories. The waste of police time was a minor add-on to the tide of human misery that the mercurial and unpleasant Labouchere had unleashed.

Yet only ten years after the Wolfenden recommendations had been shelved as 'politically impossible', the House of Commons, still containing many of the same MPs, passed the Sexual Offences Act of 1967 and repealed the Labouchere Amendment. Hart ultimately triumphed over Devlin.

The parliamentary manoeuvres which led to this extraordinary turnaround are fascinating. You can see the tectonic plates shifting before your eyes. After a Labour government squeaked home in 1964, the Labour MP Leo Abse introduced a Ten-Minute Rule Bill to decriminalize consensual and private sex between men over 21. The Commons voted down the First Reading by 178 over 159, a narrower margin than the vote four years earlier. In the Lords the following year, a similar Bill introduced by the eccentric badger's friend Lord Arran, 'Boofy', passed by 96 to 36, though still fiercely opposed by Maxwell Fyfe, now Lord Kilmuir. Back it came again to the Commons, after Labour had increased its majority in the 1966 election, and this time its first reading passed by 244 to 100. The government, seeing that the Bill now had the wind behind it, gave it parliamentary time, and the Bill sailed through both Houses, but always with less than half the members voting, the rest presumably lying low until they saw which way public opinion would swing. In fact, while all this was going on, the polls were mostly showing strong majorities in favour of decriminalization.

By contrast, before the Act, the public attitude towards homosexuality appeared to be straightforwardly punitive. In September 1957, 82 per cent were in favour of imprisonment for homosexual acts; in December 1958, Gallup found that 48 per cent backed the government's reluctance to change the law. But attitudes were to relax quite swiftly. By 1977, 58 per cent thought that sex between consenting adult men should be legal; by 1992, it was 65 per cent. Attitudes to gay marriage then began to shift, too, from 57–32 against in 1993 to 62–31 pro by 2012. Half the nation used to think that homosexual conduct was always wrong; by 2012, that figure was down to 22 per cent. The nuances were also changing. In 1983, the public thought that gays were not acceptable as teachers by a margin of 53–41 (had they never looked at their own teachers or their children's?); by 2012, 83 per cent were in favour of gay teachers, with only 14 per cent against.[15]

We may hesitantly conclude that, at the start of the period, people had a rather unthinking revulsion, without having given the issue much thought; but as voters were brought closer to the realities, they took a more nuanced and eventually more relaxed position. I have already mentioned how the memorable impact of Dirk Bogarde's performance in the film *Victim* (1961) helped to awaken public opinion to the traumatic consequences of the existing law. Certainly, there was no serious opposition in the country to the Act when it came into force, and little organized attempt to repeal it (there were a few fogeyish grumbles about the triumphalist extravagance of Gay Pride marches). MPs and sportsmen began to out themselves with increasing nonchalance. By and large, the unregenerate homophobes began to crawl into the closet which the gays had lately vacated. Within the space of a half a century, it was homophobia that had become the passion that dare not speak its name.

We need not posit at this stage a wholesale public conversion to the cause of gay rights. What was surely happening was a slow swelling of sympathy for the misery which the current law was causing to countless people, who might include a friend or neighbour whom you knew to be a law-abiding and decent person. It was to take another 30 years before the State recognized civil partnerships and accorded them most of the duties and privileges of heterosexual marriage, such as freedom from inheritance tax. It was a further ten years before the law recognized same-sex marriages in 2013. Here there was rather stiffer opposition, especially from the Church of England, which still refuses to celebrate them. When the Church in Wales did vote in September 2021 at least to bless same-sex marriages, my local vicar in South Pembrokeshire resigned and founded a breakaway Church in protest, which has attracted a sizeable congregation. Within the Conservative Party there remained until recently a large remnant of the majority that had voted for Section 28 of the Local Government Act 1988, which prohibited 'the promotion of homosexuality' by local authorities. Section 28 certainly had a chilling effect on public gay activity, but even at the time it looked like a rearguard action, and it was repealed by the Blair government in 2003, after a Commons vote of 368–76.

What the opinion polls and MPs' postbags showed was a slow but unmistakable softening in public opinion on social issues. A large number of voters, on some issues the majority, were no longer happy to see the State inflicting punishments for behaviour which they might themselves not wholly approve of but which did not seem to threaten the safety or the moral health of the nation. People were increasingly aware, too, that the State could make mistakes, ruin lives or, in the case of capital punishment, end lives after a miscarriage of justice or a disproportionate sentence. In short, public opinion was shifting more in the direction of John Stuart Mill and Herbert Hart and away from James Fitzjames Stephen and Patrick Devlin.

It took several equally hard cases to generate the momentum which led to the abolition of capital punishment in 1965. There had been vigorous campaigns against hanging for years, and even a

Royal Commission (1949–53), which hummed and hawed, pointing out the flaws in the status quo, and complaining that they had been asked 'to find some sort of practical half-way house between the present scope of the death penalty and its abolition', but that 'the object of our quest is chimerical and must be abandoned'. The chairman, Sir Ernest Gowers, a leading civil servant remembered as the author of *Plain Words*, said that what he had learned had converted him from vague support of capital punishment to strong opposition (a similar mental process affected several Home Secretaries who had the ghastly task of deciding whether or not to commute a death sentence).

During these years, three notorious executions further raised public doubts whether, even if you instinctively favoured the principle of 'a life for a life', it was possible to apply the extreme penalty with any certainty of justice: the hanging in 1950 of Timothy Evans for the murder of his wife and infant daughter, when it later emerged that his downstairs neighbour John Christie had strangled six women and eventually admitted to the murder of Mrs Evans, too; the hanging of Derek Bentley in January 1953 for murdering a policeman in the course of a burglary, although it was his accomplice Christopher Craig (who was only 16, thus too young to hang) who actually fired the shot, and all Bentley did was to shout 'let him have it, Chris' – which could have meant 'give him the gun' rather than 'kill him'. The jury recommended mercy, but neither the judge in the case, the fearsome Lord Goddard, nor the Home Secretary, the fearsome Sir David Maxwell Fyfe again, was prepared to exercise it. Both Timothy Evans and Derek Bentley were chaotic and subnormal characters. The third case, that of Ruth Ellis, raised a different set of doubts. She was a nightclub hostess who had been abused by several men, and she eventually pumped six bullets into her last, equally abusive and faithless lover, the racing driver David Blakely. The jury took only 20 minutes to find her guilty, and on 13 July 1955 she became the last woman in Britain to be hanged. The details of her sad story evoked such public interest that the issue was discussed in Cabinet, though we do not know what was said. A petition for clemency to the Home Office was signed by 50,000 people (in the internet age, that figure would surely have run into millions). Ruth's son Andy, then aged ten, committed suicide in his thirties. The trial judge, Sir Cecil Havers, sent money every year for Andy's upkeep, and the prosecuting counsel, Christmas Humphreys, paid for Andy's funeral. Thus the trial and execution of Ruth Ellis continued to trouble the conscience even of those responsible for it. The story inspired numerous films, books and plays, notably *Dance with a Stranger*, directed by Mike Newell with Miranda Richardson as Ruth.

It was to be another ten years before capital punishment was abolished, and even afterwards opinion polls continued to show strong support for the principle. Maxwell Fyfe was as hostile to abolition as he had been to homosexual liberation; it would, he said, be 'an unwise and dangerous measure, the presence of which on the statute book would be a disaster for the country and a menace to the people'. For years afterwards, backbench MPs made regular efforts to bring back capital punishment, but none of them got anywhere. In practice, the nation had lost any serious will to restore the rope.

In the same way, there had been lobbying for years to reform the stern laws prohibiting abortion under any circumstances so as to reflect the way people actually lived, most flagrantly, the fact that the poor had to resort to the uncertain skills of the back-street abortionist, while the well-off were looked after in private clinics, their illegal operations being covered under various medical euphemisms. The Abortion Law Reform Association had been founded back in 1936, but had made little headway in Parliament. The disapproval of all the Churches deterred most MPs from thinking of raising the subject. But when Harold Wilson's government took up the cause of reform, spearheaded by the Liberal MP David Steel, opposition subsided in a remarkably short time, and a Bill permitting abortion in certain widely defined circumstances passed through Parliament and has never been seriously challenged since, although the time limit of how many weeks of pregnancy termination should be permitted up to continues to be fought over.

It all happened in a remarkably brief space, but the polling evidence suggests that public attitudes towards abortion had always been flexible and attentive to circumstance. For example, in 1962, NOP (National Opinion Polls) found that 73 per cent would be in favour of allowing termination where the baby might be likely to be born with a serious deformity; 81 per cent where the pregnancy was the result of rape. Opinion was evenly divided in 1964 on the more contentious cases in which the mother could not cope with more children: 49 per cent against, 44 per cent for; by 1967, 65 per cent answered Yes to this question. Those who thought abortion should always be illegal seldom rose above a quarter of those polled.[16] Polls taken after the Act increasingly supported 'abortion on demand' and 'a woman's right to choose'. The feeling that a woman's body was her own affair was always present and often voiced forcefully in interviews. It only required these sympathies to spread more generally for the legal change to acquire the necessary momentum. The debate still continues in and out of Parliament on how late in pregnancy a termination should be carried out, and the Society for the Protection of Unborn Children, set up to oppose the 1967 Act, continues to argue its case just as passionately. In the United States, the debate rages as fiercely as ever, but in the UK the issue is largely regarded as settled.

Three of the loosenings of the law that I have already mentioned are among the most startling in all our social history: the abolition of capital punishment, the legalization of homosexuality and the legalization of abortion. In any century, these would have been spectacular innovations in the moral and legal code. For them to happen together within three years is simply mind-blowing. But there is a fourth reform, no less startling to us, but not entirely new, though it had been fought for, off and on, for at least three centuries: the recovery of the ancient freedom to divorce.

That is not how the story is usually told. The common view is that the right to divorce your spouse is something distinctively modern. But it isn't. In almost all ancient societies, legal codes permit divorce at will, and usually lay down equitable conditions for it to happen. In medieval Ireland and Wales, for example, and among the Anglo-Saxons, couples might freely divorce, after fair arrangements for the division of the goods and custody of the children. The Churches' control over divorce was only imposed painfully and over centuries and was to be relinquished no less painfully. The Renaissance humanists and the seventeenth-century Puritans were already protesting against the new repressive laws, none more forcefully than John Milton in his broadside *The Doctrine and Discipline of Divorce*. Yes, practical arrangements for the disposal of assets needed to be legally scrutinized, but in the last resort the decision belonged to the unhappy couple: 'the absolute and final hindering of divorce cannot belong to any civil or earthly power, against the will and consent of both parties, or of the husband alone.'[17] This, Milton claimed, was the true English tradition and must not be forgotten: 'Let not England forget her precedence of teaching nations how to live.' How many people who have quoted that glorious boast remember that it occurs in the introduction to a passionate plea for divorce by consent?

It was to take another three centuries for this boast to be made good. There had been reforms in the intervening years: the Matrimonial Causes Act of 1937, for example, which extended the grounds of divorce to include cruelty, insanity and desertion, as a result of A. P. Herbert's spirited campaign against 'Holy Deadlock'; and the introduction of legal aid for divorce in 1950 extended the possibility of getting unmarried to the worst off. But still divorce had to be sued for; it was not a right. Although they had been together for a decade or more, my school friend John's parents were never able to get married, because his father's first wife refused him a divorce, although the father was a prosperous banker and his mother was a leading light at the BBC.

It's easy, too, to forget now how stiff the social disapproval of divorce and divorcees used to be. Until 1955, divorcees were forbidden admission to the Royal Enclosure at Ascot, a ban which, if extended, would in time have excluded three of the Queen's four children. The Queen herself, early in her reign, had several notorious criminals strolling around the Enclosure pointed out to her and expressed surprise that they should be allowed in, and not divorcees. Officers in the better regiments had to offer their resignations to their Commanding Officers if they proposed to get divorced. Divorce ruined many a political career. Despite her rampaging affair with Robert Boothby, Harold Macmillan never thought of divorcing Lady Dorothy for fear of the political fallout. Anthony Eden's divorce would have stopped him becoming PM if he had not persuaded his wife to pretend that she was the 'guilty party'. Which did not prevent Eden, a notorious womanizer, from taking a stern line when Princess Margaret wanted to marry the divorced equerry Captain Peter Townsend, threatening to cut off her civil list allowance if she went ahead. Eden was abetted by the hard-faced Archbishop of Canterbury, Geoffrey Fisher, who was worried that the C of E was going soft on divorce. Divorced Anglicans were forbidden to remarry in church until 2002. Divorced Catholics are not even permitted to receive Holy Communion, unless they have secured an annulment of their first marriage, a devious and costly procedure only available to the well-off.

The 1969 Act was a decisive turning point. In future, couples were free to divorce after being separated for two years, if both partners agreed, or after five years if only one of them wanted to divorce. No longer did one partner have to prove the other at fault. The breakdown of the marriage was all the proof that was needed. Just as it was the couple who had freely decided to take the marriage vows, so now they were free to dissolve those vows, whatever Church or State might think. It was a remarkable recovery of human liberty.

Naturally, the Act led to a considerable increase in the number of divorces, which led its opponents to denounce the new law as a positive incitement to split. But anyone who looked around them could see perfectly well that the initial effect was mostly to expose the large number of unhappy marriages which had been dragging on under the old regime without hope of dissolution. Of course, the reform did not put an end to the unbearable pain and misery that men and women are capable of inflicting on each other. But at least the State no longer compounded the misery.

With the passing of the 1969 Act, the Permissive Society was well and truly born. If people were now free to publish or perform whatever they fancied, if they could follow their own sexual preferences without fear of arrest, if women could decide whether or not they were willing to bear a child, if men and women could choose to unmarry as freely as they had chosen to marry, then they could be said to be fully in charge of their private lives, and would henceforth have the freedom to make a success of them or mess them up without the State breathing down their necks.

The curious thing is what happened next in public debate, which was nothing very much. The term 'permissive society' was first bandied about by those who hated it, and then, as with 'Tories' and 'Methodists', by those who supported it. The collection of essays entitled *The Permissive Society*, published in 1969, was mostly written by cautious supporters of the new freedoms, such as Margaret Drabble, who believed that 'emancipation is now a reality, and we ought to be entering on the golden age of free adult sexual equality and companionship that feminists fought for'.[18] From 1960 onwards, columnists in the conservative tabloids went on warning, like Robert Pitman, of 'a long, apathetic slide into national decadence', as had happened in ancient Rome.[19] Forty years later, Lynda Lee-Potter in the *Daily Mail* was still warning that 'a lost generation' of young people needed to be saved from 'a horrific maelstrom of permissiveness'.[20] Paul Johnson, also in the *Daily Mail*, not only blamed the Twin Towers attack of 2001 on liberals for their mollycoddling of terrorists but predicted that the atrocity would 'pull down the curtain on a century of liberalism and permissiveness' and usher in a new 'Age of Reaction, when the clock was put firmly back to severity and discipline'.[21] No such thing happened or ever looked like happening. There was little or no organized resistance to the Permissive Society, apart from that generated by a lone Midlands housewife, Mrs Mary Whitehouse, and her National Viewers' and Listeners' Association. Her campaign, mostly focused on pornography and bad language on TV, attracted virtually no support from anyone of influence. As Marcus Collins points out, 'the problem with such reactionary sentiments was that anti-permissives had no usable past to which to return'.[22] Even Norman Tebbit, normally a reliable mouthpiece of the discontents of the right, cautioned against trying to 'put back the clock'.[23] All that proved was that once again Evelyn Waugh was right when he remarked that 'the Conservative party have never put the clock back a single second'. The Permissive Society was here to stay, for good or ill. In their private lives at least, men and women would be free to follow their hearts, not compelled to follow the rules. The happiness of the individual would take precedence over the preservation of public morals.

IT'S A CRIME TO DISCRIMINATE

But the so-called Permissive Society did not permit everything. On the contrary, it came down increasingly hard on discrimination, in whatever form it might crop up. If people had a right to make their own decisions in their private lives, so they had also a right to be treated equally in public matters. And very often it was the same people who had objected to the new permissive laws who also objected to the new Acts outlawing discrimination. The Race Relations Act of 1965 had already made it an offence to discriminate in public places or to promote hatred, on grounds of 'colour, race, or ethnic or national origins'. It had also created the offence of 'incitement to racial hatred'. But it specifically excluded shops and private boarding houses, so only places of public resort, such as pubs, were covered. There were successful prosecutions under the Act, such as the jailing for 18 months of Colin Jordan, leader of the British National Party. But it was generally felt that the Act was a rather feeble first response to what was clearly a growing challenge, with over a million coloured immigrants already arrived and more coming in all the time. So three years later, the Wilson government brought in another Race Relations Bill, extending the law to the crucial areas of housing and employment, the idea being to make sure that immigrants had an equal chance to make a decent life for themselves in the UK.

It was this Bill that provided the provocation for Enoch Powell's notorious 'Rivers of Blood' speech in Birmingham on

April 20, 1968. Powell himself had no doubt about the impact the speech would make. He told a friend that 'it's going to go up, "fizz" like a rocket, but whereas all rockets fall to earth, this one is going to stay up'. And it did, for a generation at least.

The speech's theme was simple. If present trends continued, within 15 or 20 years, there would be three and a half million Commonwealth immigrants and their descendants in Britain. This was transforming the country beyond recognition. The inflow must be stopped, and outflow promoted by the encouragement of voluntary repatriation. Of course, all who are in the country as citizens should be equal before the law and there should be no discrimination by public authorities. But this does not mean 'that the citizen should be denied his right to discriminate in the management of his own affairs between one fellow citizen and another or that he should be subjected to imposition as to his reason and motive for behaving in one lawful manner rather than another'.

According to Powell, the Race Relations Bill was a pernicious mistake, like 'throwing a match on to gunpowder'. The existing population found themselves 'strangers in their own country'. Ordinary English people had 'the sense of being a persecuted minority'. Powell quotes a middle-aged working man as saying that 'in this country in fifteen or twenty years time, the black man will have the whip hand over the white man'. For these inflammatory remarks, Ted Heath sacked Powell from the Shadow Cabinet, Smithfield porters marched in his defence and he became a cult hero/villain for the rest of his long life.

What I want to stress here is that the principal thrust of Powell's remarks was directed not so much on the need to stem the inflow and promote the outflow of coloured immigrants. He scarcely said a word as to how either goal was to be achieved. What he concentrated his fire on was the Race Relations Bill to outlaw discrimination and promote harmony. Discrimination in favour of one's own kind was, he implied, natural, even healthy, and we should sympathize with those who felt persecuted for doing so. He uttered not a word of sympathy for the immigrants who were thus demonized as The Other, and he showed no interest at all in what they might be feeling.

Following in Powell's footsteps, the right wing's speciality became, not to attack immigration in itself but to denounce anti-racism as an unnatural interference with the right of 'ordinary people' to prefer their ain folk. Sir Roger Scruton argued as late as 2015 that 'all coherent societies are based on discrimination: A society is an "in-group", however large and hospitable to newcomers.'[24]

Powell's memorable salvo against what was to be dubbed by its critics 'the race relations industry' was followed by a series of reactive eruptions every time the government tried to level up opportunities for the disadvantaged, culminating in the Equalities Act of 2010, which outlawed discrimination on grounds of gender, religion, sexual orientation and disability as well as colour of skin and ethnic origin. This time, the principal opponents were the Churches, who feared they might be prosecuted for refusing to sanction gay marriage or women priests. But these grumbles have lost much of their force. You have only to look at faces round the Cabinet table or in the House of Commons to see that the battle against racism is well on the way to being won.

And so was the battle against sexual discrimination. The years that followed were to see a progressive fulfilment of the views that Mill had put forward not only in On Liberty but also in The Subjection of Women (1869), which he co-wrote with his wife Harriet Taylor, who had herself published an earlier essay on the subject, The Enfranchisement of Women (1851). The argument is a simple one and to us today familiar, even stale: 'that the legal subordination of one sex to another is wrong in itself, and now one of the chief hindrances to human improvement, and that it ought to be replaced by a system of perfect equality, admitting no power and privilege on the one side, nor disability on the other'. It is not the case that there was no improvement in the position of women between 1869 and 1969. There was a great deal. It was in these years that women gained the vote, after all, at first women over 30, and then 'the flappers' vote for women over 21, in 1930. Women could now go to Oxford and Cambridge universities, though only to colleges reserved for women. They could become medical doctors and barristers (though not yet judges). But in other aspects of life, the barriers to female advancement remained daunting, still policed by stern rearguards of professional misogynists.

Mill's ultimate triumph was to encompass huge advances in liberty and openness for both sexes. The rights, feelings and aspirations of all categories of people – women and children, prisoners and lunatics, immigrants and people with disabilities – now had to be taken into proper consideration by the law and by society.

The Equal Pay Act of 1970 was one of the first fruits of this new attitude. It's hard to imagine now that men and women could be paid wildly different wages for doing the same work. The trade unions had agitated for years to name and shame workplaces where women were paid grossly inferior wages for doing work equivalent to that performed by men. The Kennedy administration in the US had already passed an Equal Pay Act in 1963. In Britain, the immediate trigger was the Ford sewing machinists' strike in 1968. The women who sewed the car seat covers at Dagenham walked out when their jobs were regraded to give them 15 per cent less than men who had previously been paid the same for work considered equivalently skilled. The question of what was and wasn't equivalent work provoked a flood of strikes and lawsuits to enforce the Act in different offices and factories.

Equal pay was only one aspect of the women's movement's demands for full equality and participation. In horse racing, for example, in the 1970s after years of struggle women gained the right to hold a trainer's licence in their own names and to ride in races against male jockeys. They were constantly told that they just weren't strong enough – an argument which received its final comeuppance when Rachael Blackmore won the Cheltenham Gold Cup, the Champion Hurdle and the Grand National in the space of two years. Athletics was equally dour about letting women in. There was no Women's Marathon in the Olympic Games until

1984 and no race for women longer than 800 metres until 1972. In 1921, the Football Association actually banned women's teams from playing on their pitches, although women's football was already hugely popular, almost as popular as it has become today. The ban lasted until 1971.

In commerce, the barriers came down equally slowly. Although women had been canny investors and merchants for centuries, they were admitted as full members of the London Stock Exchange only in 1973. About the same time, women started being admitted to the men's colleges at Oxford and Cambridge. I must confess to being surprised how tamely those crusty old misogynists submitted to the invasion. The women's colleges went unisex, too, a little more reluctantly perhaps, suspicious that their hard-won access to higher education might be jeopardized by an irruption of mansplaining know-alls. But in a year or two, it was as though single-sex colleges had never existed.

This should not prevent us from recalling what a mountain women had had to climb. The legendary constitutionalist A. V. Dicey, for example, was not alone in believing that women simply were 'physically and probably mentally weaker than men'. It was absurd to think that women could ever become police officers, governors of jails or coastguards, let alone judges and Cabinet ministers: 'women of pre-eminent goodness are often lacking in the virtues, such as active courage, firmness of judgment, self-control, steadiness of conduct, and, above all, a certain sense of justice maintained even in the heat of party conflict, which are often to be found in Englishmen even of an ordinary type.'[25]

Such inflexible male chauvinists were deaf to John Stuart Mill's argument in *The Subjection of Women* that it was impossible to know in advance what women could and could not do: 'I deny that anyone knows or can know the nature of the two sexes, as long as they have only been seen in their present relation to one another. Until conditions of equality exist, no one can possibly assess the natural differences between men and women, distorted as they have been. What is natural to the two sexes can only be found out by allowing both to develop and use their faculties freely.'

For decades, men were, by and large, reluctant to give women the chance to show their paces. Misogyny was an unlovely combination of fear and contempt that was hard to break down. Women would have to fight every step of the way. And they did. But eventually, by painfully slow degrees, sympathy seeped in. These were, after all, not alien creatures: they were mothers, sisters, daughters, wives. To go back to the race course, they had seen them out on the gallops. They knew what they could do.

There is one other thing that Mill wants to make clear. When he speaks up for liberty, he is not claiming that liberty is the only principle that matters in life. We should care what happens to our fellow human beings and do whatever we can to help them:

'It would be a great misunderstanding of this doctrine to suppose that it is one of selfish indifference which pretend that human beings have no business with each other's conduct in life and that they should not concern themselves about the well-doing or well-being of one another unless their own interest is involved ... Human beings owe to each other help to distinguish the better from the worse and encouragement to choose the former and avoid the latter.'[26]

Of course, encouragement can shade into incentive, advice into prohibition. Does not all this run perilously close to coercing people against harming themselves? Yes, of course it does, and it verges on inconsistency with Mill's guiding principle. He was, after all, no more flawless than any other philosopher. He was, in particular, blind to the terrible mayhem that malicious speech could cause, especially racial hate speech. This was partly because he was incorrigibly racist, inheriting his father's contempt for India and the Indians. In fact he introduces *On Liberty* with a blanket exclusion of 'those backward states of society', for whom 'despotism is a legitimate mode of government'.

But I don't think we can criticize him too much for inconsistency about when it is and is not legitimate for the State to protect people from harm. For, as Mill's contemporary Ralph Waldo Emerson declared, 'a foolish consistency is the hobgoblin of little minds'. The point about sympathy is that it is capable of stretching a point. Mill's principles are not free-floating absolutes. They inflect according to context and circumstance.

The Third Sentimental Revolution is not a callous free-for-all. On the contrary, it is characterized by an ongoing desire to protect the public from clear and avoidable harm, including self-harm, by any means that seem sensible and proportionate: persuasion, incentive, regulation, even prohibition. It is this unmistakable tendency of the past half-century which has been dubbed by its opponents 'the nanny state'. To which we might reply that a kind and thoughtful nanny is worth having around.

The gradual introduction of speed limits and traffic lights on the roads over the past 80 years has reduced road accidents to a fraction of their level in the 1930s, despite the huge increase in traffic. The compulsory wearing of safety belts in cars and crash helmets on motorbikes has likewise reduced the number of deaths and life-changing injuries. All these safety measures were vigorously opposed at the time of their introduction by the robust type of libertarian. The same goes for the warnings against smoking cigarettes and the gradual moves towards prohibition. Roger Scruton, so stern against the perils of immigration and diluting the nation state, was happy to accept £50,000 a year from the tobacco companies to promote the freedom to smoke tobacco. Similarly, the cause of legalizing drugs has attracted carefree libertarians for decades, despite the known perils of opioids and even of the souped-up varieties of marijuana.

My purpose here is not to defend every intervention by the State. The laws may in some cases be ill-aimed or oppressive, but what they show is that governments these days are far from indifferent to the flourishing of their citizens. Indeed, they are much more protective than governments before the war.

MURDERED FOR A SONG

And what is this background music that has been playing all this time? The same years that we have been charting the progress of all this social legislation also saw the greatest explosion of popular music in history, beginning in the early 1960s and carrying on fortissimo until the end of the century and beyond. There had been nothing like it since the sudden blossoming of the troubadours in Provence three-quarters of a millennium earlier. But this was on a global scale, magnified a thousand times by the new technologies of sound. The airwaves were soon swamped by the all-conquering twang of the electric guitar. Almost as significant as the Beatles first LP was the arrival on TV of *Top of the Pops* a year later, and on radio the advent of Radio One in 1967 to compete with the pirate radio stations which had left the poor old BBC Light Programme floundering. It is often forgotten now (certainly the BBC itself tries to forget) how suspicious the Beeb was of the new pop music. The grim shadow of Lord Reith haunted the programmers, who only now and then reluctantly allowed 20 minutes of the deplorable caterwauling on air. Vera Lynn, already voted the Forces' Sweetheart, had her radio show taken off air after the fall of Singapore in February 1942, out of fear that her sentimental songs would undermine the 'virile' nature of the troops overseas to whom she was broadcasting. Barely believably, seven years later, the BBC dropped her next show, claiming that there was no demand for her 'sob stuff'. So she took her show off to Radio Luxembourg instead. Soon the music lover also had an array of personal portable sound systems to choose from, notably the Sony Walkman from 1979 and then Apple's iPhone in 2007. So dominant did pop music become that the culture sections in the broadsheets began referring to it simply as Music, with a smaller section, usually on a later page, reserved for Classical Music.

Pop stars became not just celebrated but the new *prominenti* of society, their wealth, their break-ups, their brushes with the law all headline news. As the supply of heroes from the Second World War began to run out, even quite peripheral figures from the pop world took their place in the obituary columns, for example, the half-page allotted in *The Times* to a pop journalist whose principal achievement was to have introduced Elvis to the Beatles.[27]

What we take for granted now is that Pop Music should be almost entirely Popular Song. Again, not since the troubadours had the *vox humana* so dominated the musical scene. There was always music written for the voice, both sacred and secular: folk song and plainsong, cantatas and operas and oratorios. But the peaks of Western music were shared with if not overshadowed by instrumental music — the symphonies of Beethoven and Mozart, Bach's Brandenburg Concertos, Vivaldi's Four Seasons and so on.

By contrast, pop music is almost entirely pop song and almost entirely love song. Take the first edition of *Top of the Pops*, recorded in Manchester, and presented by Jimmy Savile (he also presented the last show in 2006 — what a terrifying run), and screened on New Year's Day 1964. It opened with Dusty Springfield singing 'I Only Want To Be With You', followed by the Rolling Stones with 'I Wanna Be Your Man' (actually written by the Beatles), and finishing with that week's No. 1, the Beatles' 'I Want To Hold Your Hand'. In its heyday, the show's viewing figures climbed to a barely credible 15 million. Never before can Desire with a capital D have been so passionately broadcast to so many people.

On their first LP, Lennon and McCartney are already exploring all the varieties of lovers' plaints through the ages: why don't you return my love? ('Please Please Me'); I've lost her and I'm doomed to unhappiness ('Misery'); love at first sight ('I Saw Her Standing There'); you're the only love I've ever had ('Ask Me Why'); I'll always be true ('Love Me Do'); treasure this letter till we meet again ('PS I Love You'); my sorrow won't last for ever ('There's A Place').

In the 200 songs they wrote and performed over the ten years until they broke up in 1970, other subjects make occasional appearances: piquant or poignant characters, such as *Lovely Rita Meter Maid*, the *Taxman*, *Nowhere Man*, and of course *Eleanor Rigby*; or general themes like the passage of time — *Will You Still Need Me, Will You Still Feed Me, When I'm Sixty-Four?*. But again and again they return to the subject of love and the boy—girl relationship. Tenderness never ceases to be the dominant theme.

Some of the songs are gay, some are sad, some aggrieved, some are consoling, none more so than 'Hey Jude'. Paul McCartney originally called the song 'Hey Jules', it being written to console the five-year-old Julian Lennon after his father had gone off with Yoko Ono. As 'Hey Jude', it retained the haunting, melancholy tone of the original

– 'take a sad song and make it better'. The song was No. 1 all over the English-speaking world and in 1968 tied the all-time record for longest run at the top of the US charts. It has gone on to become something close to an alternative national anthem. McCartney sang it at the Queen's Jubilee in 2002 and also during the last moments of the opening ceremony at the London Olympics in 2012. Yet the song has no hint of national celebration; 'Land of Hope and Glory' it isn't, still less the Marseillaise. It still carries a personal message of comfort intended for a five-year-old child.

Just before McCartney closed out 'The Party at the Palace' with 'Hey Jude', he led what might be called the royal family of rock – Rod Stewart, Joe Cocker, Queen, Eric Clapton, Cliff Richard (several of them now knighted, as are the two surviving Beatles) – in 'All You Need Is Love'. Earlier in the day, bands in towns all over the United Kingdom had also struck up 'All You Need Is Love', before church bells were rung to celebrate the fiftieth anniversary of the Queen's Coronation. The concert attracted a worldwide audience of 200 million.

But it is 'Hey Jude' that lingers in the memory, particularly when the crowd of a million in the Mall joined in that warm, witless, endless lullaby of a chorus – na -na-na-na-na ... Even the human-hand-like leaves of the plane trees along the Mall seemed to be shivering in time with the song. That day, 3 June 2002, can be ranked as one of the high points of the Third Sentimental Revolution, a day in which love, not duty or courage or patriotism, was officially recognized as the nation's core value.

Other pop groups have stayed together longer than the Beatles, some much longer. Blur, formed in 1988, is still going strong, after a long hiatus. Oasis lasted 18 years and, according to the headlines, is re-forming as I write. The Rolling Stones have gone on touring into their seventh amazing decade. Pop journalists and cultural critics are often more interested in punk and heavy metal and the other 'grittier' genres of rock music, which are deemed somehow more authentic because they are 'transgressive' in some way, as compared with the Beatles' supposedly sentimental, even bland output. But I would strongly assert that the Beatles were and remain the *decisive* pop group. It is their work which has left the most lasting impact on the emotional life of the nation, often in ways which are surprising or not immediately apparent.

Despite their simple words and often equally simple melodies, Beatles songs often seem to carry a mysterious emotional charge out of all proportion to their lack of pretension. The most bizarre, in fact horrific, example of this was the 1968 'Helter Skelter', written by McCartney in quite a different vein from 'Hey Jude'. In fact, he later said that it was his answer to those critics who said that he could only write sentimental ballads and that he was the soppy one of the four. He wanted to make 'Helter Skelter' as 'loud and dirty' as possible. He succeeded more than he could possibly have intended. Not only did 'Helter Skelter' come to be regarded as an influence on the development of heavy metal; it was also taken up by the serial killer Charles Manson, who told his befuddled followers that 'Helter Skelter' and several other songs in the Beatles so-called *White Album* of 1968 formed a coded prophecy of an apocalyptic war in the United States between racists and non-racists over the treatment of the blacks. The two sides would exterminate each other, leaving Manson and his 'Family' to emerge from their underground city and rule over the blacks, who would be too hopeless to govern the country. McCartney apologized for this weird interpretation: 'Unfortunately it inspired people to do evil deeds' — but this did not deter him or numerous other celebrated singers from continuing to belt out the blistering number.

'Helter Skelter' is not the only example recorded of a pop song provoking crazy people to commit murder. In the Philippines, the singing of 'My Way' in karaoke bars has led to numerous killings. Admittedly, even when sung by Frank Sinatra, it's a profoundly irritating song with its unabashed self-congratulation, and when sung out of tune in a crowded bar is obviously liable to lead to a punch-up, but the number of murders it has caused, now running into double figures, remains remarkable. The only multiple shooting provoked by a song seems to have occurred in Thailand in 2008, when a man in a karaoke bar shot eight people dead, including his brother-in-law, after hearing John Denver's 'Take Me Home, Country Roads' murdered once too often. But the most celebrated murder for a song took place, not in a low dive but out in the open street, and the perpetrator appears to have been quite sober at the time.

The break-up of John Lennon's marriage coincided, not only with the break-up of the Beatles but also with his new enthusiasm for left-wing politics. The first album he co-produced with Yoko Ono, in 1970, contained the fiery number 'Working Class Hero'. The song begins 'As soon as you're born, they make you feel small.' The last number on the album was 'God', which opens 'God is a concept by which measures our pain', and carries on with a list of things and people Lennon doesn't believe in, which includes magic, the Bible, Hitler, Jesus, Kennedy, Buddha, Elvis, Zimmerman (Bob Dylan) and the Beatles. The last line is 'The Dream is over.'

During this energetic left-wing phase, Lennon chummed up with the New Left group who ran the magazine *Black Dwarf*, notably Tariq Ali. After they had got to know each other, Lennon asked Tariq down to his new country house, Tittenhurst Park, Ascot, to hear his new LP. Tariq brought with him Régis Debray, who had just been released from a Bolivian jail and whom Lennon hadn't yet heard of. Tittenhurst is a superb Georgian mansion set in rolling parkland, and it was in these opulent surroundings that Lennon sang his new composition, 'Imagine', to these two celebrated firebrands. When he had finished, he asked what they thought. Tariq had a pretend consultation with Debray and the historian Robin Blackburn who had come, too, and then said, 'Yes, the Politburo approves. It can go out.' Later, when he was alone with Lennon, Tariq said he thought the song would touch people, but it was a bit too sugary and he preferred 'Working-Class Hero'. Lennon said he did, too, and himself said a few years later that you had 'to put your political message across with a little honey'. A few months afterwards, Lennon rang Tariq to say that he and Yoko were moving to the States to try and reclaim her daughter who had been kidnapped by Yoko's former husband. Tariq said, 'don't go, there are too many kooky people there'.[28]

But the song took off into the stratosphere. It was often voted the finest song of the past hundred years, and the magazine *Rolling Stone* called it 'Lennon's greatest musical gift to the world.' It was to be performed by all sorts of great artists such as Stevie Wonder and Diana Ross and was included in the closing ceremony of the London Olympics and at numerous other international events.

The piquancy of a multi-millionaire asking his audience to imagine 'a world with no possessions' did not escape some of his listeners. Elton John asked them instead to imagine six apartments, one full of fur coats and another full of shoes.

Yet Elton regularly sang 'Imagine' during his world tour of 1980, after Lennon's death. On 9 October 1990, more than a billion people are estimated to have listened to a recording of the song on what would have been Lennon's fiftieth birthday. Its vision of an entirely secular utopia has never lost its appeal: no heaven, only the sky above; no nations, no religions, no wars, no greed or hunger, only a brotherhood of man: 'Imagine all the people sharing all the world.'

Mark David Chapman had been a keen admirer of Lennon's music. Born in Texas in 1955, the son of a staff sergeant in the US Air Force, he was taking drugs and dropping out of school from the age of 14. But he pulled himself together and became a born-again Presbyterian and an outstanding counsellor at summer camps. He moved to Chicago and then worked with Vietnamese refugees at a resettlement camp in Arkansas, where again his work was said to be outstanding. He attended meetings with government officials and shook hands with President Ford. However, he dropped out of college again and attempted suicide. Then he returned to religion and was an active participant in prayer groups. It was at this time that he developed a lasting obsession with J. D. Salinger's novel *The Catcher in the Rye*. The novel's hero Holden Caulfield, with his detestation of 'phoniness' and 'crap' of every description, became his role model. Which in turn led to his anger with Lennon's hypocrisy in 'Imagine': 'He told us to imagine no possessions and there he was, with millions of dollars and yachts and farms and country estates, laughing at people like me who had believed the lies and bought the records and built a big part of their lives around his music.' How Chapman would have hated the cosy performance of 'Imagine' at Tittenhurst Park. He also objected strongly to 'God': 'I just wanted to scream out loud, "Who does he think he is, saying these things about God and heaven and the Beatles?" Saying that he doesn't believe in Jesus and things like that.' Soon he was telling his wife Gloria that he had been obsessed with killing Lennon, showing her the gun and bullets. And on 8 December 1980 he went to Lennon's apartment at the Dakota Building on West 72nd Street, and shot him in the street five times with a .38 revolver. He remained at the scene, and when NYPD police officers arrived to arrest him, he was found peacefully reading *The Catcher in the Rye*. Chapman was found guilty of murder and has since been denied parole 13 times, despite apologizing for his 'premeditated, selfish and evil crime'. He remains in jail, now aged 69.

So John Lennon was murdered for a song, or, rather, two songs, his insult to religion being just as provocative as the humbug of 'Imagine'. Obviously Chapman would seem to fit into the conventional image of a lone assassin, the sort of kook that Tariq had warned Lennon about: a solitary, unstable character, subject to psychotic episodes, drink and drugs and bouts of religious fervor. But he did have an argument, a *casus belli*, if you like. And it is an argument subscribed to, in much milder form, by many people who have been deeply annoyed by the song. For it brings together in a few skipping lines all the things that nationalist conservatives are instinctively hostile to. The manifesto of 'National Conservatism' issued by the Edmund Burke Foundation in 2024 is a menu of all the things that 'Imagine' wishes away: separate independent nation states with sternly policed borders and restricted citizenship; large and well-armed national armies; hostility to international institutions and laws; religious faith protected and entrenched by the State; the defence of private property; tight limits on immigration and on freedom of movement. No wonder that the young Catholic journalist Dan Hitchens should have remarked to the rising Tory MP Danny Kruger on their way into the London conference of National Conservatism in May 2023: 'My thesis is that this is the anti-"Imagine coalition".' Kruger agreed heartily, and in his speech proceeded to denounce the 'dystopian fantasies of John Lennon'.[29] Thus 'Imagine' still has a vigorous afterlife 50 years on, not least in the minds of those who really, really hate the song.

'Imagine' is not the only utopian ode to have achieved iconic status across the world. The year after Lennon recorded it, the European Union adopted Schiller's 'Ode to Joy' as its official anthem, in the setting which forms the final movement of Beethoven's Ninth Symphony, the Choral:

All men will brothers be
Where your gentle wings reside …
And then, in the last verse:
Be embraced all ye millions
With a kiss for all the world.

When a saxophone quartet and a soprano performed the 'Ode to Joy' on the first day of the newly elected European Parliament on 1 July 2019, Nigel Farage and the other 28 Brexit Party MPs turned their backs to face the wall, in a gesture of derision and contempt for the Parliament and all its ideals of international fraternity. This was perhaps the high-water mark of nationalist revulsion against the whole European enterprise. In the elections for the Parliament a few weeks earlier, the Brexit Party had won the joint highest number of MPs anywhere in the EU.

None the less, 'Imagine' (1971) and 'Ode to Joy' (1785) continue to be performed on all sorts of great public occasions across the globe as enduring expressions of the sentiments that millions of people feel, at least with part of their minds. Neither song pretends to be a practical political manifesto. As Ringo Starr, who collaborated on the recording of 'Imagine', sensibly pointed out a few years later: 'Lennon said "Imagine", that's all. Just imagine it.' Another commentator described it as simply 'a call to make the best world we can here and now, since this is all there is or will be'.

Whether endorsed, excused or execrated, 'Imagine' and the impact that it made on the world remain as good a marker as any of the emotional distance that was travelled in the Third Sentimental Revolution. The price that its composer paid was a horrible tribute to its effectiveness. Noël Coward says in *Private Lives*: 'Strange how potent cheap music is.' I don't think he imagined quite how potent.

TEARS ON THE TURF

When the Beatles broke up in 1970, they left behind not only 200 songs but an emotional legacy. That legacy has been diluted and vigorously contested over the next two generations, but there are still substantial residues of it in the Western mind.

It was in the early 1980s that even quite insensitive men became aware that something had happened inside their heads. The columnists were soon busily chattering about the emergence of the New Man, until they wearied of the subject, as columnists do. It was not so much that He was beginning to help with the household chores or even to change the occasional nappy. Most women reported caustically that there was little evidence of improvement on that front. But what did seem to be genuinely happening was that men were more conscious of their own feelings and were readier to discuss them. For some reason that remained unclear, they appeared to have been put 'in touch with their emotions', rather as though they had been accidentally connected to the wrong phone number. Often to their surprise, they found it quite easy to 'open up', even something of a relief.

As we have seen, this was not the first period in history when something of the sort occurred. In the First Sentimental Revolution, the troubadours sang endlessly of their feelings for their beloved and placed those sentiments at the core of their existence. The knights of Chrétien de Troyes and the other romancers engaged, often for pages of heated verse, on the subject, and appeared to be just as emotionally open as their lady loves. In the Second Sentimental Revolution, the Man of Feeling was proud of his tender sentiments and spoke of them at every possible occasion.

The Oxford English Dictionary defines the New Man as 'one who rejects sexist attitudes and the traditional male role, esp. in the context of domestic responsibilities and childcare, and who is (or is held to be) caring, sensitive and non-aggressive'. Even in that parenthesis, the OED conveys something of the scepticism that greeted the idea at the time. These psyche-changes are always greeted with suspicion and soon, often instantly, become the subject of satire. Just as medieval satirists ridiculed the soppy, romantic knights – a long tradition culminating in Cervantes and Don Quixote – and eighteenth-century hard nuts immediately started parodying *Pamela*, so the columnists of the 1980s and 1990s quickly turned the New Age Guys into figures of fun, as, in the words of Giles Coren, 'terrible limp men carrying babies around their chest. They ate vegetables and gave up drinking. They were around for a bit until they realized women didn't want to sleep with them.' Their gentle murmurs were drowned out by the hearty banter of Blokes and Lads and Men Behaving Badly.

And yet there remains an unmistakable residue of the fleeting phenomenon, most measurable in the liquid form of tears, and to be found most conspicuously, of all places, on the sports field. If real men in the old days never cried in public, real sportsmen would not have dreamed of being seen in tears. On reaching their centuries, Len Hutton or Don Bradman would acknowledge the applause by a minimal flip of his bat, scarcely a flourish. Sir Alf Ramsey barely cracked a smile as his England team went from triumph to triumph. Olympic athletes of the old school might have been made of teak for all their reaction to success or failure. The earliest case that our resident professor of lachrymology, Thomas Dixon, can find of Olympians sobbing are both of swimmers, Judy Grinham on winning the 100 metres backstroke at Melbourne in 1956, and the Japanese 200 metres relay team shedding tears of joy when winning bronze at Tokyo in 1965.[30] Perhaps being in the water for long periods helps to loosen the tear ducts. But soon the tears were flowing on the rostrum, earning the 1996 Atlanta Games the sobriquet of 'the Crying Games'. In Athens in 2004, the Old Etonian rower Matthew Pinsent shed tears 'the size of gobstoppers' as he stood on the podium. In the *Spectator*, Rod Liddle lost no time in expressing the distaste felt in some quarters:

'Eton apparently taught Matthew Pinsent very little. It is all well and good to be able to row a small boat very quickly, but nothing excuses blubbing like a baby – or, worse, a foreigner – up on the medal podium in Athens. We would all much have preferred that he had come last than triumphed and consequently subjected us all to such wet public embarrassment and humiliation. Not that he's alone among the horribly named "Team GB"; they've all been at it, sobbing their little hearts out when they win, or come second, or come last. The team headquarters must be dripping with warm salty water. We may trail Ukraine in the official medal table, but we're up there on the podium for freestyle weeping and synchronised sobbing.'[31]

Liddle called for 'a general, principled stand on emotional incontinence in men'. This was by no means the first use of the phrase. The pioneer psychiatrist Henry Maudsley in 1886 diagnosed the ecstatic enthusiasm of the Unitarian writer James Martineau (brother of Harriet Martineau) in his descriptions of Union with God as 'streams of emotional incontinence'.[32] In fact, the modern denunciations of sporting crybabies are strangely reminiscent of the criticisms that stern radicals used to make of the religious excesses of the Dissenters; for example, as we have seen, E. P. Thompson in *The Making of the English Working Class* (1963) declares, 'The box-like blackening chapels stood in the industrial districts like great traps for the human psyche ... it is difficult not to see in Methodism in these years a ritualized form of psychic masturbation.' And he claims that 'these Sabbath orgasms of feeling made more possible the single-minded weekday direction of these energies to the consummation of productive labour'[33] – a linkage for which there is scant evidence, since plenty of factory workers were not Dissenters, and plenty of Dissenters were not factory workers. But both in sport and religion, what the critics cannot abide is the ecstasy.

Rod Liddle was at least accurate in pointing out that it seemed to be irrelevant whether the competitor in question had won or lost. This was famously illustrated by the example of Andy Murray in his Wimbledon finals. Previously caricatured as the dourest type of Scot, Murray broke down in tears after losing to Roger Federer in 2012, then broke down again the following year after defeating Novak Djokovic in straight sets, thus fulfilling Rudyard Kipling's famous injunction, inscribed over the entrance to the players' dressing room on Centre Court, to treat triumph and disaster just the same, though not at all in the sense intended by Kipling, who would have been horrified by Murray's blubbing.

Again, a *Spectator* columnist, in this case Toby Young, was quick to deplore 'Murray's emotional incontinence'. When he got angry responses on Twitter, defending Murray on the grounds that it was a great achievement to reach the Wimbledon final, the first British man to do so for decades, and he was entitled to a few tears, Young retorted: 'The obvious answer is that 75 years ago it wasn't socially acceptable for men to cry in public. Murray's tears were no more "natural" than Perry or Austin's dry-eyed response. It reflects a change in social conventions and, in particular, a different conception of masculinity. Back then, it was considered unmanly to cry. Today, it isn't. And that, of course, is what I'm complaining about – the fact that it's no longer taboo for men to behave like fourteen-year-old schoolgirls.'[34]

Thomas Dixon identifies the first major breach in the sea wall protecting the nation from this briny tsunami as occurring in the FA Cup semi-final at Hillsborough on 7 April 1973, when Sunderland's manager, the rugged former miner Bob Stokoe, was seen to break down in tears at the final whistle after his unfancied team had secured a miraculous victory over Arsenal. Dixon points out that many of the Sunderland fans were in tears, too, sobbing on each other's shoulders as they chanted, 'we're gannin' to Wembley, yer bugga, we're gannin' to Wembley'. It was from this memorable afternoon that Dixon sportively pastiches Virginia Woolf's pronouncement: 'On or about April 1973 British masculinity changed.'[35]

If so, it was a change that never ceased to be derided or deplored by those who clung to the old stoic values. The most famous example of tears on the pitch was the breakdown of Paul Gascoigne towards the end of England's semi-final match against Germany in the 1990 World Cup. Gazza wept, not because England had lost but because he had just been given a yellow card for a foul tackle, which meant that he would not have been able to play in the final, had England won the semi, which they didn't. His tears were thus not a lament for his team but for himself. Which did not stop a crowd of supporters estimated at 100,000 greeting the England team at the airport on their return, although they had only finished fourth, with many of them shouting Gazza's name in unbridled adulation. Gascoigne himself was not the only one to be startled by the reception. John Barnes in his autobiography says, 'I was amazed by our reception on our return to Luton Airport. There were tens of thousands of people there to greet us, just as if we had won the World Cup. All of the squad were greeted as conquering heroes, particularly Gazza.'[36]

Gazza's tears, 1990

In the *Independent on Sunday*, no less a football fan than Salman Rushdie was withering about the whole episode:

'And those tears. *La Gazza Lacrimosa*, the Weeping Magpie. (Or, strictly speaking, ex-Magpie [Gascoigne had previously worn the black and white of Newcastle United]). Did anyone before Paul Gascoigne ever become a national hero and a dead-cert millionaire by crying? Fabulous. Weep and the world weeps with you. Gazza, the New Man, not afraid to show his pain: beautiful.' Then a further thought occurs to Rushdie: 'Gazza finds it easy to cry. He can turn on the tears, it is alleged, whenever he wants to get a little sympathy ... for example, the ungenerous thought occurs, *when he's getting booked*? Can this be true? Could he have cried deliberately, just to influence the ref ...

That's enough of that. None of that talk around here, please.'[37] Not for the first or last time, the crybaby is accused of putting it on. For those of a stoical temperament, tears are always suspect.

6 SEPTEMBER 1997

Even now, it is hard to forget the anguished wailing that broke out as soon as the little cortège came out of the gates of Kensington Palace and turned the corner into the crowded street. The papers said afterwards that they were cries of 'Diana!' and 'Bless You!', but at the time they sounded more like wordless howls of pain. Then the flowers thrown by the people standing 20 deep along the south side of the Park began to descend through the soft September air on the coffin, coming to rest in the white lilies piled high on top of it, her favourite flower. It seems to last an eternity, the slow journey along Kensington Gore, the crowd mostly quiet now, the silence broken only by the rumbling of the gun carriage and the clopping hooves of the horses. Then the stop-off at St James's Palace to pick up the two pale boys and their father and uncle and grandfather, to walk behind their mother's coffin, and then the slowdown at the gates of Buckingham Palace to allow the Queen to bow her head and perhaps shed the tears which the tabloids said she should have shed from the start – 'Show Us You Care, Ma'am', to quote the *Daily Express*. There is something awkward about these punctuations, as though they are afterthoughts to pick up members of the family who have been forgotten about in the funeral planning.

The strangeness of it all did not end when the little procession reached the Abbey. In between 'I Vow To Thee My Country' and 'Cwm Rhondda', Elton John sang a remix of 'Candle In The Wind', written as a tribute 24 years earlier to Marilyn Monroe who had also died a tragic death at much the same age as Diana. Now Elton's songwriter Bernie Taupin had deftly transposed 'Goodbye Norma Jean' into 'Goodbye England's Rose', to almost unbearable effect. And then came her brother's speech, anguished and vengeful in equal parts, against both the paparazzi and the family who had been so cold to her: 'Of all the ironies about Diana, perhaps the greatest was this – a girl given the name of the ancient goddess of hunting was, in the end, the most hunted person of the modern age.' It was one of the most remarkable funeral orations of the modern age, and when Earl Spencer had finished, no less remarkable than the wailing that had begun the funeral three hours earlier was the spontaneous applause that broke out in the congregation, then rippled out into the thousands waiting outside and on into the homes of the 32.5 million in the UK who watched it on TV, and the estimated 2–2.5 billion worldwide.

And was it all a fitting expression of a nation united in grief, the appropriate culmination to a week of mourning that had been drenched in tears and flowers? All through those fraught days, the commentators had been doing their best to reassure us. Several of the people interviewed by Mass Observation did think that this was a week that made you proud to be British. Reporting from the Mall on the eve of the funeral, the BBC journalist Jill Dando, herself to suffer an even more dreadful death than Diana 18 months later, again at much the same age as the Princess, described how 'people have been coming from all over the country to really be a symbol of the United Kingdom, a kingdom it seems so already united in grief', and she told one upset woman that 'You speak for the whole nation.'[38] It was not only the ordinary spectators who wept as the coffin passed. A young policewoman dabbed at her eyes with her handkerchief, and children too young to know anything much about Diana sobbed as they hugged their mothers' skirts. Many people described the experience as 'like losing my own family'.[39] 'The difficulty of trying to write about the public grief,' Tom Utley wrote in the Daily Telegraph, 'is that this is not public grief at all. It is private grief multiplied millions of times over. Everybody I have spoken to since Sunday feels personally bereaved as if a close relation had died.'[40]

The reality was, though, that the nation was not united. If there were 32 million in the country who watched the funeral on TV, there were over 20 million people who did not. These included, of course, a large minority of sturdy republicans who wanted nothing to do with the royal family, alive or dead. There were plenty more who didn't much care for Diana as a person. 'Rather silly, comparatively empty-headed, vain, occasionally bad-tempered, manipulative, immature' was one woman's verdict; another woman pointed out that 'hardly any mentioned her wealth, her often childish behaviour, her obvious instability or her extremely grasping divorce settlement'.[41]

But what many more felt was not so much personal antagonism to the Princess herself as an ungovernable revulsion against the overblown public hysteria after her death, in particular the enforcement of grief. As one older man told Mass Observation: 'It became quickly evident that the nation was to be media-led into self-indulgent wallowings of emotional display. An anguish previously unheard of even at the height of the Blitz. Suddenly being British meant it was all right to shed tears in public over a young woman whom few had met, and less ever having had the remotest chance of getting to know personally. What I found most disturbing to those of us who managed to remain dry-eyed, was being made to feel callously unfeeling, if not downright unpatriotic. To my mind, at least, the only lead of any dignified restraint came from the Queen, who in the end had to give way to media hysteria and herself appear on television to prove that she was suffering with "the people".'[42]

Far from the whole experience making everyone proud to be British, it had deeply embarrassed and upset a considerable proportion of the public. 'As the days and hours passed, I gradually felt like an alien in my own country.'[43] The columnists who expressed these feelings were not simply cantankerous old hacks. They spoke for thousands, if not millions. In the same issue of the *Telegraph* in which Tom Utley had described the melding of private and public grief, Boris Johnson exploded. Under the headline, 'Where Is This, Argentina?' he poured scorn on 'this Latin American carnival of grief'. Johnson was horrified by Tony Blair's 'brilliant branding' of Diana as 'the People's Princess'. But he was alarmed, too. 'Blair has seen that the big numbers are with her.' If the Tories were 'ever to be re-elected, they must study the ruthless populism of the People's Party'. Otherwise, the public would write them off as 'a pompous collection of stuffed shirts'. Decent reticent Conservatives had to swallow their nausea, wrap themselves in the Union Jack and weep along with the plebs. Cynical advice, even by

Johnson's own Olympic standards, and it was at the 2012 London Olympics that he demonstrated that he too could blub along.

Just as it is hard to exaggerate the grief undeniably felt by so many, so it is hard to exaggerate the revulsion felt by a great number of others. 'Am I alone in thinking that the country has momentarily taken leave of its senses?' A. N. Wilson asked: 'This Cult of Diana makes me shiver.'[44] Wilson, like other well-known prolific journalists, such as Nigella Lawson and Simon Heffer, had also written positive things about the nation's grief and even about Diana herself. It's as if they were having to write for two different audiences, as indeed they were.

The trauma continued to upset some columnists for a long time. Nearly eight months after the funeral, Richard Littlejohn was complaining in the Sun[45] about the proposal for a national two-minutes silence to mark the first anniversary of Diana's death. This 'latest insanity from the Lady Di industry' risked a repeat of 'the menacing mass hysteria and mob rule' visible in 'a revolting orgy of emotional incontinence and exhibitionism'. The Sun had been a consistent supporter of the Princess, but 90 per cent of Littlejohn's postbag was in favour of his renewed polemic against emotional incontinence. Four years later, the ever-mutable media, left and right alike, applauded the 'dignified' and 'restrained' public response to the death of the Queen Mother at the age of 101. The contrast, whether spoken or unspoken, was with the time when Bruce Anderson 'once felt ashamed to be British', when 'London was full of people who seemed to have lost their wits. Faces distorted by hysteria, they were shambling about blubbing and moaning ... like savages with their fetishes.'[46]

Perhaps the nation had, after all, managed to stagger through that slough of sentimentality and come out the other side, muddied and breathless perhaps but fundamentally intact. Some apprehensive observers, though, feared that the damage had penetrated deeper. A nation which could slobber so uncontrollably must have gone soft in all sorts of ways; the Diana hysteria was only the *comble* of a profound collective degeneration and derangement.

The nation was said to be suffering from 'mourning sickness', hopelessly in the grip of 'grief porn'. Carol Sarler in The Times[47] claimed that 'the cruder truth is that ersatz grief is now the new pornography; like the worst of hard-core, it is stimulated by proxy, voyeuristically piggy-backing upon that which otherwise might be deemed personal and private, for no better reason than the frisson and the quickening of an otherwise jaded pulse.' That was certainly the anguished premise of a remarkable fusillade published by the Social Affairs Unit in the February after Diana's death. We have already mentioned *Faking It: The Sentimentalisation of Modern Society*, edited by two Church of England priests, Digby Anderson and Peter Mullen, but its sustained tirade against sentimentality, written by several hands, each quivering with indignation, deserves a closer look. The editors end their introduction by asking the question: 'Is sentimentality really as widespread and central to modern society?'[48] And they give a thumping answer, which they regard as a clincher: 'There is a better answer to these questions than an argument – an event. The funeral of Diana, Princess of Wales, was sentimentality personified and canonised. In that mob grief, feeling, image and spontaneity were elevated above reason, reality, and restraint and the full extent of modern sentimentality made available for anyone with eyes to see.'[49]

In 'Diana, Queen of Hearts', the crowning essay of this collection, Anthony O'Hear, Professor of Philosophy at Bradford, amplifies the theme fortissimo: '... Diana, and what she stood for and what came through on September 6th were decadent. Feeling was elevated above reason, caring above principle, personal gratification above commitment and propriety, and what Tony Blair called "the People" above rank, tradition and history ... The culture of caring, of nicenesss, of the people, was triumphant. All the tendencies described elsewhere in this book, in education, in religion, in attitudes to culture and welfare and the self, in irrationalism and in the paramount need to confess and express one's feelings came to a head that week.'[50] What we witnessed was 'a defining moment in our history'.

According to O'Hear, Diana herself was a fitting emblem of what her death had unleashed. She was childishly self-centred, lacked any sense of duty, ran around with worthless playboys, wept at the funeral of a vulgar Italian dress designer. But what about her work for the hundred charities of which she was patron? Well, O'Hear does concede 'there is no doubt that she did quite a lot of good both for individuals and for the causes with which she was associated. Along with all her self-indulgence and muddle, she clearly wanted to make the world a better place.'[51]

But even here, Diana is seen as the symbol of everything that has gone wrong with our society: 'It is, though, in Diana's chosen role as Queen of Hearts that her and our sentimentality presents itself in its purest form.'[52] Her charity work, too, was fatally poisoned by sentimentality, even or perhaps especially in her two most celebrated causes.

'Her choice of AIDS as one of her six favoured activities is highly significant ... As things are in the world today, in favouring it as publicly as Diana did, one is expressing a calculated refusal to be judgmental about the activities which bring AIDS about.'[53] In other words, it would have been better if she had not implicitly condoned homosexual practices and if she had instead avoided such a tainted cause and stuck to lepers.

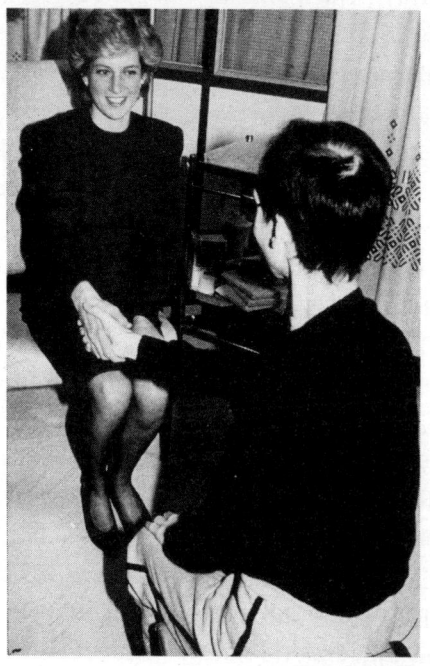

Princess Diana shakes hands with AIDS patient, Middlesex Hospital, April 1987

Yet any impartial observer of the sort imagined by Adam Smith would, I think, judge the campaign against AIDS to have been one of the more admirable episodes in the history of public health in Britain. By taking it up so promptly and wholeheartedly (over the initial reservations of the Prime Minister), the Health Minister, Norman Fowler, ensured that the AIDS victims who were already mortally ill were properly looked after and that the retroviral treatments were speedily developed and rolled out. Thousands of lives were saved, and 'the gay plague' (which, of course, was not confined to gays) began to become a horrific memory. In April 1987, Princess Diana had opened the first purpose-built AIDS ward in Britain, at the Middlesex Hospital, where, without gloves, she shook hands with a patient, helping to dispel the fear, widespread at the time, that HIV could be spread by touch. She also became patron of the Mildmay Hospital in Shoreditch, a religious foundation which specialized in AIDS treatment. She visited the hospital 17 times, often at night, to comfort the patients – you cannot help thinking of Florence Nightingale, another controversial, often difficult character, doing her nocturnal rounds in the military hospital at Scutari – the Lady with the Lamp. In March 1997, Diana went to South Africa and met Nelson Mandela, who said after her death that 'when she stroked the limbs of someone with leprosy or sat on the bed of a man with HIV/AIDS and held his hand, she transformed public attitudes and improved the life chances of such people'. Not just a vacuous, self-centred Sloane, then.

Professor O'Hear is equally damning about Princess Diana's visit to Bosnia and her campaign against landmines, which he sees as another example of 'the sentimentality often found with well-meaning people when confronted either with evil or with intractable conflicts of interest. Of course, ethnic strife is appalling, as are the effects of landmines. But an angel is powerless against inflexible wills, particularly if one or both is an evil will, each with claims of right and tradition. There are occasions where placing landmines may be the lesser evil. It is sentimental to avoid the roots of a problem, and it is sentimental to think that there is no problem which cannot be solved with a bit of good will on both sides.'[54]

'Lesser evil'? Lesser than what? Innocent women and children being blown to bits at random or maimed for life seems quite evil enough to be going on with. And is an angel really so powerless? What O'Hear neglects to mention is that Diana's efforts were part of an international effort to secure a convention against the planting of landmines. That campaign bore practical fruit in the shape of the Ottawa Treaty signed in the year of Diana's death, 'the Convention on the Prohibition of the Use, Stockpiling, Production and Transfer of Anti-Personnel Mines and on their Destruction'. To date, 164 nations have signed the Treaty, though not China, Russia and the United States. So not just a sentimental gesture, then.

In these tirades against sentimentality, we can, I think, now and then detect a hint of desperation or perhaps fear at the way the world is going. There is at least a certain consistency in the way O'Hear and his fellow contributors hunt down the faintest whiff of the S— word wherever they can find it. In literature, for example, the redoubtable Leavisite critic Ian Robinson lays into Dickens, Thackeray and even George Eliot (normally a heroine to the followers of Dr Leavis), for their 'tearful gushing'. Only their hard-boiled passages escape censure: 'In these cases it is always the emotional bits, never the satirical, that are false or fake.'[55] Robinson quotes with hearty approval D. H. Lawrence's scorching remarks on the 'faked feelings' of John Galsworthy: 'It is when he comes to sex that Mr Galsworthy collapses finally. He becomes nastily sentimental. He wants to make sex important, and he only makes it repulsive. Sentimentalism is the working off on yourself of feelings you haven't really got.'[56]

Yet is Lawrence himself really any better as a novelist? He's a wonderful essayist, biting, ironic and insightful, but when he tries to create other people on the page, the effect is so often dull and hollow. As Anthony Powell concluded, after steeping himself in Lawrence's fiction: 'As a novelist, with all his force, he is never wholly at ease with the medium. He himself is the only character who ever truly emerges.'[57]

Robinson tells us with great emphasis that 'Serious writing requires irony. Sentimentality is unironic.'[58] This is an interesting reprise, three-quarters of a century later, of Ortega y Gasset's contention that 'the first consequence of the retreat of art upon itself is a ban on all pathos'. The tongue has to be always firmly lodged in the cheek. Every poem, painting or piece of music must be 'flavoured with a dash of irony'.[59] In the masterworks of modern art, the irony has entered the soul. Yet is irony enough to make a great novel? Surely what makes Dickens and Thackeray, and even Bennett and Galsworthy, at their best great novelists, is that they are both ironic and sentimental, often on the same page, persuading us by a combination of distance and empathy that this is what life is really like. Like Chaucer and like Shakespeare, in fact.

In matters of religion, too, the contributors to *Faking It* appear anxious to cut down the display of feeling to the barest minimum. The editors argue that 'when Christianity is emptied of doctrine, tradition and rules, all that remains is sentimentality'.[60] All that the 'rootless, nebulous togetherness' of the happy-clappy services has to offer are woolly jumpers and woolly minds. According to Peter Mullen, 'Traditional Christianity is robust and unsentimental.'[61] This assertion would have come as a surprise to Friedrich Nietzsche. He loathed Christianity precisely because it appealed to the softer feelings and glorified the weak and powerless in defiance of the realities of life. He particularly hated the Beatitudes in the Sermon on the Mount, which are indeed one long, softhearted paean. And was Nietzsche so wrong?

What about the shortest verse in the Bible? John 11.35: 'Jesus wept.' Note that He weeps because others are weeping, just the kind of sentimental contagion that was deplored at the funeral of Princess Diana. Mary Magdalen is weeping because her brother Lazarus has died and Jesus was not there to save him: 'when Jesus therefore saw her weeping, and the Jews also weeping which came with her, he groaned in the spirit, and was troubled, and said, where have ye laid him? They said unto him, Lord, come and see.' It's only then that Jesus weeps. He also weeps in Luke 19.41. In this case, he weeps for Jerusalem and the cruel fate that lies in store for the city, which he will not be there to witness – again the sort of tears for remote events which are so sharply criticized these days.

And what does St Paul say? Try his advice to the Galatians, chapter 5.22–3: 'But the fruit of the Spirit is love, joy, peace, long-suffering, gentleness, goodness, faith, meekness, temperance: against such there is no law.' Surely more than a soupçon of sentimentality there.

In fact, an impartial observer coming fresh to the New Testament might conclude precisely the opposite of Peter Mullen: that if you take out of the Church the codes of discipline and the liturgies and the priests and the rituals, what you are left with is the core of Christianity, its appeal to the intimate inner feelings which is the peculiar essence of the faith.

Instead, readers of *Faking It* are told to shiver at 'God's wrath and indignation' as we 'acknowledge and bewail our manifold sins and wickedness' and declare that 'the remembrance of them is grievous unto us: the burden of them is intolerable'. If we are getting married, we must pay attention to the parson's stern injunction: 'I require and charge you both, as ye will answer at the dreadful day of judgment when the secrets of all hearts shall be disclosed.'

The Social Affairs Unit's call for a revival of doctrine, discipline and the fear of punishment is not confined to the religious sphere. In an earlier volume of essays, *This Will Hurt: The Restoration of Virtue and Civil Order*,[62] Digby Anderson leads another team of contributors who compete to offer the strictest remedies for 'the grievous moral disorder' which the redoubtable Gertrude Himmelfarb claims in her preface we are now suffering from.[63] Rabbi Daniel Lappin recommends that we go back to ostracizing bastards and stigmatizing their single mothers.[64] Graeme Newman deplores the reduction in the range of punishments that used to be available, such as branding, the pillory, the scold's bridle, and, of course, corporal and capital punishment.[65] Professor Newman is on record as advocating a return to flogging, but here he does not specify which items on his enticing menu he would plump for. He concludes only that if we are to make criminals accept responsibility for their actions and repair the moral damage that they have done, 'it will certainly mean revisiting and perhaps up-dating penalties once discarded as barbaric'.[66] Or adding to the list from new technologies, such as tasering perhaps?

Instead of throwing up our hands in pious horror at these suggestions, we might perhaps jot down a few statistics. In the 30 years since these books were published, the rate of homicide in the UK has declined sharply. So have the rates of burglary, robbery and juvenile delinquency. Firearms offences are down from 25,000 in 2003 to under 10,000 in 2022 (though knife crime has risen in recent years). Violence against the person has more than halved since 1994. Just about the only category of crime that has increased, and sharply, too, is rape, but this is clearly due to the greater readiness of society to understand the full extent of the sexual and domestic violence that women suffer and the greater readiness of women to report the crime. The outrage which provoked the most powerful sentimental responses in the First and Second Sentimental Revolutions – in Chaucer's *Troilus and Criseyde* and in Richardson's *Pamela* and *Clarissa* – is still provoking equally powerful reactions in our own day.

All the same, if we are in the depths of a grievous moral crisis and our penal system and our religious practice have been fatally undermined by the new sentimentality, it doesn't seem to have had much effect on the crime rate. If we are going to hell in a handcart, temporarily at least, the handcart seems to be stuck in reverse gear. Of course, men and women go on doing terrible things to one another, more often men to women. Divorce, desertion and disease continue to exact their toll. But is it so wrong for the State to go on trying, however ham-fistedly, to pick up the casualties, rather than chastise them for their misdeeds and misfortunes?

Let me, at this late stage, make clear the obvious fact that there are many occasions in life when the tougher virtues are indispensable: in times of war and plague, in illness and bereavement, in divorce and desertion. Then the four virtues which Plato sets out so clearly in *The Republic*[67] – Justice, Temperance, Fortitude and Wisdom – need to be deployed, often for long periods and under stresses which may seem unbearable. The Church adopted those four classical virtues as her Cardinal Virtues, which was not such a stretch, as the same four are also to be found in the Book of Wisdom (8.7). Then in the fourth century, St Ambrose and St Augustine added three more, the so-called Theological Virtues, taken from First Corinthians 13: Faith, Hope and Charity – or Love, which is a better translation of the original Greek *Agape*. Thus were born the Seven Heavenly Virtues.

But this was not the end of the story. As the concept of the Seven Deadly Sins evolved, so the Church felt it necessary to enumerate seven virtues in opposition, and so were born the Seven Remedial or Contrary Virtues, promulgated by Pope Gregory the Great in AD 590. This latter septet has a very different, softer feel to it: Castitas, Temperantia, Caritas, Diligentia, Humanitas, Patientia, Humilitas – Chastity, Temperance, Love, Diligence, Kindness, Patience, Humility. Only one item on this list, Temperance, is carried over from Plato's quartet. Yet it is this list which to us today seems to incapsulate the tradition that is specifically, perhaps uniquely Christian, with its emphasis on meekness, modesty and kindness, the tradition that anti-Christians like Goethe, Nietzsche and Lawrence have always loathed. If the Seven Contrary Virtues have a bias, it is undeniably a sentimental one.

I am not suggesting that Gregory's virtues have achieved a permanent domination over Plato's. The struggle continues. In fact, we are experiencing an impassioned phase of the struggle at the moment. It is hard to ignore or to separate out the rancorous currents of anger boiling up on the right: anger against immigrants and Islam, against LGBT and Transgender advocates, against 'cultural Marxism', against trendy vicars, and against 'the feminization of society' which has allegedly led to a corresponding 'crisis of masculinity' among young men. All these resentments are poured into the steaming cauldron which calls itself 'anti-woke', and whose stirrers such as Douglas Murray and Jordan Peterson draw huge audiences across the English-speaking world. What they seem to have in common is a certain unforgiving hardness and withholding of sympathy from minorities of any description.

It all began 20 years ago with the outcry against 'political correctness gone mad'. What had been intended as mere politeness towards people who had been abused or given sneering nicknames, such as 'Paki' or 'cripple', was now said to have gone too far and to be stifling freedom of speech. This panic went viral during the last years of the Tory government in Britain, whose leaders and attendant columnists could talk of nothing but the 'wokerati' and 'cancel culture'. What is clear is that underlying the whole intifada is a loathing of what I have called the Third Sentimental Revolution, and the fury is a backhanded tribute to its success.

What does it look like in action, this Third Sentimental Revolution? Let us look back at a golden September evening in Paris in 2024. Its origins lay in Britain. In 1944, Dr Ludwig Guttmann had opened a spinal injuries unit at Stoke Mandeville Hospital. Four years later, he organized an archery competition for 16 injured servicemen and women to coincide with the 1948 London Olympics. This developed into the Paralympic Games and then also the Winter Paralympics, which today both take place every four years alongside the other Olympics and feature hundreds of disabled athletes competing in dozens of sports in front of ever-growing crowds. The Paris Paralympics sold two and a half million tickets with record viewing figures on TV. The golden finale on 7 September was the Blind Football final at a packed Stade Tour Eiffel. *Blind football.* In the penalty shoot-out between France and Argentina, the crowd went wild when the first four players all scored, guided only by officials banging the sides of the goals with metal sticks, the goalies being the only sighted players on the pitch. Could there be a more spectacular demonstration of human resourcefulness, or of the transformation in attitudes towards the disabled – from the old mockery and neglect to respect and heartfelt admiration?

I want to end this long journey by putting the argument in a stronger form than I would have dared at the beginning. Certainly I set out in a contrarian spirit, to question the accepted scorn for sentimentality, but I did so a little hesitantly, venturing only to suggest that sentimentality might have its uses, that there might be some benefit to individuals and to society in letting one's feelings flow, even overflow. What the sterner critics dismiss as futile mawkishness might actually stir people to practical benevolence.

Now, as we come towards the end of the Third Sentimental Revolution and look back over the cathedrals and hospitals of the thirteenth century, the humanitarian reforms of the second half of the eighteenth century, and the libertarian and compassionate advances of the last third of the twentieth century, I want to press the case more firmly. Sentimentality is not just an occasionally useful spur to action; it is indispensable to human flourishing. A society that is incapable of sentimentality is thereby shrivelled, a harder, lesser place. Slopping over irrigates the human heart. I cannot help thinking of my favourite quotation from P. G. Wodehouse: 'as the car drove in at the gate, we struck a bumpy patch, and I could hear the milk of human kindness sloshing about inside him.' Of all the phrases that Wodehouse draws from Shakespeare, 'the milk of human kindness' is easily the most frequently deployed – no less than 40 times, all derived from that single cutting remark of Lady Macbeth to her husband: 'Yet do I fear thy nature; / It is too full of the milk of human kindness / To catch the nearest way.'[68]

Whenever the sentimental tendency gains ascendancy, there are practical and measurable consequences in the real world. For a tear *is* an intellectual thing.

Picture Credits and Permissions

Every effort has been made to track down the copyright holders of the photos used in the book.

p.ii Vintage 1898 photograph by Victorian photographer Oscar Gustave Rejlander. *A Night Out. Homeless* depicts a young boy on the streets of London. © photo-fox / Alamy Stock Photo

p.xv 'The Death of Little Nell' by George Cattermole, from The Old Curiosity Shop, 1902 © Chronicle / Alamy Stock Photo

p.9 'Tristan drinking the love potion' from Livre de Messire Lancelot, by Gautier de Moap, 1470 © Bibliothèque nationale de France

p.27 The Isenheim altarpiece by Matthias Grünewald, 1512–16 © Artefact / Alamy Stock Photo

p.33 Henry III by Matthew Paris © The Picture Art Collection / Alamy Stock Photo

p.38 Westminster Abbey, the interior © Steve Vidler / Alamy Stock Photo

p.44 Ruins of Walsingham Abbey © Greg Balfour Evans / Alamy Stock Photo

p.56 Headless figures of St Margaret of Antioch, Fingringhoe, Essex and the Coronation of the Virgin, West Front, Wells Cathedral © Anonymous

p.64 Samuel Richardson by Joseph Highmore, c. 1747 © Art Collection 2 / Alamy Stock Photo p.65 Pamela Fainting by Joseph Highmore, 1743–4 © National Gallery of Victoria, Melbourne. The Felton Bequest, 1921. Image courtesy National Gallery of Victoria, Melbourne

p.101 The Man of Feeling by Thomas Rowlandson, 1788 © ARTGEN / Alamy Stock Photo

p.107 The Foundling Hospital by L. P. Boitard, 1753 © Iconographic Archive / Alamy Stock Photo

p.111 The Four Stages of Cruelty: Stage One: boys being cruel to small animals by William Hogarth, 1751 © GRANGER - Historical Picture Archive / Alamy Stock Photo

p.130 Mary Wollstonecraft by John Opie, 1797 © Art Collection 2 / Alamy Stock Photo

p.134 The Edith Cavell Monument © Loop Images Ltd / Alamy Stock Photo

p.143 The Death of General Wolfe by Benjamin West, 1770 © IanDagnall Computing / Alamy Stock Photo; The Death of General Gordon by G. W. Joy, 1893 © Classic Image / Alamy Stock Photo

p.152 'The Death of Paul Dombey' from Dombey and Son Harry Furniss/Bridgeman Images © Look and Learn / Bridgeman Images

p.160 The Death of Uncle Tom by Thomas W. Strong, 1853 © GRANGER - Historical Picture Archive / Alamy Stock Photo

p.171 'Cosette with her broom' from Les Misérables, Émile Bayard © Pictorial Press Ltd / Alamy Stock Photo

p.176 The Blind Girl by John Everett Millais, 1856 © 19th era / Alamy Stock Photo

p.188 The Empty Chair by Luke Fildes, 1870 © ARTGEN / Alamy Stock Photo

p.189 Gauguin's Chair by Vincent van Gogh, 1888 © steeve-x-art / Alamy Stock Photo

PICTURE CREDITS

p.190 The Doctor by Luke Fildes, 1891 © photosublime / Alamy Stock Photo

p.195 Science and Charity by Pablo Picasso, 1897 © Album / Alamy Stock Photo

p.197 First Communion, 1896, Pablo Picasso (1881, 1973), Museu Picasso Museum, Barcelona, Catalonia, Spain. © Album / Alamy Stock Photo

p.203 The Menin Road by Paul Nash 1919 © IanDagnall Computing / Alamy Stock Photo

p.204 La Patrie by C. R. W. Nevinson, 1916 © Penta Springs Limited / Alamy Stock Photo

p.205 Guernica by Pablo Picasso, 1937 © Peter Eastland / Alamy Stock Photo

p.216 The Beatles receive their MBEs, 1965 © Photo by Jeff Hochberg/ Getty Images

p.219 BUM by Pauline Boty, 1966 © The Estate of Pauline Boty, courtesy of Whitford Fine Art, London.

p.251 Gazza's tears, 1990 © Photo by David Cannon/Allsport/Getty Images

p.260 Princess Diana shakes hands with AIDS patient, Middlesex Hospital, April 1987 © Photo by Anwar Hussein/WireImage

Text permissions
p.4 From Dawn to Dawn, Troubadour Poetry by A. S. Kline, TRANSLATOR Copyright © 2009.

pp.208–9 Lyrics from the song, 'Little Boxes'
Words and music by Malvina Reynolds. Copyright 1962 Schrodrer Music Co. (ASCAP). Renewed 1990. Used by permission. All rights reserved.

p.215 'Annus Mirabilis' in High Windows © Philip Larkin, printed with permission of Faber and Faber

Notes

INTRODUCTION

1. Mackenzie, *The Man of Feeling*, p. xv.
2. Anderson and Mullen, eds, *Faking It: The Sentimentalisation of Modern Society*, p. 5.
3. Gareth Roberts, 'World War Twee', *Spectator*, 7 December 2024.
4. quoted Lacey, M. J., and Wilkin, P. (2005), *Global Politics in the Information Age*, p.11.
5. Kingsley, *The Water Babies*, ch. I.
6. ODNB, Juliet Hacking, 'Oscar Gustav Rejlander'.
7. *Observer*, 4 November 2023.
8. Oscar Wilde, *De Profundis*, pp. 636, 640 (*Letters*, p. 501).
9. Dixon, *Weeping Britannia*, p.156, quoting from Vyvyan Holland, *Son of Oscar Wilde*, pp. 53–4.
10. 'On Kitsch and Sentimentality', *Journal of Aesthetics and Art Criticism*, Winter 1991, 8–9.
11. De Rougemont, *Love in the Western World*, p. 5.
12. Pottle, *The Idiom of Poetry*, esp. pp 4–6. For drawing my attention to this brilliant discussion of shifts in literary sensibility, I am indebted to Zachary Leader's invaluable *Ellmann's Joyce*, Yale, 2025 (pp. 58 and 373n).

CHAPTER ONE: THE FIRST SENTIMENTAL REVOLUTION

1. Lewis, *The Allegory of Love*, p. 2.
2. Ibid., p. 11.
3. Morris, *The Discovery of the Individual*, p. 108.
4. Ibid., p. 114.
5. De Rougemont, *Love in the Western World*, p. 74.
6. Ibid., p. 75.

7 Ibid., p. 122.
8 Lewis, The Allegory of Love, p. 4.
9 Huizinga, The Waning of the Middle Ages, p. 119.
10 Morris, The Discovery of the Individual, pp. 115–16.
11 Lewis, The Allegory of Love, p. 150.
12 Morris, The Discovery of the Individual, pp. 116–17.
13 De Rougemont, Love in the Western World, pp. 358–9.
14 Kline, From Dawn to Dawn: Troubadour Poetry, p. 18.
15 Béroul, The Romance of Tristan, p. 48.
16 Ibid., p. 50.
17 Ibid., p. 74.
18 Ibid., p. 142.
19 Ibid., pp. 88–9.
20 Ibid., p. 88.
21 Ibid., p. 44.
22 Chrétien de Troyes, Arthurian Romances, trans. W. W. Kibler, p. 161.
23 Lewis, Allegory of Love, p. 29.
24 Chrétien de Troyes, pp. 131–5.
25 Ibid., pp. 169–70.
26 Ibid., p. 225.
27 Ibid., p. 259.
28 Romance of the Rose, p. 220.
29 Ibid., p. 45.
30 Ibid., p. 46.
31 Ibid., p. 47.
32 Ibid., p. 67.
33 Lewis, The Allegory of Love, p. 116.
34 Romance of the Rose, p. 12.
35 Lewis, The Allegory of Love, p. 135.
36 Huizinga, The Waning of the Middle Ages, p. 120.
37 Ibid., p. 385.
38 Ibid., p. 127.
39 Ibid., pp 131–2.
40 Romance of the Rose, p. 223.
41 Ibid., p. 304.
42 Ibid., pp. 332–3.
43 Ibid., p. 335.
44 Chaucer, Troilus and Criseyde, I, 25–6, in Nevill Coghill's springy translation into modern English.
45 Ibid., V, 116–17.
46 Ibid., V, 152.

47 Ibid., III, 171–3.
48 Ibid., III, 176–7.
49 Ibid., III, 179.
50 Chaucer, *Canterbury Quintet*, ed. Michael Murphy, p. 22.
51 Powell, *Some Poets, Artists, & 'A Reference for Mellors'*, pp. 7–9.
52 Ibid., p. 8.
53 *Canterbury Tales*, lines 3233–48.
54 Matarasso, trans., *Aucassin and Nicolette and Other Tales*, pp 24–5.
55 Jones, *Chaucer's Knight*, p. xx.
56 Ibid., p. xxi.
57 *Henry V*, II.3.
58 De Rougemont, *Love in the Western World*, p. 165.
59 Etchegoyen, *L'Amour divin*.
60 Quoted de Rougemont, *Love in the Western World*, pp. 161–2.
61 Morris, *The Discovery of the Individual*, p. 23.
62 De Rougemont, *Love in the Western World*, p. 187.
63 Luke 2.7.
64 De Rougemont, *Love in the Western World*, p. 111.
65 Ibid.
66 Mâle, *The Gothic Image*, pp. 272–4.
67 Quoted Duffy, *The Stripping of the Altars*, p. 161.
68 Ibid., p. 165.
69 Mâle, *The Gothic Image*, pp. 292–3.
70 Ibid., ch. IV.
71 Duffy, *The Stripping of the Altars*, p. 181.
72 Ibid., p. 182.
73 Huizinga, *The Waning of the Middle Ages*, p. 155.
74 Ibid., pp. 217–18.
75 Dixon, *Weeping Britannia*, p. 20.
76 Ibid., p. 18.
77 Ibid., p. 21.
78 Carpenter, *Henry III: The Rise to Power and Personal Rule*, p. 167.
79 Ibid., p. 211.
80 Ibid., p. 282.
81 Ibid., p. 294.
82 Carpenter, *Henry III: Reform, Rebellion, Civil War, Settlement*, p. 242.
83 De Rougemont, *Love in the Western World*, p. 354.
84 Carpenter, *Henry III: The Rise to Power and Personal Rule*, p. 262.
85 Britnell, *The Commercialisation of English Society 1000–1500*, pp. 102–3.

86 Hermann Levy (1943), 'The Economic History of Sickness and Medical Benefit Before the Puritan Revolution', *Economic History Review*, 13.1, 42–57; Hartley and Elliot, *Life and Work of the People of England*, p. 19 et ff; Barry G. Gale (1967), 'The Dissolution and the Revolution in London Hospital Facilities', *Medical History*, Jan. 11(1), 91–6.
87 Quoted, Carpenter, *Henry III: Reform, Rebellion, Civil War, Settlement*, p. 160.
88 Morris, *The Discovery of the Individual*, pp. 73–5.
89 Ibid., p. 89.
90 *Foreign Policy*, Jan.–Feb. 2003.

CHAPTER TWO: THE NEW STONY AGE

1 *The New Oxford Book of Sixteenth-Century Verse*, 1991, pp. 550–1. Possibly written by Philip, Earl of Arundel, condemned to death for his Catholicism, died in the Tower of London and canonized in 1970 as St Philip Howard, one of the Forty Martyrs of England and Wales.
2 Quoted, Aston, *Broken Idols of the Reformation*, p. 209.
3 Duffy, *The Stripping of the Altars*, p. 279.
4 Levy, 'The Economic History of Sickness and Medical Benefit Before the Puritan Revolution', *Economic History Review*, 1943, 13.1, 42–57; Hartley and Elliot, *Life and Work of the People of England*, p. 19; Gale, 'The Dissolution and the Revolution in London Hospital Facilities', *Medical History*, 1967, Jan. 11(1), 91–6.
5 Duffy, *The Stripping of the Altars*, pp. 494–5.
6 Dixon, *Weeping Britannia*, pp. 33–4.
7 Ibid., pp. 34–5.
8 Smith, *An Inquiry into the Nature and Causes of the Wealth of Nations*, p. 128.
9 Levy, 'The Economic History of Sickness and Medical Benefit Since the Puritan Revolution', *Economic History Review*, 1944, 14.2, 135–60.
10 Weber, *The Protestant Ethic and the Spirit of Capitalism*, ch. V.
11 Ibid., p. 97.
12 White, ed., *Journal of William Dowsing*, p. 6.
13 Ibid., p. 15.
14 Holroyd, ed. and trans., *Michael Angelo Buonarroti*, p. 213.
15 Ibid.
16 Ibid.
17 Ibid.
18 Ibid.
19 Huizinga, *The Waning of the Middle Ages*, p. 307.
20 Ibid., p. 318.

21 Ibid., pp. 294–5.
22 Lecture to the Royal Institution, 1836.
23 Montaigne, *Essays*, II, xii, 291.

CHAPTER THREE: THE SECOND SENTIMENTAL REVOLUTION

1 ODNB, John A. Dussinger, 'Samuel Richardson'.
2 *Clarissa*, Preface
3 *Clarissa*, Letter 224.
4 Richardson, *Pamela*, Letter I.
5 Ibid., p. 234.
6 Ibid., p. 84.
7 Ibid., p. 126.
8 Ibid., p. 163.
9 Ibid., p. 186.
10 Ibid., p. 248.
11 Ibid., p. 290.
12 Ibid., p, 433.
13 Quoted Eagleton, *The Rape of Clarissa*, p. 13.
14 *Pamela*, p. xxi.
15 Todd, *Sensibility: An Introduction*, p. 75.
16 Eagleton, *The Rape of Clarissa*, p. 77.
17 Schmidt, *Richardson, Rousseau und Goethe*, p. 19.
18 Ibid., p. 6.
19 *Pamela*, p. xvi.
20 Boswell, *Life of Johnson*, 6 April 1772; see also Mullan, *Sentiment and Sociability*, pp. 98–9.
21 6 April 1772; see also Mullan, *Sentiment and Sociability*, pp. 98–9.
22 Richardson, *Clarissa*, p. 123.
23 *Richardson's Correspondence*, ed. Anna Barbauld, 1804, IV, 282.
24 Richardson, *Clarissa*, Introduction, p. 24.
25 Ibid., p. 1499.
26 Eagleton, *The Rape of Clarissa*, p. 50.
27 Richardson, *Clarissa*, pp. 65–6.
28 Ibid., p. 48.
29 Ibid., p. 72.
30 Ibid., pp. 1214–15.
31 Ibid., pp. 1133–8.
32 Ibid., p. 885.
33 Ibid., p. 1143
34 Ibid., p. 897.

35 Lerner, *Love and Marriage*, pp. 201–2.
36 Ibid., p. 201.
37 Eagleton, *The Rape of Clarissa*, p. 101.
38 Lerner, *Love and Marriage*, p. 211.
39 Ibid., p. 205; Richardson, *Clarissa*, IV, p. 497.
40 Richardson, *Clarissa*, p. 1388.
41 Mullan, *Sentiment and Sociability*, p. 59.
42 Ibid.
43 Ibid., p. 58.
44 Stone, *The Family, Sex and Marriage in England, 1500–1800*, p. 163.
45 Quoted Eagleton, *The Rape of Clarissa*, p. 66.
46 Ibid., p. 65.
47 Ibid., p. 64.
48 Ibid., pp. 73–4.
49 Quoted Mullan, *Sentiment and Sociability*, p. 109.
50 Dixon, *Weeping Britannia*, pp. 73–4.
51 Hempton, *Methodism*, p. 33.
52 E. P. Thompson, *Making of the English Working Class*, pp. 404–5.
53 Ibid., p. 406.
54 Todd, *Sensibility: An Introduction*, p. 23.
55 Ibid., pp. 49–50.
56 Ibid., p. 95.
57 Rousseau, *Julie, ou la Nouvelle Héloïse*, Book IV, III, p. 426.
58 Ibid., Book V, VI, p. 453.
59 Safranski, *Goethe: Life as a Work of Art*, p. 209.
60 See Jeffrey R. Collins, 'The Church Settlement of Oliver Cromwell', *History*, 2002, vol. 87, 285.
61 See, for example, Neil McKendrick et al., *The Birth of a Consumer Society*, and Britnell, *The Commercialisation of English Society, 1000–1500*.
62 Hume, *A Treatise of Human Nature*, p. 415, see also Mullan, *Sentiment and Sociability*, p. 19 et ff.
63 Ibid., p. 605.
64 Smith, *The Theory of Moral Sentiments*, p. 3.
65 Ibid.
66 Ibid., p. 499.
67 Raphael, *Adam Smith*, p. 93.
68 Quoted ibid., p. 111.
69 1959; originally published in 1934 as *Logik der Forschung*.
70 Smith, *The Theory of Moral Sentiments*, p. 224.
71 Ross, *Life of Adam Smith*, p. 181.

72 Dixon, Weeping Britannia, p. 100.
73 Ibid., p. 98.
74 Quoted Mullan, Sentiment and Sociability, p. 123.
75 Mackenzie, The Man of Feeling, p. xv.
76 Ibid.
77 Mullan, Sentiment and Sociability, p. 123.
78 Todd, Sensibility: An Introduction, p. 146.
79 Mackenzie, The Man of Feeling, pp. 4–5.
80 Ibid., p. 72.
81 Marx, trans Moore and Aveling, Capital, vol. I, ch. xxv, n. 107.
82 Mackenzie, The Man of Feeling, p. 76.
83 Mullan, Sentiment and Sociability, p. 118.
84 The Lounger, no. 10, 18 June 1785; Mackenzie, The Man of Feeling, p. 102.
85 Todd, Sensibility: An Introduction, p. 131.
86 Mullan, p. 135.
87 Quoted, Todd, p. 135.
88 Stone, The Family, Sex and Marriage in England, 1500–1800, p. 163.
89 Ibid., pp. 162–3.
90 Mount, Jem (and Sam), p. 425.
91 Gentleman's Magazine, June 1801.
92 McKendrick et al., The Birth of a Consumer Society, p. 302.
93 Ibid., p. 304.

CHAPTER FOUR: MANLINESS RULES OK

1 Todd, Sensibility: An Introduction, p. 128.
2 Ibid., p. 134.
3 Quoted ibid., p. 122.
4 Ibid., p. 135.
5 Ibid., p. 140.
6 A Letter to the Duke of Newcastle, with some remarks touching the French Revolution, 1792, pp. 81–2, quoted Dixon, Weeping Britannia, p. 116.
7 Letter to Richard Fitzpatrick, 30 July 1789, in Lord John Russell, Life and Times of Charles James Fox, 1859, vol. II.
8 Hague, William Pitt the Younger, p. 272.
9 Dixon, Weeping Britannia, p. 110.
10 Ibid.
11 Carlyle, Works, ed. Traill, 3.3.I.
12 Ibid., 1.2.VII.
13 Wollstonecraft, A Vindication of the Rights of Woman, pp. 357, 319.

14 Todd, *Sensibility: An Introduction*, p. 139.
15 *The Watchman*, 25 March 1796.
16 Todd, *Sensibility: An Introduction*, p. 145,
17 Wollstonecraft, *A Vindication of the Rights of Woman*, p. 180.
18 Christine de Pizan, *The Book of the City of Ladies*, trans. Rosalind Brown-Grant (1999), p. 5.
19 Wollstonecraft, ibid., p. 113.
20 Ibid., p. 119.
21 Ibid., p. 100.
22 Ibid., p. 283.
23 14 March 1826.
24 Peter Sabor, 'Finished up to Nature': Walter Scott's review of *Emma*, *Persuasions*, no. 13, 1991, 88–99.
25 Tomalin, *Jane Austen: A Life*, p. 71.
26 Biographical Notice of Ellis and Acton Bell, 1850, quoted Brontë, *Wuthering Heights*, p. 4.
27 Quoted Dixon, *Weeping Britannia*, p. 150.
28 Ibid., p. 203.
29 Jon Wilson, *India Conquered*, pp. 138–9.
30 Mount, *Tears of the Rajas*, pp. 212–15.
31 Ibid., p. 343.
32 Ibid., p. 380.
33 Ibid., pp. 442–3.
34 Kaye and Malleson, *History of the Indian Mutiny*, vol. 1, p. 109.
35 *All the Year Round*, 18 February 1871, p. 273.
36 Stowe, *Uncle Tom's Cabin*, pp. 96, 114.
37 Sassoon, *Siegfried's Journey*, p. 78.
38 Quoted Dixon, *Weeping Britannia*, p. 214.

CHAPTER FIVE: MR POPULAR SENTIMENT

1 Trollope, *The Warden*, p. 12.
2 Ibid., p. 135.
3 Ch. Five.
4 Ibid.
5 Ibid., p. 99.
6 Ibid., p. 156.
7 Ibid.
8 Ibid., p. 154.
9 Ibid., p. 155.
10 Collins, ed., *Dickens: The Critical Heritage*, p. 569.

11 Saturday Review, 17 December 1859.
12 'Mr Dickens as a politician', Saturday Review, 3 January 1857, iii, pp. 8–9.
13 Saturday Review, 8 May 1858, v, pp. 474–5.
14 Ibid.
15 Edinburgh Review, cvi, 1857, pp. 124–56.
16 Literary Studies, 1879, ii, pp. 184–220; reprinted from National Review, October 1858, vii, pp. 458–86.
17 Bagehot, English Constitution, p. 276.
18 Ibid., p. 266.
19 Ruskin, 'Fiction Fair and Foul', in The Ethics of the Dust, p. 182
20 Ibid., p. 187.
21 Ibid., p. 184.
22 Fortnightly Review, February 1872, xvii, pp. 141–54.
23 Huxley, Vulgarity in Literature, pp. 54–9.
24 Stowe, Uncle Tom's Cabin, p. 412.
25 Ibid., p. 166.
26 Baldwin, Notes of a Native Son, pp. 17–18.
27 Stowe, Uncle Tom's Cabin, p. 299.
28 Baldwin, Notes of a Native Son, p. 14.
29 Quoted Kirkham, The Building of Uncle Tom's Cabin, p. 111.
30 Stowe, Uncle Tom's Cabin, p. 409.
31 Orwell, ed. Orwell and Angus, Collected Essays, vol. IV, 2 November 1945, pp. 21–2.
32 Wilson, Patriotic Gore, p. 134.
33 Stowe, Uncle Tom's Cabin, pp. 213, 207.
34 Tompkins, Sensational Designs, pp. 122–3.
35 Ibid., p. 124.
36 Ibid., p. 217.
37 Ibid., p. 145.
38 Stowe, p. xxii.
39 Eastman, Aunt Phillis's Cabin,, p. 4.
40 Ibid., pp. 6–8.
41 Ibid., p. 124.
42 Ibid., p. 132.
43 Ibid., p. 29.
44 Ibid., p. 129.
45 Ibid., p. 32.
46 Stowe, p. 99.
47 Eastman, p. 133.
48 L. Frank Baum, Aberdeen Saturday Pioneer, 3 January 1891.

49 Eastman, *Aunt Phillis's Cabin*, p. 63.
50 Behr, *The Complete Book of Les Misérables*, p. 50.
51 *Guardian*, 21 September 2010.
52 *Journal*, April 1862 (Laffont, 1989), vol I, pp. 808–9.
53 *Le Boulevard*, 20 April 1862
54 Dunlop, *The Shock of the New*, p. 30.
55 Whistler, *The Gentle Art of Making Enemies*.
56 Ruskin, *Fors Clavigera*, letter 79, June 1877.
57 Lamartine, *Oeuvres Complètes*, vols XIV–XV; see also Trousson, *Lamartine critique des Misérables*.
58 *Oeuvres Complètes*, vols XXI–XXII.
59 Robert Hughes, *The Fatal Shore*, 1986, p. 581 and n.
60 Hugo, trans. Rose, *Les Misérables*, p. 261.
61 Ibid., pp. 422, 423.
62 Ibid. p. 432.
63 Ibid., pp. 101–2.
64 Gide, *Victor Hugo, Hélas!*, pp. 8–9.
65 Ibid., pp. 12–13.
66 Ibid., pp. 34–5.

CHAPTER SIX: THE GREAT ESTRANGING

1   Bell, *Art*, p. 9.
2   Ibid.
3   Ibid., p. 11.
4   Ibid.
5   Ibid., p. 12.
6   Ibid., p. 10.
7   Ibid.
8   Ortega y Gasset, *The Dehumanization of Art*, p. 21.
9   Ibid., p. 22.
10 Ibid., p. 27.
11 Carey, *The Intellectuals and the Masses*, p. 74.
12 Bell, *Art*, p. 13.
13 Richardson, *A Life of Picasso*, vol. I, pp. 80–82.
14 Ibid., pp. 70–2.
15 Woolf, 'Mr Bennett and Mrs Brown', 18 May 1924.
16 Virginia Woolf, 'Old Bloomsbury', written 1920–1, but published in *Moments of Being* (1976), pp. 195–6.
17 Dunlop, *The Shock of the New*, p. 226.

18 Carey, *The Intellectuals and the Masses*, pp. 163–4.
19 Ibid., p. 157.
20 Ibid., p. 153.
21 Ortega y Gasset, *The Dehumanization of Art*, p. 5.
22 Ibid., p. 4.
23 Ibid., pp. 47–8.
24 Ibid.
25 Nash, *Outline: An Autobiography and Other Writings*.
26 Delaroche's remark was taken as the title of a pioneering Arts Council exhibition of early photography in 1972, co-curated by my cousin and brother-in-law Tristram Powell, to whose memory this book is dedicated.
27 Yeats, *On the Boiler*.
28 Barnett and Scruton, *Town and Country*, p. 322
29 Ortega y Gasset, *The Dehumanization of Art*, p. 10.
30 Nietzsche and Mencken, *The Anti-Christ*, p. 6.
31 Ibid., pp. 9–10.
32 Ibid., p. 11.
33 Quoted Carey, *The Intellectuals and the Masses*, pp. 196–7.

CHAPTER SEVEN: THE THIRD SENTIMENTAL REVOLUTION

1   Hennessy, *Having It So Good*, p. 510.
2   Ibid.
3   Graham Stewart, 'The Accidental Legacy of a Homophobic Humanitarian', *The Times*, 2 October 2000.
4   Kynaston, *Family Britain*, p. 370.
5   House of Lords, 4 December 1957.
6   Hennessy, *Having It So Good*, p. 509.
7   Devlin, *The Enforcement of Morals*, pp. 13–14.
8   'Immorality and Treason', *Listener*, 30 July 1959.
9   Hart, *Law, Liberty, and Morality*, p. 22.
10 Ibid., p. 79.
11 Mill, *On Liberty*, ch. 1.
12 Stephen, *Liberty, Equality, Fraternity*, p. 165.
13 Ibid.
14 Stephen, *A History of the Criminal Law of England*, II, pp. 81–2, cited in Hart, *Law, Liberty, and Morality*, p. 64.
15 Ben Clements and Clive D. Field, 'Public opinion towards homosexuality and gay rights in Great Britain', *The Public Opinion Quarterly*, Summer 2014, vol. 78, no. 2, 523–47.

16 Ben Clements and Clive D. Field, 'Abortion and public opinion in Britain – a 50-year retrospect', *Journal of Beliefs and Values*, vol. 39, 2018, 41.
17 See Mount, *The Subversive Family*, p. 211–12.
18 Collins, ed., *The Permissive Society*, p. 27.
19 Ibid., p. 3.
20 Lynda Lee-Potter, *Daily Mail*, 20 March 2002.
21 Paul Johnson, *Daily Mail*, 15 September 2001.
22 Collins, ed., *The Permissive Society*, p. 32.
23 Norman Tebbit, *The Times*, 23 November 1993.
24 Roger Scruton, 'The Future of European Civilisation: Lessons for America', lecture to Heritage Foundation, October 2015.
25 See Ferdinand Mount, *The British Constitution Now*, p. 57.
26 Mill, *On Liberty*, ch. 4.
27 'Chris Hutchins', *The Times*, 6 August 2024.
28 Ali, *Street Fighting Years*, pp. 250–4; *Jacobin*, 12 December 2020; *Guardian*, 2 February 2010.
29 *First Things*, 19 May 2023.
30 Dixon, *Weeping Britannia*, pp. 400–401.
31 Rod Liddle, 'Big Girls Don't Cry. Nor Do Conservatives', *Spectator*, 26 August 2004.
32 Maudsley, *Natural Causes and Supernatural Seemings*, pp. 300–1.
33 Thompson, *The Making of the English Working Class*, pp. 404–6.
34 Toby Young, 'When Did Tears Become Compulsory?', *Spectator*, 14 July 2012.
35 Dixon, *Weeping Britannia*, p. 263.
36 Gascoigne, *Gazza: My Story*, p. 154.
37 Salman Rushdie, 'The Boy, the Butcher and the Wizard of Gaz', *Independent on Sunday*, 18 November 1990.
38 Thomas, *Diana's Mourning*, p. 8.
39 *Sun*, 8 September 1997.
40 Tom Utley, *Daily Telegraph*, 3 September 1997.
41 Thomas, *Diana's Mourning*, p. 52.
42 Ibid., pp. 109–10.
43 Ibid., p. 110.
44 Ibid. p. 166.
45 Richard Littlejohn, *Sun*, 19 April 1998.
46 Bruce Anderson, *Independent*, 8 April 2002.
47 Carol Sarler, *The Times*, 7 September 2007.
48 Anderson and Mullen, eds, *Faking It*, p. 18.
49 Ibid.

50 Ibid., pp. 189–90.
51 Ibid., p. 188.
52 Ibid.
53 Ibid.
54 Ibid., p. 189.
55 Ibid., p. 125.
56 Ibid., p. 121.
57 Anthony Powell, *Under Review*, p. 178.
58 Anderson and Mullen, eds, *Faking It*, p. 126.
59 Ortega y Gasset, *The Dehumanization of Art*, pp. 47–8.
60 Anderson and Mullen, eds, *Faking It*, p. 12.
61 Ibid., p. 112.
62 Anderson, ed., *This Will Hurt*.
63 Ibid., p. x.
64 Ibid., ch. 7.
65 Ibid., ch. 4.
66 Ibid., p. 49.
67 Plato, *The Republic*, IV.432.
68 *Macbeth*, I. v.

Further Reading

(Place of publication London, except where stated)

Ali, Tariq (1987), *Street Fighting Years*. Collins.
Anderson, Digby, ed. (1995), *This Will Hurt: The Restoration of Virtue and Civil Order*. Social Affairs Unit.
Anderson, Digby and Mullen, Peter, eds. (1998), *Faking It: The Sentimentalisation of Modern Society*. Social Affairs Unit.
Arts Council (1972), *'From Today Painting Is Dead': The Beginnings of Photography*. Catalogue of the Exhibition at the Victoria and Albert Museum.
Aston, Margaret (2016), *Broken Idols of the Reformation*. Cambridge: Cambridge University Press.
Bagehot, Walter (1867), *The English Constitution*. World's Classics (1928).
Baldwin, James (1955), *Notes of a Native Son*. New York; Penguin Modern Classics (2017).
Barbauld, Anna, ed. (1804), *Richardson's Correspondence*. Richard Phillips.
Barczewski, Stephanie (2016), *Heroic Failure and the British*. New Haven: Yale University Press.
Barnett, Anthony and Scruton, Roger (1998), *Town and Country*. Jonathan Cape.
Beatles, The (1993), *The Beatles Lyrics*. Milwaukee, Wisconsin: Hal Leonard.
Behr, Edward (1989), *The Complete Book of Les Misérables*. New York: Arcade.
Bell, Clive (1916), *Art*. Chatto & Windus.
— (1928), *Civilisation*. Chatto & Windus.
Béroul, Alfred Ewert, ed. (1939), *The Romance of Tristan*. Oxford: Basil Blackwell.
Béroul, trans. Alan S. Fedrick (1970), *The Romance of Tristan*. Penguin Classics.

Boswell, James (1992), *The Life of Samuel Johnson*. Reprinted, Everyman.
Boyle, Nicholas, *Goethe: The Poet and the Age*, vol. I (1991); vol. II (2000). Oxford: Clarendon Press.
Brewer, John (1996), *The Pleasures of the Imagination: English Culture in the Eighteenth Century*. HarperCollins.
Britnell, Richard H. (1993), *The Commercialisation of English Society, 1000–1500*. Cambridge: Cambridge University Press.
Brontë, Emily, *Wuthering Heights*. W. W. Norton (2019).
Bruckner, M. T., Shepard, L. and White, Sarah, ed. and trans. (2000), *Songs of the Women Troubadours*. Routledge.
Carey, John (1992), *The Intellectuals and the Masses*. Faber & Faber.
Carlyle, Thomas (1896–9), *Works*, ed. H. D. Traill. Chapman & Hall.
Carpenter, David (2015), *Magna Carta*. Penguin Classics.
— (2020), *Henry III: The Rise to Power and Personal Rule, 1207–1258*. New Haven: Yale University Press.
— (2023), *Henry III: Reform, Rebellion, Civil War, Settlement, 1259–1272*. New Haven: Yale University Press.
Cervantes, Miguel de, *Don Quixote*, trans. John Rutherford. Penguin Classics (2000).
Chaucer, Geoffrey, *Romaunt of the Rose*, trans. (2016), Leopold Classics.
Chaucer, Geoffrey, *The Canterbury Tales*, trans. Nevill Coghill (1951), Penguin Classics (2003).
Chaucer, Geoffrey, *Troilus and Criseyde*, trans. Nevill Coghill (1971), Penguin Classics (2004).
Chaucer, Geoffrey, *Canterbury Quintet. The General Prologue & Four Tales*, ed. Michael Murphy. New York: Conal & Gavin (2000).
Collins, Marcus, ed. (2007), *The Permissive Society and Its Enemies*. Rivers Oram Press.
Collins, Philip, ed. (1971), *Dickens: The Critical Heritage*. Routledge & Kegan Paul.
Cunningham, Valentine (1975), *Everywhere Spoken Against: Dissent in the Victorian Novel*. Oxford: Oxford University Press.
Devlin, Patrick (1965), *The Enforcement of Morals*. Oxford: Oxford University Press.
Dickens, Charles (1848), *Dombey and Son*.
Dickens, Charles (1870), *The Mystery of Edwin Drood*.
Dickens, Charles (1841), *The Old Curiosity Shop*.
Diderot, Denis (1762), *Éloge de Richardson*. Paris.
Dixon, Thomas (2015), *Weeping Britannia*. Oxford: Oxford University Press.
Dowsing, William (1786), *The Journal of William Dowsing*. Woodbridge.

Duffy, Eamon (1992), *The Stripping of the Altars*. New Haven: Yale University Press.
— (2001), *The Voices of Morebath*. New Haven: Yale University Press.
Dunlop, Ian (1972), *The Shock of the New*. Weidenfeld & Nicolson.
Eagleton, Terry (1982), *The Rape of Clarissa*. Minneapolis: University of Minnesota Press.
Eastman, Mary H. (1852), *Aunt Phillis's Cabin*. CreateSpace (2016).
Eliot, George (1871–2), *Middlemarch*.
Etchegoyen, Gaston (1923), *L'Amour divin: essai sur les sources de sainte Thérèse*. Paris.
Fielding, Henry (1741), *Shamela*.
— (1742), *Joseph Andrews*.
Ford, George H. and Lane, Lauriat, Jr (1961), *The Dickens Critics*. Ithaca, New York: Cornell University Press.
Frascina, Francis and Harrison, Charles (1982), *Modern Art and Modernism: A Critical Anthology*. Harper & Row.
Gascoigne, Paul with Davies, Hunter (2004), *Gazza: My Story*. Hodder Headline.
Gide, André (2002), *Hugo, hélas!*. Fontfroide, Narbonne, France: Éditions Fata Morgana.
Goethe, Johann Wolfgang von (1774), *Die Leiden des Jungen Werthers*.
— (1777), *Der Triumph der Empfindsamkeit*.
Goody, Jack (1983), *The Development of the Family and Marriage in Europe*. Cambridge: Cambridge University Press.
Hague, William (2004), *William Pitt the Younger*. HarperCollins.
Hall, Joseph, *Bishop Hall's Hard Measure*, in *The Shaking of the Olive Tree* (1660, reprinted 1710).
Hart, H. L. A. (1963), *Law, Liberty and Morality*. Oxford: Oxford University Press.
Hartley, Dorothy and Elliot, Margaret (1925), *Life and Work of the People of England*, vol. I, *The Eleventh to Thirteenth Centuries*. B. T. Batsford.
Hempton, David (2005), *Methodism*. New Haven: Yale University Press.
Hennessy, Peter (2006), *Having It So Good*. Allen Lane.
Highmore, Joseph (1963), *Paintings by Joseph Highmore*. LCC, Kenwood.
Holland, Vyvyan (1954), *Son of Oscar Wilde*. Oxford: Oxford University Press.
Holroyd, Charles, ed. and trans. (2023), *Michael Angelo Buonarroti by Francisco de Holanda*. Alpha Editions.
Homans, George C. (1941), *English Villagers of the Thirteenth Century*. Cambridge, Mass.: Harvard University Press.
Hughes, Robert (1986), *The Fatal Shore*. Collins Harvill.

Hugo, Victor, trans. Julie Rose (2009), *Les Misérables*. Vintage.
Huizinga, Johan (1924), *The Waning of the Middle Ages*. Reprinted, Cluny Media (2018).
Hume, David (1740), *A Treatise of Human Nature*. Reprinted, Oxford (1978).
Huxley, Aldous (1930), *Vulgarity in Literature*. Chatto & Windus.
Jones, Terry (1980), *Chaucer's Knight*. Weidenfeld & Nicolson.
Kaye, J. W. and Malleson, G. B. (1888–9), *History of the Indian Mutiny*. W. H. Allen, 6 vols.
Keen, Maurice (1990), *English Society in the Later Middle Ages, 1348–1500*. Allen Lane.
Kingsley, Charles (1863), *The Water Babies*. Reprinted, Allen & Unwin (1978).
Kirkham, E. Bruce (1977), *The Building of Uncle Tom's Cabin*. Knoxville Tennessee: University of Tennessee Press.
Kline, A. S., trans. (2009), *From Dawn to Dawn: Troubadour Poetry*. CreateSpace.
Lamartine, Alphonse de (1845), *Oeuvres Complètes*. Paris.
— (1863), *Fior d'Aliza*. Paris.
Leavis, F. R. (1948), *The Great Tradition*. Chatto & Windus.
Leavis, F. R. and Leavis, Q. D. (1970), *Dickens the Novelist*. Chatto & Windus.
Lerner, Laurence (1979), *Love and Marriage: Literature and Its Social Context*. Edward Arnold.
Lewis, C. S. (1936), *The Allegory of Love*. Oxford: Oxford University Press.
Lieven, Dominic (2022), *In the Shadow of Gods: The Emperor in World History*. Allen Lane.
Locke, John (1689), *A Letter Concerning Toleration*. Reprinted, A. Murray (1870).
Lorris, Guillaume de and Meun, Jean de, trans. Frances Horgan (1994), *The Romance of the Rose*. Oxford: Oxford World's Classics.
Mackenzie, Henry (1771), *The Man of Feeling*. Oxford, World's Classics (1987).
Macpherson, C. B. (1962), *The Political Theory of Possessive Individualism*. Oxford: Clarendon Press.
Mâle, Emile (1913), *The Gothic Image*. J. M. Dent.
Marinetti, F. T., *Selected Writings*, ed. R. W. Flint (1972). New York: Farrar, Straus and Giroux.
Marx, Karl, trans Samuel Moore and Edward Aveling (1889), *Capital*. Reprinted, Allen & Unwin (1938).
Matarasso, Pauline, trans. (1971), *Aucassin and Nicolette and Other Tales*. Penguin Classics.
Maudsley, Henry (1886), *Natural Causes and Supernatural Seemings*. Reprinted, Watts (1939).
McKendrick, Neil, Brewer, John and Plumb, J. H. (1982), *The Birth of a Consumer Society: The Commercialization of Eighteenth-Century England*. Europa.

Mill, John Stuart (1859), *On Liberty*. Reprinted, Penguin (2006).
Mill, John Stuart and Mill, Harriet Taylor (1869), *The Subjection of Women*. Reprinted, Penguin (2006).
Morris, Colin (1972), *The Discovery of the Individual, 1050–1200*. New York: Harper & Row.
Mount, Ferdinand (1982), *The Subversive Family*. Jonathan Cape.
— (1998), *Jem (and Sam)*. Chatto & Windus.
— (2015), *The Tears of the Rajas*. Simon & Schuster.
Mullan, John (1988), *Sentiment and Sociability: The Language of Feeling in the Eighteenth Century*. Oxford: Oxford University Press.
Nash, Paul (1949), *Outline: An Autobiography*. Faber & Faber.
Nietzsche, Friedrich (2017), *The Will to Power*. Penguin Classics.
Nietzsche, Friedrich and Mencken, H. L. (2015), *The Anti-Christ*. New York, Tribeca Books.
Nye, Joseph S., Jr (2004), *Soft Power*. New York: Public Affairs.
Ortega y Gasset, José (1930), *The Revolt of the Masses*. Reprinted (1994) New York: Norton.
— (1948), *The Dehumanization of Art and Other Essays*. Princeton, New Jersey, Princeton University Press.
Orwell, George, ed. Sonia Orwell and Ian Angus (1968), *Collected Essays*. Four vols, Secker & Warburg.
Oxford Dictionary of National Biography (2004). Oxford: Oxford University Press.
Plato, trans Benjamin Jowett, (1908), *The Republic*. Oxford: Oxford University Press.
Pottle, Frederick A. (1941), *The Idiom of Poetry*. Ithaca NY: Cornell University Press
Powell, Anthony (1991), *Under Review*. Chicago: University of Chicago Press.
— (2005), *Some Poets, Artists and 'A Reference for Mellors'*. Timewell Press.
Powicke, Maurice (1953), *The Thirteenth Century 1216–1307*. Oxford: Oxford University Press.
Raphael, D. D. (1985), *Adam Smith*. Oxford: Oxford University Press.
Renton, Alex (2018), *Stiff Upper Lip*. Weidenfeld & Nicolson.
Richardson, John, *A Life of Picasso*, vol. I (1991), vol. II (1996). Jonathan Cape.
Richardson, Samuel (1740), *Pamela: or, Virtue Rewarded*. Oxford: Oxford World's Classics (2001).
— (1747–8), *Clarissa: or, The History of a Young Lady*. Penguin Classics (1985).
Ross, Ian Simpson (1995), *The Life of Adam Smith*. Oxford: Oxford University Press.

Rougemont, Denis de (1940), *Love in the Western World*. Princeton, New Jersey, Princeton University Press (1983 edn).

Rousseau, Jean-Jacques (1761), *Julie, ou La Nouvelle Héloïse*. Paris: Flammarion (1967).

Ruskin, John (1871–84), *Fors Clavigera*. Legare Street Press (2022).

— (2016), *The Ethics of the Dust, etc*. Palala Press.

Safranski, Rüdiger (2013), *Goethe: Life as a Work of Art*. New York: Norton/Liveright.

Sassoon, Siegfried (1945), *Siegfried's Journey*. Faber & Faber.

Schmidt, Erich (1875), *Richardson, Rousseau und Goethe: Ein Beitrag zur Geschichte des Romans im 18 Jahrhundert*. Forgotten Books (2018).

Smith, Adam (1759), *The Theory of Moral Sentiments*. Penguin Classics (2009).

— (1776), *An Inquiry into the Nature and Causes of the Wealth of Nations*. Everyman (1975)

Solomon, Robert C. (2004), *In Defence of Sentimentality*. Oxford: Oxford University Press.

Stephen, James Fitzjames (1873), *Liberty, Equality, Fraternity*. Smith Elder.

Stone, Lawrence (1977), *The Family, Sex and Marriage in England, 1500–1800*. Weidenfeld & Nicolson.

Stowe, Harriet Beecher (1852), *Uncle Tom's Cabin*. Wordsworth Classics (1995).

Tawney, R. H. (1926), *Religion and the Rise of Capitalism*. Penguin Books (1948).

Thomas, James (2002), *Diana's Mourning: A People's History*. Cardiff: University of Wales Press.

Thompson, E. P. (1963), *The Making of the English Working Class*. Victor Gollancz.

Todd, Janet (1986), *Sensibility: An Introduction*. Methuen.

Tomalin, Clare (1997), *Jane Austen: A Life*. Viking.

Tompkins, Jane (1985), *Sensational Designs: The Cultural Work of American Fiction 1790–1860*. Oxford: Oxford University Press.

Trollope, Anthony (1855), *The Warden*. Penguin Classics (2012).

Trousson, Raymond (1995), *Lamartine critique des Misérables*. Brussels: L'Académie royale de langue et de littérature françaises de Belgique.

Troyes, Chrétien de, trans. W. W. Kibler (1991), *Arthurian Romances*. Penguin Classics.

Viereck, Peter (1941, 1961), *Meta-Politics: The Roots of the Nazi Mind*. New York, Knopf.

Voragine, Jacobus de (1998), *The Golden Legend*. Penguin Classics.

Weber, Max (1905), *The Protestant Ethic and the Spirit of Capitalism*. Penguin Books (2002).
Whistler, James Abbott McNeill (1878), *The Gentle Art of Making Enemies*.
Wilde, Oscar (1897), *De Profundis*.
Wilson, Edmund (1962), *Patriotic Gore*. New York: W. W. Norton.
Wilson, Jon (2016), *India Conquered*. Simon & Schuster.
Wollstonecraft, Mary (1790), *A Vindication of the Rights of Woman* and *A Vindication of the Rights of Men*. Oxford: Oxford World's Classics (1994).
Woolf, Virginia (1928), *Mr Bennett and Mrs Brown*. Hogarth Press.
— (1976), *Moments of Being*. Chatto & Windus.
Yeats, W. B. (1939), *On the Boiler*. Dublin: Cuala Press.

Acknowledgements

At Bloomsbury I am so grateful for the thoughtful comments and editing of Tomasz Hoskins, Octavia Stocker and Sarah Jones. The debt which I owe to those scholars who have identified the great sentimental revolutions and the reactions against them is obvious. But I must record my special gratitude to those writers who have actively transformed my understanding of their periods: John Carey, David Carpenter, Thomas Dixon, Eamon Duffy, Terry Eagleton and Janet Todd.

Index

Note: page numbers in *italic* indicate illustrations.

Ab la dolchor del temps novel (William of Aquitaine) 4
abortion 98, 220, 230–1
'Advice of the Old Woman' 11–12, 15
'Aesthetic Hypothesis, The' (Bell) 190–1
After Strange Gods (Eliot) 212
Aldersgate Day 79–80
Ali, Tariq 246
alienation effect (*Verfremdungseffekt*) 192
All the Year Round (magazine, Dickens) 139
Amesbury Abbey 45
Anderson, Bruce 258
Anderson, Digby ix–x, 259, 263, 264
Anglicans/Anglicanism 51, 52, 117
animal rights 110–13
'Annus Mirabilis' (Larkin) 215–16
Anti-Christ, The (Nietzsche) 209–10
anti-Semitism 209, 210–12
Aquinas, Thomas 28–9
Aristotle 94
art, new movements in 195–6, 201
Art (Bell) 191–2
'Artist and Empire' Tate exhibition 142
Arts Council 218
ataraxia 60–1, 81, 155, 183–4
Aucassin and Nicolette 21–2
Auguries of Innocence (Blake) 112
Aunt Phillis's Cabin; or, Southern Life as it is (Eastman) 166–7, 169, 170
Austen, Jane 131–2
Autobiography (Mill) 136
Autobiography (Trollope) 147, 148–9

Bagehot, Walter 153–4
Baldwin, James 158, 159, 162

Barczewski, Stephanie 141–4
Barnes, John 254
Barwick, J`ohn 55
Baudelaire, Charles 174
Baudrillard, Jean x
Baum, L. Frank 170
Beatles 216, 242–6, 249
Beatriz, Comtessa de Dia 5
Beethoven, Ludwig van 194, 249
Bell, Clive xviii, 190–1, 192, 193–4, 200
Benedict, St 38–9
Benjamin, Floella 218
Benn, Gottfried 198
Bennett, Arnold 198–9, 200, 206
Bentham, Jeremy 105, 112, 115–116
Bentley, Derek 229
Berlepsch, Emilie von 88
Bernard of Clairvaux, St 28, 32
Bernart de Ventadorn 3
Béroul 3, 6–9
Billington, Michael 172
Bishop Hall's Hard Measure, written by himself upon his Impeachment of High Crimes and Misdemeanours for defending the Church of England (Hall) 54
Blake, William 104, 112, 161
Blanchard, Sophie 128
Bleak House (Dickens) 82, 155, 157
Blind Girl, The (Millais) 176, 176
Boccaccio, Giovanni 20, 40
Bodenham, Cecily 44–5
Bogarde, Dirk xii–xiii, 227
Bond, Edward 217
Book of the City of Ladies, The (Christine de Pizan) 130
Boothby, Robert 223, 233

Boswell, James 69
Boty, Pauline 218–19, 219
Boublil, Alain 171–2
Bradshaigh, Lady 63, 67, 71, 75, 79
Brady, Mathew 206
Brandt, Bill 207
Braque, Georges 196, 201–2
Braverman, Suella xii
Brecht, Bertolt 192
Brexit Party 249
Brontë, Charlotte 132, 133, 135
Brontë, Emily 134–5
Brooke, Rupert 145, 146
Browne, Thomas 55
Buchan, John 145
BUM (Boty) 219, 219
buona figliuola, La (opera buffa) 68
buona figliuola maritata, La (opera buffa) 68
'Burbank with a Baedeker, Bleistein with a Cigar' (Eliot) 211–12
Burke, Edmund 99, 125
Burns, Robert 99

Calvin, John 50, 54
Canterbury Tales, The (Chaucer) 19–21, 23, 40
Capa, Robert 207
capital punishment, campaign against 228–30
Carey, John 193, 199, 200
Carlyle, Thomas 126, 149
Cartwright, John 116–17, 124, 128
Cathy Come Home (Sandford) xii
Cato Street Conspiracy 128
Cavell, Edith 134, 134, 146
censorship 216–220
Cervantes, Miguel de 23–4
chante-fables 21–2
Chapman, Mark David 247–8
Chaucer, Geoffrey 12, 16–21, 23, 40, 76
Chesterfield, Lord 12
Chrétien de Troyes 3, 9–11, 25, 250
Christianity 53, 209–10, 263–4, 265–6
Christine de Pizan 130
Christopherson, John 47
Churchill, Winston 145–146
Clarissa, or the History of a Young Lady (Richardson) 64–5, 67–8, 72–7
Clarkson, Thomas 117, 119
Cligès (Chrétien de Troyes) 9–11
Cobbold, Lord 217
Cockburn, Henry 103
Coleridge, Samuel Taylor 127

Collins, Marcus 234–5
Colonna, Vittoria 58
Communist Manifesto, The (Marx and Engels) 207
Confessions (Rousseau) 86
Connolly, Cyril 208
Constable, John 60, 110
copycat suicides (Werther Effect) 87
Coram, Thomas 107–8
Coren, Giles 251
Cornwallis Code 137
Cours Familier de Littérature (Lamartine) 177–8
Coward, Noël 249
Cowper, William 118
Cranmer, Thomas 50
Crimean War 133–4, 206–7
Criterion, The (Eliot) 208
Crofton Boys, The (Martineau) 136–7
Cromwell, Oliver 51, 90–1
Cromwell, Thomas 44, 45–6, 48–9
'Cywydd y cedor' ('Hymn to the Vulva', Mechain) 5–6

Dando, Jill 256
Darwin, Charles xi–xii
Day in the Death of Joe Egg, A (Nichols) xiii
De Profundis (Wilde) xiii, xiv
death xiv, xv, 31–6, 50, 78, 255–8
Decameron (Boccaccio) 40
Dehumanization of Art, The (Ortega y Gasset) 193, 200–1
Delaroche, Paul 206
Delille, Jacques 181
Denis the Carthusian 32
Denning, Lord 223
Devlin, Patrick 224–5, 226
Diana, Princess of Wales 255–62, 260
'Diana, Queen of Hearts' (O'Hear) 259–62
Dickens, Charles xiv, 71, 82, 139, 149–57, 162–3, 187
Dickens the Novelist (Leavis) 156
Diderot, Denis 72–3, 79, 86
discrimination 235–240
Dissenters 120–121, 252
Dissolution of the Monasteries 44–9
divorce 220, 231–3
Dixon, Thomas 100, 126, 251, 253
Doctor, The (Fildes) 187, 188, 189–91, 190
Dombey and Son (Dickens) 82
Douglas, Lord Alfred xiv
Dowsing, William (Smasher Dowsing) 55–7

INDEX

Drabble, Margaret 234
Duffy, Eamon 31, 48, 50

Eagleton, Terry 67–8, 74, 76, 78
East India Company (EIC) 119, 135–6, 137–8
Eastman, Charles Alexander 169–70
Eastman, Mary Henderson 166–9, 170
Eastman, Seth 169
Eden, Anthony 233
Edmund Burke Foundation 248
EIC (East India Company) 119, 135–6, 137–8
Eliot, George 82, 103, 133
Eliot, T. S. 200, 207, 208, 211–12
Ellis, Ruth 229–30
Éloge de Richardson (Diderot) 72–3, 86
Emerson, Ralph Waldo 240
Emma (Austen) 131, 132
emotional incontinence 252–3, 258
Empty Chair, The (Fildes) 188, 188
Enfranchisement of Women, The (Mill) 237
Engels, Friedrich 207
Essay Concerning Human Understanding, An (Locke) 91–2
Essays (Montaigne) 60
'Estat ai en greu cossirier' (Beatriz, Comtessa de Dia) 5
Etchegoyen, Gaston 25
Evans, Timothy 229
Exhortation to all menne to take hede and beware of rebellion (Christopherson) 47
Expression of the Emotions in Man and Animals, The (Darwin) xi–xii

Faking It: The Sentimentalisation of Modern Society (Anderson and Mullen) ix–x, 259, 263, 264
Farage, Nigel 249
Faringdon, Hugh 45
feminism 75–6, 131
Fenton, Roger 206–7
Ferguson, Niall 41
Ferrer, St Vincent 32
Fiction Fair and Foul (Ruskin) 155
Fielding, Henry 69–70, 71
Fildes, Luke 187–8, 188, 189–91, 190
Fior d'Aliza (Lamartine) 179
First Communion (Picasso) 196, 197
First Sentimental Revolution 1–42, 250
  invention of love 1–24
  Passion of Christ 24–31
  social progress 36–42
  tears 31–6
Fisher, Geoffrey 233
Flaubert, Gustave 23–4, 89, 173–4, 182
Florio, John 60
Fontevraud Abbey 35–6
Football Association 239
Foundling Hospital, London 107–8, 107, 110
Four Stages of Cruelty, The (Hogarth) 110–11
Fowler, Norman 261
Francisco de Holanda 57–8
French Revolution 124–7
Fry, Elizabeth 115
Futurism 203–4, 212–14

Gainsborough, Thomas 60, 108
Galsworthy, John 198, 200, 262
Garrison, William Lloyd 159
Gascoigne, Paul 253–5, 254
Gauguin's Armchair (van Gogh) 188, 189
Gauthier, Léon 172
Gautier, Théophile 185
Gellert, Christian 68
'Gerontion' (Eliot) 211–12
Gerson, Jean 14
Gibson, Edmund 82
Gide, André 184–5
Gillespie, Rollo 141–2
Gillray, James 100–1
'God' (Lennon) 246–9
Goethe, Johann Wolfgang von 68, 79, 84, 86–89, 123
Golden Legend, The (Voragine) 30
Goldoni, Carlo 68
Goncourt brothers 173
Gordon, Charles George 141, 142
Gower, John 23
Gowers, Ernest 229
Great Tradition, The (Leavis) 156
Greenberg, Clement xviii, 205
Grenfell, Francis and Riversdale 145, 146
Grenfell, Julian 145, 146
Griffith-Jones, Mervyn 217
Grünewald, Matthias 26–7, 27
Guernica (Picasso) 205–6, 205
guilds: patron saints 30
Guttmann, Ludwig 267
Guy, Thomas 109
Gwalior, Maharaja of 138

Hair! (rock musical) 218
Hall, Joseph 54–5

Handel, George Frideric   108
Hard Times (Dickens)   156, 157
Hardy, Thomas   45
Hart, Herbert   224–5, 226
health care   38–9, 49, 107–10, 107
Héloise   3
'Helter Skelter' (Beatles)   245
Henley, W. E.   138–9
Henry III, King of England   33, 33–5, 36–7, 39, 40, 41–2
Henry V (Shakespeare)   24
Henry VIII, King of England   45–6, 49
Herbert, A. P.   220, 232
Herebert, William   28
'Hey Jude' (McCartney)   243–4
High Renaissance   57–61
Highmore, Joseph   64, 65, 68, 108
Himmelfarb, Gertrude   264
'History of Astronomy' (Smith)   97–8
History of Sir Charles Grandison, The (Richardson)   67
History of the Criminal Law of England, A (Stephen)   225
History of the French Revolution (Carlyle)   126
History of the Indian Mutiny (Kaye)   138
Hitchens, Dan   248
Hitler, Adolf   210–11
Hobbes, Thomas   92, 94
Hogarth, William   108, 110–11, 111
Hoggart, Richard   217
Holland, Cyril   146
Holland, Vyvyan   146
'Holy Deadlock' campaign   220, 232
Homeless/Poor Jo/Night in Town (Rejlander)   iiii, xi, 206
homelessness   xi–xii, 53
homosexuality   xii–xiii, 98, 106, 220, 222–8, 260–1
hospitals   39, 49, 107–10
Houseless and Hungry (Fildes)   187
Howard, John   114–16
Hughes, Thomas   136–137
Hugo, Victor   155, 170–4, 177–9, 180, 181–5, 193
Huizinga, Johan   3, 14, 29, 31, 59–60. 155
Hume, David   94, 96, 112
Huxley, Aldous   101, 156
Hyderabad, Nizam of   138
Hymn to the Virgin, A   28
'Hymn to the Vulva' ('Cywydd y cedor,' Mechain)   5–6

iconoclasm   47, 51–5, 56
'If' (Kipling)   139–40
'Imagine' (Lennon)   243, 246–8, 249
indifferentism   xviii–xix
Ingenious Gentleman Don Quixote of La Mancha (Cervantes)   23–4
intelligentsia   151, 200, 207–8, 209, 212, 213
'Invictus' (Henley)   138–9
irony   201, 263
Isenheim altarpiece   26–7, 27

James II, King of England   91
Jean de Meun   12, 14–16, 25
Jefferson, Thomas   116, 168
Jenkins, Roy   216
Jenny Wade of Gettysburg (Eastman)   168–9
John, Elton   247, 255
John of Beverley, St   29–30
Johnson, Boris   257–8
Johnson, Paul   234
Johnson, Samuel   69
Jones, Inigo   61
Jones, Terry   19, 20, 22–3
Joseph Andrews (Fielding)   70
Joy, G. W.   142, 143
Joyce, James   xiii–xiv
Jude the Obscure (Hardy)   45
Julian of Norwich   29–30
Julie (Rousseau)   84–6, 89

Kapital, Das (Marx)   102
Kaye, John   138
Kempe, Margery   32
Key to Uncle Tom's Cabin, A (Stowe)   158
King, Francis   172
King, Martin Luther   161
Kingsley, Charles   xi, 82–3, 134
Kingsley, Mary   134
Kipling, Rudyard   136–7, 139–41, 252
Knight of the Cart, The (Chrétien de Troyes)   10, 11
'Knight's Tale, The' (Chaucer)   19–20
Knox, John   50
Kokoschka, Oskar   201–2
Kruger, Danny   248
Kuhn, Thomas   97–8

Lac, Le (Lamartine)   177
Lady Chatterley's Lover (Lawrence)   217
Lamartine, Alphonse de   177–80, 182
Lambert, John   51
'Lament for Walsingham, A'   43

INDEX

Lange, Dorothea 207
Lappin, Daniel 264
Larkin, Philip 215–216
Lassberg, Christel von 87–8
Lawrence, D. H. 199, 200, 217, 262
Lead Belly xv
Leavis, F. R. 77, 156
Leavis, Q. D. 77, 156
Legend of Good Women (Chaucer) 16
Leicester, Lord 102
Leiden des Jungen Werthers, Die (*The Sorrows of Young Werther*, Goethe) 68, 86–7, 88–9
Lennon, John 243, 245–9
Lenz, Jakob 68–9
Lerner, Laurence 75–6
Les Mis (musical) 170–2, 184: see also *Misérables, Les* (Hugo)
Letters on Toleration (Locke) 91–2
Leviathan (Hobbes) 92
Lewes, George Henry 151, 154–5, 156, 157
Lewis, C. S. 1, 10, 13
Lewis, Wyndham 200, 203–4, 210–11
Liberty, Equality, Fraternity (Stephen) 152, 225
Liddle, Rod 251–2
Life of Pamela, The 71
Lincoln, Abraham x–xi, 158
'Little Boxes' (song) 208–9
Little Dorrit (Dickens) 157
Littlejohn, Richard 258
Locke, John 91–3
London Corresponding Society 117, 128
Louis IX, King of France (St Louis) 34–5, 39
Lounger, The (journal) 103
love, invention of 1–24
Low, John 137–8
Lynn, Vera 242

Macaulay, Catharine 129, 133
Macbeth (Shakespeare) 268
McCartney, Paul ix, x, 243–5
McCullin, Don 60, 207
MacDiarmid, Hugh 212
Mackenzie, Henry 78, 99–104
Macmillan, Harold 221–2, 224, 233
Madame Bovary (Flaubert) 89
Mâle, Émile 29
Malevich, Kazimir 196
Mallarmé, Stéphane 193
Man of Feeling 83, 105, 250
Man of Feeling, The (Mackenzie) 78, 99–103
Mandela, Nelson 261

Manifesto of Futurism (Marinetti) 145, 213–14
manliness 123–46, 210–11
  men and 135–46
  women and 129–35, 146
Manson, Charles 245
Mantel, Hilary 48
Marinetti, Filippo Tommaso 145, 203, 212–14
Martin, Richard 112–13
Martineau, Harriet 136–7
Marx, Karl 102, 207
Mary, A Fiction (Wollstonecraft) 105, 123–4
Matisse, Henri 199–200
Maudsley, Henry 252
Maxwell Fyfe, David 222, 223, 226, 229, 230
Mechain, Gwerful 5–6
Méditations (Lamartine) 177
Mein Kampf (Hitler) 210
Mencken, H. L. 209–10
mental illness 119–20, 221
Messiah, The (Handel) 108
Methodists/Methodism 79–82
Michelangelo Buonarroti 57, 58, 59, 61
Middlemarch (Eliot) 82, 103
Mill, Harriet Taylor 237
Mill, James 136
Mill, John Stuart 136, 225, 237, 238, 239, 240, 241
Millais, John Everett 176, 176, 187
'Miller's Tale, The' (Chaucer) 20–1
Misérables, Les (Hugo) 170–4, 177–9, 180, 181–4, 185
Mitrailleuse, La (Nevinson) 204–5
modernism xviii, 157, 192–3, 201–14
Montaigne, Michel de 60
Montfort, Simon de 36, 39
Monthly Review, The 100, 101
More, Thomas 30
Morris, Colin 1, 26, 41
Mount, Richard 105–6
Mullan, John 77–8, 101, 104
Mullen, Peter ix–x, 259, 263, 264
Müller, Max 136
Murray, Andy 252–3
Mussolini, Benito 210–11, 213
Mystery of Edwin Drood, The (Dickens) 187

Nanine, ou le Préjugé vaincu (Voltaire) 68
Napoleon Bonaparte 87, 127–8
Nash, Paul 202–3, 203, 206
National Conservatism manifesto 248

Native Americans   169–70
Neoliberalism   xviii
Neville, Richard   44–5
Nevinson, C. R. W.   203–5, 204, 206
New Critics   xviii
New Left   xviii
New Man   250
Newbery, John   112
Newman, Graeme   264–5
Newton, John   117–18
Newton, Thomas   166
Nicholas Nickleby (Dickens)   157
Nichols, Peter   xiii
Nietzsche, Friedrich   207, 209–10, 263
Nightingale, Florence   109, 133–4
Nocturne in Black and Gold – the Falling Rocket (Whistler)   175
Notes of a Native Son (Baldwin)   158
Notre-Dame de Paris (Hugo)   155
novels of sentiment   63–79, 83–9
Nye, Joseph   41

'Ode to Joy' (Schiller)   249
Oh Calcutta! (revue)   218–19
O'Hear, Anthony   259–60, 261
'Old Bloomsbury' (Woolf)   197–9
Old Curiosity Shop, The (Dickens)   xiv, xv, 156–7
Old Wives' Tale, The (Bennett)   199
Oliver Twist (Dickens)   155, 157
Olney Hymns (Newton and Cowper)   118
Olympic Games   238–9, 251–2, 258, 267
On Liberty (Mill)   225, 240
'On Richardson's Portrait' (Gellert)   68
Orison to the Blessed Virgin (Herebert)   28
Ortega y Gasset, José   193, 200–1, 205–6, 208–9, 263
Orwell, George   156, 163
Ottawa Treaty   262
Oudh, King of (Wajid Ali Shah)   138
Our Lady's Song   28
Outram, James   138

Pamela: or Virtue Rewarded (Richardson)   63, 65–7, 68–71, 72, 73, 123
Paris, Matthew   33, 34, 41
Paris, Treaty of   39
Parker, Matthew   50
Passion of Christ   24–31, 51–2
Paths of Glory (Nevinson)   204–5
Patria Mia (Pound)   211
Patrie, La (Nevinson)   204–5, 204, 206
Perceval (Chrétien de Troyes)   25

Permissive Society   234–5
photography   206–7
Picasso, Pablo   194–5, 195, 196, 197, 199–200, 205–6, 205
Pickwick Papers, The (Dickens)   82, 157
Pinsent, Matthew   251
'Pitié, La' (Delille)   181
Pitt, William   125
Plato   265–6
Poems of Currer, Ellis and Acton Bell, The (Brontë sisters)   135
poor relief system   52
Popper, Karl   98
popular music   215–16, 241–5
Pottle, Frederick   xviii
Pound, Ezra   211
Powell, Anthony   19, 20, 85, 180, 262
Powell, Enoch   221, 235–7
Powicke, Maurice   40
Pre-Raphaelite Brotherhood   175–7
Prévost, Abbé   68, 72–3
Pride and Prejudice (Austen)   132
primitive art   192
Pritchett, V. S.   78
Private Lives (Coward)   249
Puritans/Puritanism   51, 52, 53, 83

Quakers/Quakerism   61, 117, 119, 120–1
Quarterly Review   131
Quatre Lettres sur La Nouvelle Héloïse (Voltaire)   86
Quiller-Couch, Arthur   138–9

racial discrimination   235–7
Raimbaut of Orange   5
Ranworth church, Norfolk: Lady Altar   30–1
Raphael, David   97
Ratcliffe, Michael   172
Reading Abbey   45
'Recessional' (Kipling)   140
Red Rag, The (Whistler)   174–5
Reformation   53, 57
reforms   xi–xiii, 104–21, 215–41
Rejlander, Oscar Gustav   ii, xi–xii, 206
Renaissance   57–61
Renton, Alex   139
Republic, The (Plato)   265–6
Revolt of the Masses, The (Ortega y Gasset)   209
Rewards and Fairies (Kipling)   140
Richardson, John   195, 196
Richardson, Samuel   64, 63–79, 103, 123, 132
Robert d'Arbrissel   35–6

Roberts, Andrew 120
Roberts, Gareth x
Robespierre, Maximilien 126
Robinson, Ian 262, 263
Robinson, John 217
Roman Catholicism xviii–xix, 93, 233
Roman de la Rose 11–16
Romance of Tristan, The (Béroul) 6–9
Romaunt of the Rose, The (Chaucer) 12, 14, 16
Rougemont, Denis de xvii, 1–2
Rousseau, Jean-Jacques 84–6, 89, 126
Rowlandson, Thomas 100, 110
Royal Academy of Art 110
Royal African Company 163–4
Royal Humane Society (previously Society for the Recovery of Persons Apparently Drowned) 113–14
Rushdie, Salman 254–5
Ruskin, John 155, 175–6
Russell, Bertrand 200

Safranski, Rüdiger 88–9
St Paul's Cathedral 61, 141
saints 29–30
Sand, George 182
Sarler, Carol 258–9
Sassoon, Siegfried 145–6
Saturday Review 151
Saved (Bond) 217
Schiller, Friedrich 249
Schmidt, Erich 69
Science and Charity (Picasso) 194–5, 195
Scott, Walter 131–2, 155
'Scottsboro Boys, The' (Lead Belly) xv
Scruton, Roger 208, 237, 241
Seafarer, The 6
Second Sentimental Revolution 63–121
  animal rights 110–13
  Man of Feeling 250
  mental illness 119–20
  novels of sentiment 63–79, 83–9
  romance and religion 79–83
  Scottish Sympathizers 94–103
  social reform 104–21
  sympathy 94–107
  toleration 90–4
Seeger, Pete 208–9
sensibility: and social reform 104–7
sentimentality: and reform x–xiii
Servites 29
sexual discrimination 237–40
sexual equality 237, 238
Shaftesbury Abbey 45

Shaftesbury Society xi
Shakespeare, William 24, 45, 268
Shamela (Fielding) 69–70
Shaw, George Bernard 207–8 217–18
Sickert, Walter 204
slavery 117–19, 157–68
Sluter, Claus 59–60, 61
Smasher Dowsing (William Dowsing) 55–7
Smith, Adam 52–3, 95–6, 97–8, 99, 103, 112
Social Affairs Unit 259, 264
social reform
  Second Sentimental Revolution 104–21
  Third Sentimental Revolution 215–41
Society for the Recovery of Persons Apparently Drowned (later Royal Humane Society) 113–14
Society of Authors 216
Soldaten, Die (Lenz) 68–9
Solomon, Robert xvi
Son of Oscar Wilde (Holland) 146
Song of Roland 2
Sorrows of Young Werther, The (*Die Leiden des Jungen Werthers*, Goethe) 68, 86–7, 88–9
Stalky & Co. (Kipling) 136–7
Stephen, James Fitzjames 151–3, 225
Stevas, Norman St John- 216–17
Stone, Lawrence 78, 101, 105
Stowe, Calvin 158
Stowe, Harriet Beecher x–xi, 139, 157–66, 167–8
Stuart, Lady Louisa 100
Subjection of Women, The (Mill) 237, 239
suburbia 207–9, 211, 212
suicide 87–8, 89, 113–14, 221–2
sympathy x, xvi, 94–107, 196, 254–5
  Second Sentimental Revolution 112, 115, 119
  Third Sentimental Revolution 221, 228, 240–1

Take Your Choice! (Cartwright) 116
'Tale of Melibeus' (Chaucer) 23
Tale of Two Cities, A (Dickens) 151–2
Tate, Henry 187
Tate galleries 187, 201
Taube, A (Nevinson) 204, 205
tears xiv, 31–6, 50, 51–2, 80–3, 84, 99–100, 255–8
  in Bible 263–4
  in sport 251–4
Tebbit, Norman 235
Teresa of Ávila, St 25